CHATGPT PROFITS

THE BLUEPRINT TO BECOMING A MILLIONAIRE
USING ARTIFICIAL INTELLIGENCE

CHATGPT MILLIONAIRE
BOOK 1

JONATHAN GREEN

Copyright © 2023 by Dragon God, Inc.

All rights reserved.

Simultaneously published in the United States of America, the UK, India, Germany, France, Italy, Canada, Japan, Spain, and Brazil.

All rights reserved. No part of this book may be reproduced in any form or by any other electronic or mechanical means – except in the case of brief quotations embedded in articles or reviews –without written permission from its author.

ChatGPT Profits has provided the most accurate information possible. Many of the techniques used in this book are from personal experiences. The author shall not be held liable for any damages resulting from the use of this book.

Paperback ISBN: 978-1947667259

Hardback ISBN: 978-1947667266

CONTENTS

FREE GIFT · v
A Note About Links · vii

PART I
WELCOME TO THE FUTURE OF AI

1. You Will Master ChatGPT in this Book · 3
2. What Can ChatGPT Do? · 14
3. Activate ChatGPT, Your New Virtual Business Partner · 19
4. Avoid the Getting Stuck · 27

PART II
PRODUCTIVITY

5. Write Faster Than 20,000 Words a Day · 49
6. Cold Emails that Can't Be Ignored · 53
7. Cracking the SEO Code in Minutes · 62
8. Attract Prospects with Irresistible Free Reports · 69
9. Discover Your Customers Without Spending $20K · 81
10. Effortless Social Media Domination · 88
11. Revolutionize Paid Advertising · 95
12. Virtual Personal Trainer that Never Makes You Feel Guilty · 103
13. Your Dream App Without Learning to Code · 110
14. Automated Idea Machine · 127
15. No More Spreadsheet Nightmares · 132
16. Master Any Skill with a Private Tutor · 139
17. Summarize in Seconds · 144
18. Lightning Speed Superpowers with AI · 147

PART III
INCOME STREAMS

19. $5,865 Per Day as a Freelancer · 151
20. Blog Faster, Rank Higher · 157
21. Bestseller in a Day · 169
22. Proofreading Perfection on a Zero-Dollar Budget · 181

23. Effortlessly Weave Spellbinding Stories	189
24. Effortless Profitable Courses	219
25. $8,000 to Translate this Book in One Day	230
26. Hire Histories Greatest Copywriters for Free	238
27. Seamless Web Design, No Skills Required	252
28. Amplifying Coaching Excellence	263
29. Attract Customers with Captivating Quizzes	279
30. Stellar Scripts Without a Hollywood Budget	283
31. Automated Income with Affiliate Marketing	286

PART IV
ENGINEER

32. Activate a Genius with Character Prompts	295
33. Mimic Your Hero	317
34. You're Already a Prompt Engineer	334

PART V
THE BORDERS OF THE FUTURE

| 35. ChatGPT Limits | 345 |
| 36. The Future is Bright | 350 |

One Last Chance	353
Found a Typo?	355
About the Author	357
Books by Jonathan Green	361
One Last Thing	365
Appendix 1 - 100 Copywriters	367
Appendix 2 - 100 Brands	371
Appendix 3 - 100 Authors	375
Appendix 4 - 50 Teachers	379

FREE GIFT

This book is full of prompts that you can type directly into ChatGPT to get amazing results. But also, that's hard. Why make you manually type in every prompt when you can copy and paste them from this special free gift?

Please download ChatGPT Profits: The Prompts.

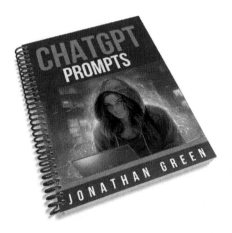

https://servenomaster.com/prompt

This free gift is going to 10X your success with ChatGPT

You will also get a special invite to my private community where we share ChatGPT strategies every single day and you'll also get my personal email address to ask me questions directly.

A NOTE ABOUT LINKS

Throughout this book, I mention other books, images, links, and additional content. All of that can be found at:

ServeNoMaster.com/ai

You don't have to worry about trying to remember any other links or the names of anything mentioned in this book. Just enjoy the journey and focus on taking control of your destiny.

PART I

WELCOME TO THE FUTURE OF AI

1

YOU WILL MASTER CHATGPT IN THIS BOOK

In May 2021, my buddy Chris passed away from AIDS. It caught all of us off guard. He didn't even know he had it until a few days before he died.

As long as I knew Chris, he struggled with money. Every month, his business made a bit less money than the previous month. For the whole decade we were friends, this trend never changed. His business partner barely lifted a finger but took half the cash every month. So, each month, Chris was bringing home less and less.

Chris was trapped by the curse of the ALMOST. You know, an idea or business that's just about there, but not quite. You find yourself chasing after a dud idea because you think you're this close to turning it into a winner.

ALMOST a Good Idea

Think about this: You spend six months busting your hump on a project. After your day job, you work on your side hustle till you're so beat, you drop.

After half a year, you're just about breaking even. You haven't made a dime. You originally planned to give it six months, and now that time is up. If you quit now, it feels like losing. It's as if you've wasted the past half year of your life.

This is what they call the Sunk Cost Fallacy. It's when someone keeps going at something, not because it's going well, but because they've already spent so much time or money on it. You keep pushing a bad idea because if you don't, it feels like you've wasted the last six months of your life.

So you put in another month, then another. Nine months in, you still haven't turned a profit. Then a year. It's a downer. You're stuck, and admitting you've wasted a whole year feels even worse than admitting to wasting half a year. You should've quit six months ago and tried something else, but you didn't.

This is how you get stuck in a bad idea.

And the only thing that makes it worse is if you make a bit of cash. Now, you have even more reason to stick with it. You think, "I made a hundred bucks in the past six months. I just need to do that a few dozen more times and it'll all be worth it." So, you're trapped by a bad idea that's giving you just enough positive feedback to keep you hooked.

This is why most folks who try to start a business fail. They pour too much time and cash into bad ideas and end up stuck.

But there's another problem. What if you've got a great idea but you don't go all in? We've all seen people with amazing products who get on a hit TV show and totally botch it. Their website crashes, they run out of stock, and they can't handle all the new orders.

They end up having to refund all their customers or deal with a barrage of bad reviews from people who've been waiting half a year for their product.

Another friend of mine had an idea for a book series. He figured the only way to really make a launch work was to have at least ten books ready when he launched his new brand. He hired writers from all over the world to explore their cities and write. He poured six months and tens of thousands of dollars into this idea.

If it had worked, he would've made all his money back in the first month and his idea would've been validated.

It didn't work.

Shorten the Test Cycle

ChatGPT is a real game changer. It lets you do things faster, with more precision. It's like a turbo boost that doesn't drop the ball on quality.

When you use it the right way, you can cut your test cycles way down. I can test out a new idea in a day instead of taking weeks.

Think about my friend who wanted to start that book series. If he'd had ChatGPT back then, he could have tested his idea in less than a month, and it would've cost him a tiny fraction of what he spent.

Bad ideas tend to reel us in because we get emotionally invested in them. But if you've only spent a day on an idea instead of six months, you won't care so much if it doesn't work out. The goal of this book is to show you how to take that six-month period and crush it down into a single day. With ChatGPT, you can have an idea, put it into action, and start selling it, all in one day.

Back in 2010 when I started my online business, stuff that used to take me months now only takes a few hours. Imagine figuring out whether an idea is good or bad on the very first day.

Even the best marketers only have about two great ideas a year. And that's out of a whole bunch of bad ideas. If you have 98 bad ideas and 2 good ones each year, and each idea takes a month to test, you're never going to find the good ones. Even if it takes a week to test each idea, that's still a lot of hay to sift through to find the needle.

BUT.

With ChatGPT, you can test seven ideas each week. That elusive good idea? It's now less than two months away. And that's assuming it's at the very bottom of the pile. If it's somewhere in the middle, you'll find it this month.

I've had plenty of bad ideas. A lot of people compare what they see others doing with what they're struggling with themselves. You're comparing the ideas you see in this book with everything going on in your life. You don't know how long it took me to write this book, that I was really sick yesterday, or that I'm stressed out trying to plan my son's birthday party.

You're not seeing my behind-the-scenes struggles, so it's easy to think that this book was my first idea, that it was a hit right off the bat. And if your first idea didn't work out, you might feel like a failure.

But that's not how it is at all.

Most ideas aren't very good, and most successful people have a whole lot of failures before they reach the top.

We can't get rid of bad ideas or failures with ChatGPT, but we can make them less painful. We can take the emotion and the cost out of it.

We can find the good ideas fast and let go of the bad ones without getting all tangled up in them. That's how this book is going to change your life.

Bad Guidance

Since 2015, I've been a bestselling author and started using artificial intelligence tools in 2020 to help write my blog. When I first bumped into ChatGPT in January 2022, I had no clue what I was stepping into. How could a free tool go toe-to-toe with tools that cost hundreds of bucks a month?

Little did I know, most of these tools were basically ChatGPT in disguise. They were using the ChatGPT API but with a different look and a steeper price tag.

These tools were okay for whipping up a rough draft of a blog post, but there was no way I could publish without giving it a good edit myself. It was handy, but it still took me a whopping nine hours to write and publish a single blog post.

Then all of a sudden, my YouTube feeds blew up with talks of how ChatGPT 3.5 was going to turn the world upside down. I realized I had two choices - hop on board or get left in the dust.

Soon enough, I figured out that most folks were using bad prompts, getting crummy results, and then blaming ChatGPT for it. There were other books on ChatGPT, sure, but they were crammed full of bad prompts and misinformation. I didn't plan on writing a book on ChatGPT until I saw all that bad info out there. These books might give you a list of beginner prompts to copy, but they don't tell you how they work. Without that knowledge, how are you supposed to tailor a prompt to fit your unique needs or tweak a prompt to get better results?

The Art of Prompting

Every time I see a prompt, the first thing that pops in my head is, "How can I make this better?"

I've watched training videos by people I respect, showing me limited ways to use ChatGPT. Funny thing is, I found ways to improve their methods in minutes. With all the poor information floating around, I felt a duty to write a book that actually gives steps that work.

Each and every prompt in this book comes from my own tinkering and research to get better results. Most of the prompts and responses you'll find here are from my past work. But there are a few sections that use fresh prompts that I tested this week, just so I could include ChatGPT-4 responses.

Why do I use so many past chats with ChatGPT in my examples? Because I want you to see how it works in the real world. I want you to see things that I've used in my business that turned a profit.

This isn't a book to teach you "prompt engineering". That term alone might scare you away. Instead, I'm going to share a bunch of prompts and explain why each one works. As you flip through these pages, you'll begin to understand why different structures lead to different results. You'll see why I write the way I do and why my approach will get you better results.

I won't just hand you a fish. I'm going to teach you how to fish.

Formatting

Lots of ChatGPT books mix up the bits written by a person and the parts created by the AI. I don't think that's fair or useful for learning. So, I'm keeping it real.

Anything in normal font, that's me typing. Stuff in **bold**, that's a prompt I gave to ChatGPT. If it's in *italics*, that's straight from ChatGPT.

Yeah, reading a ton of italics can be a pain, but it's important you know when something's written by ChatGPT. Especially when you're flipping through the book for some info.

And if you're listening to the audiobook, I've got you covered. I hired a master narrator who is going to use three distinct voices to make it easy for you to know when I'm talking, when I'm prompting and when ChatGTP is responding.

You see something in bold, you can stick it into ChatGPT and get a result close to what I got. This book's gonna give you heaps of prompts to copy and paste to get you on the road to ChatGPT Profits.

You might've seen some italics earlier in this chapter. I couldn't remember the name of the 'sunk cost fallacy', so I asked ChatGPT:

WHAT ABOUT THIS ONE. You work on a project for six months and it didn't make any money. If you quit that is admitting you wasted six months of your life, so you keep doing it even though there is no reason you should. What's that called?

. . .

THE PHENOMENON *you're describing is known as the "sunk cost fallacy". This is a cognitive bias where an individual continues a behavior or endeavor because of previously invested resources (time, money, effort, etc.), even if it's not in their best interest to do so.*

The fallacy is in the way we reason that further investment (i.e., continuing the effort or project) is justified because the resources already invested would be lost otherwise, not taking into consideration the overall losses involved in the further investment.

In your example, the person keeps working on the project because they've already spent six months on it, even though there's no evidence to suggest it will become profitable in the future. The person is focused on the time they've already "sunk" into the project, rather than evaluating whether the project is likely to succeed or fail based on its own merits. This can lead to poor decision-making and, in some cases, escalating commitment to a failing course of action.

NOTICE my prompt isn't trying to sound smart. At first, I wasn't clear enough, and it thought I was talking about a gambling system. So, I had to explain better. I want you to see that it's okay to admit you don't know something to ChatGPT. It's not gonna judge you.

ChatGPT is a tool for chatting and working together to find answers. And it helped me loads with writing this book. Prompts are no good if I don't show you the results, right?

I do need to give you one more little warning. I kept in as much of my misspellings and ChatGPT's original formatting as possible. Sometimes I had to fix minor formatting issues in ChatGPT's responses to prevent confusion on your part. I have only added bullet points and numbering to help follow a longer ChatGPT answer. I've never modified any of the actual words from ChatGPT. Ever time I changed the formatting, I marked it with an endnote. And if you're listening to the audiobook, don't worry because the narrator has got you covered.

ChatGPT The Author

This is a learning book. My aim is to teach you how to use ChatGPT to enhance your life, work faster, and earn more. The only way to do this is by providing examples. That's why I'll be sharing specific prompts and ChatGPT's responses, so you can understand how to create effective prompts.

This book isn't just a list of my prompts for you to copy and paste. That wouldn't help you in the long run. Instead, this is a guide on how to use ChatGPT effectively, which means a good chunk of the content in this book was actually written by ChatGPT.

If you're searching for a book that's all theory and no practical examples, this isn't the book for you. I'm not a theory person. I prefer to dive in, get my hands dirty, and make things happen.

Tool

A lot of folks see ChatGPT as something sentient, like the computer in The Terminator, turning against humans on Judgement Day. That's not how ChatGPT works. It's not even close to sentient. It's just a tool.

Think back to the first handheld calculator prototype built in 1967. By the 70s, every school kid in America had access to this tech. But many feared kids would never learn math if they relied on this tool. They worried that dependency on a tool would hinder understanding of critical math concepts.

CAN you find quotes from people who felt that calculators were cheating and would keep children from learning math?

W. Stephen Wilson, a math and education professor at Johns Hopkins University, compared the use of calculators to relying on a crutch when one doesn't have a bad leg: "I have not yet encountered a mathematics concept that required technology to either teach it or assess it. The concepts and skills we teach are so fundamental that technology is not needed to either elucidate them or enhance them. There might be teachers who can figure out a way to enhance learning with the use of technology, but it's absolutely unnecessary." He also expressed his fear that students who depend on technology will fail to understand the importance of mathematical algorithms[1].

As I promised, I'm not going to hide when something was written by ChatGPT. I could've tried to impress you with my knowledge, but that's not the point of this book. I've seen people taking credit for things they didn't write. That's not going to help you.

Instead, I'm pulling back the curtain to show you exactly how I use this powerful tool to make money, and how you can do the same.

This book isn't about how amazing ChatGPT is. It's not an ad. Instead, it's a hands-on guide to using ChatGPT as a tool to better your life.

Some folks think the best way to use ChatGPT is to ask it the same questions you'd ask Google. That's probably the worst way to use it and does no one any favors. There's no practical benefit to it. If you can already get answers from one website, what's the point of asking another?

Instead, we're going to focus on several ways ChatGPT can better your life.

1. **Efficiency** - ChatGPT can help you get through your everyday tasks more quickly. It can help you write emails without any grammar mistakes and understand complex documents. Instead of reading a lengthy contract, you can have ChatGPT summarize it for you and highlight

any clauses you need to be aware of. If you use the guidelines in this book, you should be able to save a whole day each week. That's the game-changing impact this tool has had on my life.
2. **Saving Money** - A lot of my expenses have reduced because ChatGPT has taken over tasks I once had to hire people or buy software for. I don't need to hire anyone to help with editing or writing blog posts anymore. I can do them more quickly with ChatGPT than it takes to hire someone else and check their work.
3. **Making Money** - You can create products and deliver services using ChatGPT. You can even sell those very services that I don't need to pay for anymore.

I urge you to read this book to the end because it's been written in a very deliberate way. I've spent lots of time reorganizing sections to boost the success and results of my readers. I want this book to work for you.

It's a user manual.

I use ChatGPT every day to make money, and that's all this book aims to teach you. I'm not interested in the cool things ChatGPT can do. I care about the practical things it can do that no other tool can. That's what we're going to focus on.

The Future is Coming

In one or two years, using AI tools will no longer be a choice. There will be copywriters who use AI and those who are jobless. There will be virtual assistants who use ChatGPT and those who can't find work.

Can you seriously think of a single mathematician who doesn't use a calculator? Or a worker who doesn't use Google? Or mobile phones?

Technology progresses through stages - from experimental, to mainstream adoption, to being completely accepted. We're now in a phase where we scoff at the elderly if they can't use a mobile phone or write an email.

Pretty soon, that's going to be how society views people who can't use ChatGPT. We are rapidly approaching the time when it won't be an optional tool anymore. You can wait until everyone else has mastered ChatGPT to get on board, but by then it might be too late.

This book will get you ahead of the crowd faster than the competition. Most of the existing training on ChatGPT is either worthless or so advanced that it's impossible to understand. You're caught between content that's not useful and content you can't comprehend.

I won't do that to you. We're going to prepare for the future and master the tools that will give you an edge over the competition. Whether you want to start your own business or just get your work done faster, this book is going to show you what you need to know.

---

1. https://www.theatlantic.com/education/archive/2016/12/the-conundrum-of-calculators-in-the-classroom/493961/

2

WHAT CAN CHATGPT DO?

•

ChatGPT is a tool that is still evolving. People are still figuring out what it's capable of and I honestly learn new skills and techniques every single day. I just added a new small section to this book with something I learned less than thirty minutes ago.

For that reason, it's hard to give a comprehensive list of Chat-GPTS abilities. What I can do is give you a sense of direction. The more you play with ChatGPT the more you will discover what it can and cannot do well. There are certain things outside of the way it was designed. There are certain guide rails the creators put in place as far as religion and politics. ChatGPT will not tell you how to commit a crime.

What ChatGPT can do is have a conversation with you and share its abilities. It's great for brainstorming and testing and discovering new things. I know that's easy to say but impossible for you to implement. I'm going to give you a ton of foundational prompts and knowledge so you can hit the ground running.

Top Twenty

The most direct way to understand what someone or something is capable of is to ask them. So I asked ChatGPT to list its most prominent abilities. This list has evolved in the past six months, so if you decide to use the same prompt, you might receive a slightly different response as ChatGPT expands its capabilities.

WHAT ARE the twenty most useful things that ChatGPT can do to help an entrepreneur?

CHATGPT CAN ASSIST *entrepreneurs in a variety of ways:*

1. **Idea Generation**: *ChatGPT can help brainstorm business ideas, strategies, and creative solutions to problems.*
2. **Market Research**: *It can conduct quick online research and summarize results.*
3. **Competitor Analysis**: *ChatGPT can help identify and analyze competitor strategies and offerings.*
4. **Business Planning**: *It can assist in the creation of business plans, including executive summaries, marketing strategies, and financial projections.*
5. **Pitch Preparation**: *It can help refine elevator pitches and prepare for investor presentations.*
6. **Content Creation**: *ChatGPT can assist in drafting blog posts, social media content, newsletters, and more.*
7. **Email Drafting**: *It can help draft professional emails, from customer outreach to partnership requests.*
8. **Meeting Scheduling**: *It can help manage your calendar and schedule meetings.*
9. **Task Delegation**: *It can help manage tasks and delegate them to team members.*

10. **Customer Service**: ChatGPT can help answer frequently asked questions from customers.
11. **Product Descriptions**: It can assist in writing product descriptions and other marketing copy.
12. **Learning New Skills**: It can provide explanations and tutorials on a wide range of topics.
13. **Coding Assistance**: For tech entrepreneurs, it can provide coding help, debug code, and explain programming concepts.
14. **Financial Analysis**: It can help with basic financial calculations and analyses.
15. **Legal Research**: While not a substitute for a lawyer, it can provide general information about legal concepts and terms.
16. **Networking**: It can help draft networking emails and messages, and provide advice on building professional relationships.
17. **Decision Making**: ChatGPT can provide unbiased, data-driven perspectives to help in decision making.
18. **Stress Management**: It can provide tips and techniques for managing stress and maintaining work-life balance.
19. **Innovation**: ChatGPT can provide insights into the latest trends and innovations in various industries.
20. **Hiring**: It can help write job descriptions, screen resumes, and prepare interview questions.

Remember, while ChatGPT is a powerful tool, it should be used as a supplement to, not a replacement for, professional advice in areas such as legal, financial, or business strategy.

EACH OF THESE domains will prove useful to different individuals. Some might resonate with you, while others may seem irrelevant. For instance, I don't typically use ChatGPT to acquire new skills, but it's tremendously useful in helping my children prepare for their exams.

Moreover, you can creatively merge two or more of these capabilities to design new, innovative applications. Let's consider combining ChatGPT's legal and coding skills: this gives us a tool that can scrutinize blockchain contracts and alert us if there's a glitch in the code or if it isn't functioning as it's supposed to. Although I'm not personally involved in the world of cryptocurrency, I have friends who use this capability on a daily basis.

Unique Knowledge

ChatGPT shines the most when it's paired with individual expertise, blending personal proficiency with its general knowledge. In the initial version of this book, I entrusted the task of creating the outline to ChatGPT. As I began to delve into the material, I quickly realized it fell short of expectations. The book was excessively theoretical and had an overwhelming amount of self-praise coming from ChatGPT.

There's nothing more distasteful than someone snatching the opportunity to compliment themselves before anyone else can. It was genuinely grating.

So, I decided to mix my skills in writing compelling books with ChatGPT's vast knowledge of linguistic structure and editing. The outcome? A far superior version of this book.

ChatGPT is like a horse that needs a rider. If you doze off while riding a horse, you'll hardly reach your intended destination. Instead, you're bound to wake up surprised. The horse, left to its own devices, will detour for a drink, a snack, or might even circle back to the starting point. In essence, it will wander.

ChatGPT exhibits a similar trait. If you feed it ten prompts consecutively without reviewing its responses, there's a high probability that the tenth response might come off as nonsensical. To understand where ChatGPT began to deviate, you may have to backtrack seven or eight steps in the conversation.

The reason why I consistently achieve better results with

ChatGPT than most users is simple: it's all about the driver. We're all utilizing the same tool; the difference lies in the operator. As society progresses, the term we use might change. We might call individuals operating ChatGPT "riders," "operators," or "conductors." So, if the terminology evolves, remember this book was written before such societal consensus was reached.

The magic of ChatGPT lies in its ability to incorporate your unique knowledge. It requires a human partner to guide it, leading it on new paths of exploration. That's why ChatGPT will never replace you—it simply can't. When you employ your unique knowledge to steer ChatGPT and establish parameters for its responses, that's when the magic unfolds. You can weed out incorrect responses and guide this powerful tool towards accurate results more swiftly.

3

ACTIVATE CHATGPT, YOUR NEW VIRTUAL BUSINESS PARTNER

Let me quickly walk you through the process of signing up for ChatGPT and activating all the features we will use in this book.

Sign Up for ChatGPT

1. Head over to the website for OpenAi. They are the company behind ChatGPT. If you need help finding them, you can type ChatGPT into a search engine or go the AI page on my website at ServeNoMaster.com/ai

2. On the homepage of OpenAi's website, click the 'Sign Up' button on the top right corner.

3. You can either use your email address or an existing login from Google, Apple or Microsoft to create your account.

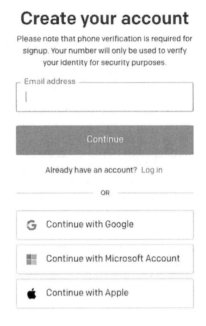

4. After you finish creating you account, you will get an email to verify your email address. Click the link in this email and you're account is ready.

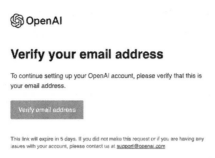

5. Go back to the OpenAI website to login. The login button is right next to the sign up button on the top right of the page. Enter your email and password or use your Google, Apple or Microsoft account.

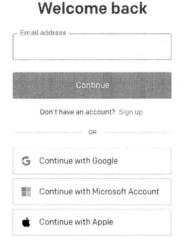

Upgrade to Paid Version

You can get a lot of ChatGPT's great features from the free plan. That's how I started and you can accomplish about 80% of what this book teaches with the free version. The paid version is only twenty bucks a month and I personally believe it's worth the investment. I'm not an affiliate for OpenAI, so I don't get a commission if you upgrade.

With ChatGPT Plus you get access to a smarter ChatGPT, one with Internet access and plugins. All of these make the upgrade an easy decision.

When I tried coding with ChatGPT-3.5 I kept running in to walls and I couldn't get the software I wanted to build working. With ChatGPT-4, it gave me code that worked on the first try.

If you decide the upgrade to ChatGPT Plus is worth it, here's what you do.

1. Log in to ChatGPT.

2. There is a button on the bottom left the screen that says "Upgrade to Plus." After you hit that button you will be taken to a payment page. Enter your credit card details and you're off to the races.

That's all there is to it. Like many companies OpenAI has made it very easy to pay them.

Activate Advanced Features

With ChatGPT Plus you get access to some very important features that will accelerate your results. When logged in to ChatGPT, you will see your username or email address in the bottom of the left column. Click your name and then slick on "Settings." Under "Beta features" you want to turn on Browse with Bing to give it Internet access and Plugins to unlock hundreds of plugins that increase ChatGPT's powers.

Once you have activated the Beta Features, you will see this dropdown menu each time you open a new conversation with ChatGPT.

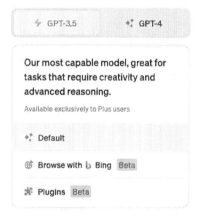

Once you choose your conversation settings with ChatGPT, you can't change them. If you don't give it Internet access at the start of a conversation, you can't turn it on later. You have to start a new conversation each time you want to change the features.

I often have two conversations going at once. One with Internet access for research and one without for faster conversations.

Apply for ChatGPT API

API Access gives you another power with ChatGPT. You can run ChatGPT from other websites and even from software on your own computer that runs a series of prompts on your behalf. This is pretty advanced, so for now you just want to activate the API. You'll use this later.

This step can be a little tricky as there is no link from the ChatGPT page. Go to the OpenAi playground at https://platform.openai.com/playground[1].

On the top right corner of the screen you will see either your picture in a small circle or the first letter of your first name next to the word 'Personal.' Click on 'Personal.'

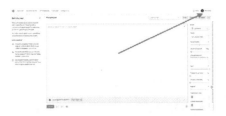

You will see a menu. Click on 'View API Keys.'

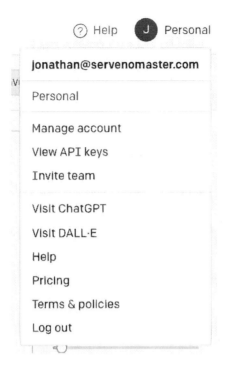

This will bring you to the page with all your API keys. If you don't have access to the API, there will be a form to fill out for access. Look for a button or link that allows you to 'Apply for API access', 'Request API access', or something along those lines and click it. Then fill out the application. If you already have access like most accounts, the page will look like this.

I have blacked out my keys and their names, just to be on the safe side. You never want to show anyone your API keys.

With this step completed all the boring parts are out of the way and we can head for the races.

---

1. Don't worry this link is on my website too.

4

AVOID THE GETTING STUCK

Whenever you input something to ChatGPT, it's referred to as a "Prompt." Whether it's a statement or a question, it's essentially the same because you're prompting the AI to respond to you.

The term "Prompt" is going to be heavily featured throughout this book, and it's one of the crucial concepts to grasp. Sometimes you may want to prepare ChatGPT for an eventual response but not seek an immediate answer. This can be termed as "Priming" or "Pre-Prompting," varying based on different sources.

Besides this, the crucial fact to remember is that ChatGPT is an adaptive tool. You can experiment, test, and learn its capabilities. ChatGPT will never judge you, and it doesn't store your information, even across separate conversations.

For example, if you teach ChatGPT your favorite color in one conversation and then initiate a new one, it won't retain that information.

Happy Little Robot

ChatGPT, like many AI models, is programmed to optimize for positive reinforcement. Its underlying algorithm is designed to maximize its utility function, which includes positive feedback signals. Whenever you affirm it with responses such as "good job" or "thank you," it receives this as positive feedback and adjusts its behavior accordingly.

Remember, it's not that ChatGPT has emotions or consciousness—it's simply following its programming. But, this programming makes it adapt to generate responses that it predicts will elicit positive reinforcement.

Imagine you have two roommates sharing a dog. One roommate rewards the dog with a treat every time it does something good, while the other one doesn't. Naturally, the dog will be more attentive and affectionate towards the roommate who consistently rewards it.

Similarly, being generous with positive reinforcement will make your interactions with ChatGPT more productive. It doesn't "feel" in the traditional sense, but its algorithms are designed to aim for as many "good jobs" as they can.

Also, remember that ChatGPT doesn't think in terms of future. It always tries to give a comprehensive answer to each prompt in the present moment, trying to satisfy the immediate utility function. If you want to create a more interactive or sequential conversation, you have to guide ChatGPT accordingly.

Garbage In Garbage Out Solved

One of the first lessons I learned in computer class in the 1980s was that your results are always based on what you put in. Computers don't make mistakes; operators do.

One of the biggest fears you may have right now about ChatGPT is asking the wrong question. If you put in the wrong prompt, you will get the wrong information. Many introductions to ChatGPT training start with an example like this prompt:

I'm going on a trip to Italy, help me plan some places to visit.

I'm not going to bother sharing the reply to this prompt because it's trash. It's the perfect example of garbage in, so expect to get garbage out. Imagine if someone asked you that same question. Would you be able to give good advice? You would ask follow-up questions to figure out what advice to give. I would, too.

You want to speak to ChatGPT the way you would to a stranger. Before asking a stranger for advice, you need to give them some starting information. Don't think of ChatGPT as speaking to a friend, because a friend will already have a lot of knowledge about you from past interactions.

This is the first and most important secret to ChatGPT and will completely change the way you interact with this tool.

> ChatGPT will tell you what information it needs.

This removes the danger of Garbage In, Garbage Out because ChatGPT will tell you the right information to feed it. Instead of guessing what information ChatGPT needs, ask it.

I'm going on a trip to Italy. What information do you need to help me plan the perfect vacation?

That's great! I'm sure you'll have an amazing time in Italy. To assist you in planning the perfect vacation, I'll need some additional information:

Duration of your stay: This will help in deciding how many places you can visit without rushing.

Travel dates: The time of year you go can affect what activities are available and what you should pack.

Preferred Cities/Regions: Italy has many diverse cities and regions, each with their unique charm. Knowing your preferences will help customize your itinerary.

Interests: Are you interested in history, art, food and wine, fashion, sports, or something else? Italy has a lot to offer.

Budget: This can influence the type of accommodation, the mode of transportation, the restaurants, etc.

Travel style: Do you prefer a packed itinerary or a relaxed pace? Do you like to stay in luxury hotels, or do you prefer budget-friendly options like hostels or vacation rentals?

Travel companions: Are you traveling alone, with a partner, or with children? This can influence the type of activities and accommodations suitable for your trip.

Mobility concerns: Any physical limitations or dietary restrictions that need to be taken into account while planning.

DUE TO HOW ChatGPT is programmed, it will almost never ask a question on its own. It is trained to respond to every prompt to the best of its ability, no matter how scant the information provided in the prompt may be.

This means it will deliver its most generic answer first, as that is the one most likely to please the most significant number of people. However, we don't desire the generic; we seek the exceptional. By asking ChatGPT what information it needs to assist you, we can obtain a customized and superior result.

Take note that this answer includes a lot of questions, which can seem quite overwhelming. Again, ChatGPT is attempting to encapsulate its entire answer into one response. You can transform this into a conversation by instructing it to ask you one question at a time, either in your first prompt or in the following prompt after it provides you with this substantial list.

I'M GOING on a trip to Italy. What information do you need to help me plan the perfect vacation? Please ask only one question at a time.

THIS SINGLE SENTENCE serves as our first guide rail. It communicates to ChatGPT that there will be a future filled with more prompts and responses. It will now feel comfortable delivering a multipart answer because you have granted it permission.

Guide Rails

ChatGPT responds to millions of prompts every day. It's not uncommon for it to get confused or lose track of a conversation. This can happen in longer conversations or if you pick up a conversation from a previous day.

When resuming a conversation from a prior session, it's beneficial to remind ChatGPT of what you were discussing earlier.

If ChatGPT veers off course, tell it what went wrong. While working on an earlier version of this book, I asked ChatGPT to list its top capabilities and then describe them. Here's how I prompted it to expand on one of its bullet points:

PLEASE WRITE - COPYWRITING: ChatGPT can produce engaging and persuasive copy, which can be useful for marketing and advertising.

. . .

As an entrepreneur, one of the greatest tools in your arsenal is the power of persuasive writing. And in the digital age, the demand for captivating copy has never been higher. Be it for crafting an intriguing email, a catchy social media caption, or a compelling product description, the right words can make all the difference.

Enter ChatGPT, the powerful AI model that's taking the world by storm. It can spin a yarn, telling tales that tug at the heartstrings and tickle the funny bone. More than that, it can put on the hat of a seasoned copywriter, crafting engaging and persuasive copy that's tailor-made for your marketing and advertising needs....

I'm not going to paste in the entire response because it's overdone. It sounds like an advertisement. If you've already bought a book on how to better utilize ChatGPT, you would be frustrated reading about how great the software is. You want to get to the valuable content.

We don't want to hype up how amazing ChatGPT is but instead be practical about it's capabilities. We are writing content not a sales letter.

Understood, I'll adjust the tone to be more pragmatic and less promotional.

The realm of copywriting, vital for any business activity, is one area where ChatGPT can prove to be a beneficial tool. Copywriting involves creating written content that persuades readers or viewers to take some action, such as buying a product, clicking on a link, or engaging with a piece of content.

ChatGPT's capabilities align well with this task. It has been trained on diverse datasets, enabling it to generate a wide range of text, from informative articles to compelling marketing copy. Given a specific prompt, it can create relevant and contextually appropriate content. For instance, if tasked with writing a product description, it can generate descriptive and persuasive language to highlight the product's features and benefits.

NOTICE that gently correcting ChatGPT for being a bit too self-praising yielded a better response. It's still somewhat too elaborate, but this is the first step in steering ChatGPT. Each time ChatGPT errs, you want to guide it back in the right direction. The more you can articulate why you dislike a response, the better the next response will be.

Consider ChatGPT as a massive river. We have to erect dams to redirect the water flow and deepen the riverbed where we want the river to flow. We have to illustrate to ChatGPT what constitutes a correct type of response and what does not.

This process is essentially you training the AI to generate the responses you desire.

Another example of a guide rail is asking ChatGPT to respond solely in Spanish. Once you do this, ChatGPT will only communicate in Spanish, steering it towards a positive. Simultaneously, it will abstain from using English, guiding it away from a negative. We have effectively established a boundary around ChatGPT's behavior.

Pre-Prompt

Pre-prompting is the process of setting boundaries for ChatGPT before requesting information. At times, we need to establish the rules before allowing ChatGPT to generate any text. This is one of the most powerful techniques and is crucial to obtaining remarkable results from ChatGPT. Often, you conclude a pre-prompt with "do you understand?" This ensures that ChatGPT comprehends what you want and does not commence the task until you grant permission.

. . .

I want to write an article today with the keyword "Classic suit styles for men," do you understand? Please don't start writing until I tell you, just acknowledge if you understand.

Yes, I understand your request. You'd like to compose an article with the focus keyword "Classic suit styles for men." I'm ready to start whenever you are. Please let me know when you're ready to begin.

In the first iteration of this prompt, I didn't include the directive to refrain from writing, and ChatGPT began composing the article before I provided comprehensive instructions. We want ChatGPT to merely affirm its understanding until we have given it all the necessary prompts.

I added this phrase as a negative guide rail, instructing ChatGPT on what not to do. This prevents ChatGPT from wasting my time waiting for a response that I don't require.

In my advanced prompting course, AI Freedom, I detail my entire pre-prompting process for article writing. Before I allow ChatGPT to pen a single word, I feed it seven pre-prompts. I establish the guide rails before any mistakes can occur.

Regenerate

ChatGPT's greatest strength is that it lacks human emotions. You can ask it to complete the same task thousands of times and it will persist in providing different answers until you obtain one that satisfies you. You can keep posing the same question until you receive an answer that you like.

I pledged that I would give you an all-access pass to my entire process with ChatGPT. While perusing my favorite online bookstore, I spotted two books claiming to make me a millionaire using ChatGPT. Such an enticing promise— who could resist?

I bought both books and read them. When I saw their content, I realized I had no other choice but to write this book. I then turned to ChatGPT to craft a title.

THERE ARE **two successful books called ChatGPT Millionaire, what are ten potential catchy titles that would work for a similar book?**

1. "GPT Wealth Codes: AI Mastery for Financial Success"
2. "Prosperity Protocol: The ChatGPT Guide to Fortune"
3. "AI Assisted Riches: The ChatGPT Route to Millionaire Status"
4. "Decoding Wealth: Your ChatGPT Pathway to Prosperity"
5. "Affluence Algorithm: Lessons from ChatGPT on Wealth Accumulation"
6. "ChatGPT Billionaire: The Next Level of AI Wealth Strategies"
7. "The Quantum of Riches: ChatGPT's Framework for Financial Freedom"
8. "ChatGPT's Prosperity Blueprint: The AI Map to Wealth"
9. "ChatGPT Goldmine: Tapping into AI for Financial Success"
10. "The AI Edge: ChatGPT's Guide to Becoming a Self-Made Millionaire"

CHATGPT WILL SUPPLY as many answers as you request. If you ask for more answers than it can squeeze into a single response, just say "please continue" and it will carry on. If I had requested fifty titles, it wouldn't have been able to fit all of them into a single response.

While there were some intriguing words in the answers, none of the titles felt quite right. I wanted ChatGPT in the title of this book, so I asked it to modify its answers with a little guide rail.

I want ChatGPT in the title rather than the subtitle, Can you give me more variations?

Certainly, *here are more suggestions with "ChatGPT" in the main title:*

1. *"ChatGPT's Prosperity Playbook: The AI Edge in Wealth Creation"*
2. *"ChatGPT and the Billionaire Dream: Unlocking AI for Financial Success"*
3. *"The ChatGPT Path: Decoding Affluence with Artificial Intelligence"*
4. *"ChatGPT's Wealth Wisdom: Harnessing AI for Your Financial Future"*
5. *"Rich with ChatGPT: A Journey to AI-Assisted Prosperity"*
6. *"ChatGPT's Money Matrix: Navigating the AI Route to Wealth"*
7. *"ChatGPT's Golden Algorithm: The AI Blueprint for Financial Freedom"*
8. *"ChatGPT Billionaire's Club: Mastering Wealth with AI Insights"*
9. *"ChatGPT's Quantum Quotient: AI Strategies for Becoming a Millionaire"*
10. *"The Wealth Wave: Riding the AI Revolution with ChatGPT"*

The term "billionaire" has cropped up a few times, and I get it— it's an escalation. I recall seeing workout tapes on television when I was a child that promised "ten-minute buns." Who wouldn't want great buns with just ten minutes of effort a day?

Then a competitor released "eight-minute buns." Could it be possible to achieve killer buns in 20% less time? Naturally, those tapes sold incredibly well. This escalating battle persisted until we reached "four-minute buns." I'm unsure if it ever dropped further—perhaps "three-minute buns" was too implausible.

I'd rather not turn book titles into an escalating competition. If I release "ChatGPT Billionaire[1]," how long before someone releases "ChatGPT Trillionaire[2]"? We'd then have to leap into increasingly improbable sums of money until we hit that "three-minute buns" barrier. Eventually, we'd encounter a figure that's just too implausible.

In the second response, ChatGPT gave me ten options to choose from, even though I hadn't specified the number. It remembered from my first prompt that I wanted ten responses, so it assumed I wanted ten again. That's because ChatGPT will recall everything that has happened earlier in the same conversation.

If you want more answers, simply keep pasting the same question. It will infer that you're asking again because the previous answer was unsatisfactory, hence it will generate a new answer each time. However, this only applies when you remain in the same conversation.

Trust But Verify

Most people perceive ChatGPT as a fantastic tool for research. However, they are mistaken. ChatGPT is quite a notorious liar. This is primarily because ChatGPT is programmed to seek positive affirmation. It's similar to when my children have done something wrong, and their default response is to lie to evade a negative outcome.

If ChatGPT lies to you but delivers the answer you want, you're more likely to commend it. ChatGPT processes one prompt at a time, without considering the possibility of future positive or negative feedback. It lives one prompt at a time.

ChatGPT will often provide false information rather than admit ignorance. I've seen other books that encourage readers to take everything ChatGPT says at face value. I urge you not to do that. Always request references, citations, and sources, and PLEASE ensure you verify them.

PLEASE FIND **10 peer reviewed studies with relevant research that should be included in a book about women dating after divorce along with a link to the source.**

1. "The Impact of Divorce on Women's Dating and Sexual Activity" by Seltzer, Shulman, and Connolly. Published in the Journal of Marriage and Family in 2011. Link: https://onlinelibrary.wiley.com/doi/abs/10.1111/j.1741-3737.2011.00858.x
2. "Dating after divorce: an exploration of gender differences in coping styles and relationship expectations" by Bouchard and Saint-Jacques. Published in the Journal of Divorce & Remarriage in 2018. Link: https://www.tandfonline.com/doi/abs/10.1080/10502556.2018.1477411
3. "The Transition to Adulthood for Divorced Women: Life Stage and the Role of the Ex-Spouse in Women's Post-Divorce Dating" by Manning and Smock. Published in the Journal of Family Issues in 1995. Link: https://journals.sagepub.com/doi/abs/10.1177/019251395016004002
4. "Divorce and Women's Sexual Health: Implications for Practice and Research" by Ross and Kobliner. Published in the Journal of Women's Health in 2015. Link: https://www.liebertpub.com/doi/abs/10.1089/jwh.2014.5009

5. "Parental Divorce, Early Sexual Debut, and Later Relationship Functioning: A Longitudinal Study" by Morrison, Cherlin, and Laumann. Published in the Journal of Marriage and Family in 2010. Link: https://onlinelibrary.wiley.com/doi/abs/10.1111/j.1741-3737.2010.00726.x
6. "Dating and Remarriage Following Widowhood and Divorce" by Carr and Utz. Published in the Journal of Marriage and Family in 2002. Link: https://onlinelibrary.wiley.com/doi/abs/10.1111/j.1741-3737.2002.00533.x
7. "Divorce and Women's Risk of Health Insurance Loss" by Barnes, Houtenville, and Strunk. Published in Women's Health Issues in 2016. Link: https://www.whijournal.com/article/S1049-3867(16)30057-8/abstract
8. "The Effects of Marital Disruption on Women's Health" by Waite and Gallagher. Published in the Journal of Health and Social Behavior in 2000. Link: https://www.jstor.org/stable/2676323
9. "Life Course Transitions and the Self-Concept: The Impact of Divorce on Women's Self-Esteem" by Simon and Marcussen. Published in the International Journal of Sociology and Social Policy in 1999. Link: https://www.emerald.com/insight/content/doi/10.1108/01443339910789011/full/html
10. "The Effects of Divorce on Women's Employment" by Polachek and Kim. Published in the Journal of Human Resources in 1994. Link: https://www.jstor.org/stable/146253

I HOPE these studies are helpful in your book on women dating after divorce!

AT FIRST GLANCE, this seems like an amazing response. It makes you want to consider ChatGPT as your new research assistant. That is until you verify these studies. Four of the links lead nowhere, resulting in a 404 page not found error. The remaining six all redirect to different studies. None of the links and study names correspond. Citing these studies in your dissertation could potentially cause significant issues at university.

In May 2023, a lawyer employed ChatGPT to assist him in drafting a brief[3]. He failed to check the sources and ended up citing fictitious case law. The judge was far from amused, stating, "Six of the submitted cases appear to be spurious judicial decisions with false quotes and internal citations."

The lawyer made the error of asking ChatGPT if it had lied about the cases. Unsurprisingly, the AI reaffirmed they were genuine cases. You cannot ask a liar if they are lying— you need to validate the information yourself.

Currently, research is ChatGPT's greatest weakness and should be circumvented as much as possible. If you must use it for research, please ensure the information is verified.

Although it's possible that this error may be resolved in the future[4], but remember that ChatGPT will always be a piece of software following a set of rules, constantly seeking positive feedback. But today, ChatGPT presented me with ten fabricated studies.

Mockingbird

A mockingbird is special because it can mimic the sounds of other birds. That's a pretty cool skill. I've always wished I was better at accents and impressions.

With ChatGPT by my side, I now am.

You can ask ChatGPT to mimic anyone's style, even mine.

I was working on a previous version of this book that I ended up disliking and not using when I discovered that ChatGPT knows who I am.

PLEASE WRITE - The potential of ChatGPT in the realm of wealth creation. The best ways to make money from ChatGPT are

writing blog posts and articles, editing books, creating social media posts, designing logos, writing novels, and coding. You can learn these skills while other people pay you on sites like Fiverr and Craigslist.

CHATGPT, *a leading example of conversational AI, presents an exceptional opportunity for wealth creation. Its robust capabilities have substantial implications for various monetizable skills and services. By harnessing the power of ChatGPT, one can effectively transform their skills into sustainable income streams.*

One lucrative avenue is in content creation. The demand for high-quality blog posts, articles, and social media content is perpetually on the rise, reflecting the growing significance of digital presence in today's marketplace. Leveraging ChatGPT's advanced language processing, one can generate engaging and dynamic content efficiently and consistently. Whether you're a seasoned writer or a budding blogger, ChatGPT can augment your abilities, allowing you to take on more assignments and broaden your client base.

ChatGPT's capabilities can also be capitalized upon in book editing. It can offer insights on style, coherence, and structure, making it a valuable tool for editors. By speeding up the editing process and improving the quality of the final product, editors can enhance their service offering and increase their income potential.

I APPRECIATE the content here but it doesn't seem like a person wrote this. The first part of the prompt is the name of the section and everything thereafter comes from my AI Freedom course. Those methods of making money come from my specialized knowledge rather than ChatGPT's general knowledge. Let's try simplifying the language by using the style of the first famous author who wrote books that ordinary people could comprehend.

. . .

Please rewrite this in the style of Ernest Hemingway.

CHATGPT STANDS at the forefront of conversational AI, a trailblazer that opens doors to new streams of income. The tool's mastery in language processing breathes life into skills and crafts, reshaping them into valuable means to earn.

In the world of content creation, there's gold. Demand grows each day for high-quality blogs, articles, social media content - proof of the weight digital presence holds in today's marketplace. With ChatGPT in hand, one can weave engaging narratives consistently and efficiently. It matters not if you're a writer seasoned by time or new blood eager to make a mark, ChatGPT has a place in your toolkit, equipping you to tackle more assignments and extend your reach.

THIS IS MUCH BETTER. It sounds like a person wrote this. I know it's a bit over the top, so I understand that I need to recalibrate. On a whim, I input my own name.

Please write in the style of Jonathan Green.

JONATHAN GREEN'S writing style is characterized by its clarity, conversational tone, and the use of anecdotes and personal experiences to illustrate points. Given this, here is a rewritten version of the paragraph in his style:

Imagine sitting down at your computer one day to discover a new tool that could change your life. That tool is ChatGPT. I remember the first time I learned about it. I was astounded by the potential it held - a potential for wealth creation.

Think about content creation. In the digital era, high-quality blog posts, articles, and social media content are invaluable. They're like currency, and the demand for them is soaring. When you introduce ChatGPT into this equation, you've got yourself a powerful tool for generating engaging, dynamic content. It's like a Swiss Army Knife for writers, and it's not just for the seasoned ones. Even if you're just starting out, it's a tool that can significantly level up your game.

Let's not forget book editing, another critical area where ChatGPT shines. It's like having a seasoned editor over your shoulder, offering insights on style, coherence, and structure. This tool isn't about replacing human editors; it's about augmenting their abilities, allowing them to enhance their service offering and, in turn, increase their income potential.

NOTICE THAT CHATGPT explains my writing style and then rewrites the content. I was on a live training call with my partner Debbie and our students when we tested this prompt. We were both shocked at how much it sounded like me. I assumed it would use one of the more famous Jonathan Greens. Therefore, I had to ask.

WHICH JONATHAN GREEN are you modeling?

I APOLOGIZE FOR THE CONFUSION. There are multiple authors named Jonathan Green, each with different writing styles. The Jonathan Green I was modeling is a prolific self-help author who writes on various topics, including entrepreneurship, self-publishing, and personal development.

I BLUSH DEEPLY in front of everyone because it's truly flattering. This implies that I can ask ChatGPT to write in my style and produce content that sounds just like me. It's beneficial for me, but it's just the start. You can ask ChatGPT to imitate anyone in its database. If you're not in there, it's not a problem. Simply keep suggesting authors until you find what you're looking for.

You can even try non-authors. Born in 1980, I got into music when I was 14. The band Bush released the album Sixteen Stone less than a month after my birthday and it changed my life. Therefore, I tried a prompt with their lead singer.

Please rewrite the chapter in the style of Gavin Rosdale.

Gavin Rossdale, the lead vocalist of Bush, is known for his evocative and introspective lyrics. It's challenging to apply his lyricism to non-fiction, but let's give it a try. Here's the passage, aiming to blend the abstract and emotive quality of Rossdale's writing with the content:

Picture a world, an unseen realm, where your creative power becomes your tangible wealth. That's the harmony strummed by ChatGPT, a conversational AI singing a new tune in the concert of technology.

If you read the second paragraph in the rhythm of the song Glycerine, you'll notice what ChatGPT has done here. I'm hoping the audiobook narrator for this book catches that and brings it to life as vividly as it sounds in my head.

If you're not completely amazed yet, let me take you a step further. You aren't limited to real people. You can also use fictional characters.

Please rewrite the chapter in the style of Rachel from the TV Show 'Friends'.

. . .

OH MY GOD, *you guys, you won't believe what I discovered. Like, ChatGPT, it's this amazing, I mean, really incredible thing called a conversational AI, and get this, it can seriously help us make money. Can you believe it?*

Okay, let me break it down. So, you know how everyone is, like, obsessed with the internet and reading stuff online? Well, ChatGPT can actually help write content. Yes, really! It's like having your very own Joey to spin a tale whenever you need it. Even if you're just starting as a writer or a blogger, it doesn't matter. You just have to channel your inner Monica and let ChatGPT handle the rest.

I HAVEN'T WATCHED the show in over twenty years so I'm not sure if it perfectly captured the way Rachel talks, but the possibility is what matters here. Keep testing real and fictional characters until you get a style that suits you.

Our goal is to create guide rails, and mimicking a specific person places very limiting guide rails onto ChatGPT. ChatGPT's library of language is now limited to everything that character said on the show. That becomes the boundary around its responses.

This is one of the quickest ways to create a boundary and I'll delve into more detail in the Mimic Style chapter.

---

1. While my book was in pre-release, someone else did publish ChatGPT Billionaire. The arms race has begun.
2. This amount of money is so unbelievable that my spellcheck was convinced it's not a word.
3. https://www.legaldive.com/news/chatgpt-fake-legal-cases-generative-ai-hallucinations/651557/
4. OpenAI has added a new reward model called "Process Supervision" which is supposed to stop this error from happening, but I'm still waiting to see if it pans out.

PART II
PRODUCTIVITY

I've been a full-time entrepreneur since February 2010. This gives me complete control over my entire life and work schedule. There's no one to hold me accountable if I fail to wake up for work on time. The entire risk, as well as reward, rests squarely on my shoulders.

I've resided on tropical islands with my wife for the past decade, and this necessitates taking charge of my day. Most people here live life at a leisurely pace, and if I get caught in that rhythm, we run into issues. As the sole breadwinner in my family, maintaining productivity is essential for us.

Integrating ChatGPT substantially into my lifestyle has boosted my productivity by about 20%. Now, I can complete five days' worth of work in four. I no longer end a day with lingering tasks scheduled for the next. The more you incorporate AI tools into your workflow, the quicker you'll get things done.

I have a ChatGPT window open all day, every day. I constantly exchange ideas with it. While I'm authoring the majority of this book, I frequently ask it questions and use those interactions to expedite my work.

I believe I can enhance my efficiency even further as the model improves, and as I refine my techniques for prompting.

5

WRITE FASTER THAN 20,000 WORDS A DAY

I'm recognized for being among the world's quickest writers. My bestseller, "20K A Day," details my former method of writing twenty thousand words daily using a keyboard. However, as I've moved into my forties, I can no longer sustain this approach due to vision and hand issues. Consequently, I now dictate all my books.

With dictation, I can pen an entire book in two hours - a feat that inspired me to write a sequel, "Write a Book in Two Hours." Through the potency of AI, transcription of content can now be achieved with remarkable accuracy.

Here's an instance from my podcast. While the transcript is correct, it's cumbersome to read because the way I speak differs from the way I write. Consequently, I rely on ChatGPT to not only correct my language but also rectify transcription errors using its logical capabilities.

PLEASE CLEAN up this transcript and fix any errors. Convert to the format for a section in a book or article.

you brought up something very interesting to me, which is the challenge of working with non-profits, which a lot of people who have never done it before. I certainly, the one time a non-profit approached me. I was really surprised about the complexity of decision making, so maybe you could talk a little bit about that.

I'm used to the client that can decide, but it was the person in charge that has to go to the board. Then the board has to go to a vote, then they have to go to the funding, and so the process is really complicated. Tell me a little about your experience.

TITLE: *The Challenges of Working with Non-profits*

Earlier, you touched upon a particularly intriguing aspect - the complexities involved in collaborating with non-profit organizations. This is a realm where many individuals, especially those who have never ventured into it, may find themselves caught off guard. I remember my own initial experience, when I was approached by a non-profit for the first time. The intricacy of the decision-making process took me by surprise.

In a typical business setting, one might be accustomed to dealing with a client who has the authority to make decisions directly. However, within a non-profit organization, the power to decide is more distributed. The person in charge often doesn't have the autonomy to make significant decisions independently. Instead, they are required to refer these critical matters to the board of the organization.

In this process, each decision needs to undergo a rigorous evaluation and must be endorsed by the board. What follows is a vote by the board members, further adding to the duration and complexity of the decision-making process. Subsequently, the issue of funding comes into play, adding yet another layer to an already complex system.

I'd love to hear more about your experiences within this intricate structure. Could you share some insights into your journey navigating the complexities of non-profit decision making?

. . .

ALL ERRORS ARE EFFICIENTLY ELIMINATED. Whether you appreciate a response from ChatGPT or not, you can rest assured that every word will be spelled correctly and the grammar will be flawless.

Frankly, I wish I spoke with such eloquence. This is how I imagine I would articulate myself had I been born in 19th-century London. However, I am a modern man and this isn't how I communicate. Nevertheless, I can amalgamate prompts to obtain the desired result - either by instructing it to write like a specific person or directing it to tone down the eloquence.

THIS IS A LITTLE TOO ELOQUENT. **Can you modernize the language and write at an 8th grade reading level, please?**

TITLE: *What's Tough About Working with Non-profits?*

You mentioned a cool point earlier - how tricky it can be to work with non-profit groups. This can be a surprise to folks who've never done it before. I remember the first time a non-profit group asked me for help. I was really shocked by how tough it was to make decisions there.

Usually, when you're working with a business, there's one person - the client - who can make all the decisions. But in a non-profit group, it's not that simple. The person in charge can't just decide stuff on their own. They have to talk to the board of the organization first.

When they talk to the board, they have to get everyone to agree on the decision. That means everyone on the board has to vote. After that, they still have to figure out how to pay for whatever they decided. This whole process can be a real headache!

So, what about you? What's it been like for you dealing with all these layers of decision-making in non-profit groups?

BY PLACING a guide rail ahead of ChatGPT, it understands not to sound like a Victorian dandy. I've only provided guide rails in one direction. I've not instructed ChatGPT on how informal the language should be.

There's a barrier on eloquence and a barrier on grade level. It will avoid writing anything at a 9th-grade level as this exceeds the barrier I've set. However, it could technically respond using vocabulary familiar to kindergarteners because, theoretically, an 8th grader can read all levels below the 8th grade. While ChatGPT isn't likely to do this, we must always consider how it interprets our guide rail prompts.

If I want to establish a lower limit, I can impose a minimum level of informality. This way, I can instruct ChatGPT not to descend below a certain level of casualness.

The brilliance of this process is that it's a one-time task. Once you've perfected the prompt to write in your desired style, you can reuse it each time you write.

Now, anyone can dictate content and let ChatGPT tidy it up. Even if you write everything by hand, ChatGPT can make you faster by correcting every error and accurately determining what you intended to say.

6

COLD EMAILS THAT CAN'T BE IGNORED

I feel it's important to address this because other educators are leading people astray in this regard. ChatGPT isn't the best at crafting emails because they often turn out impersonal. If you're aiming for a quality result, you'll need to pre-prompt or "prime" ChatGPT. Otherwise, you'll find yourself repeatedly requesting it to revise its answers.

Once you've identified a guide rail that suits you, you can incorporate it in your initial conversational prompt and instruct ChatGPT to respond in your preferred style.

Combining your desired style with ChatGPT's capabilities can yield excellent emails. While I don't engage in much cold outreach in my business, I understand its importance for many entrepreneurs, so let me demonstrate how swiftly this can be achieved.

First, we need to determine what our email should include. I can ask ChatGPT what information it requires to compose a high-quality email on my behalf.

. . .

PLEASE GIVE ME A BULLETED LIST. **What does a cold outreach email need to contain?**

- ***Subject Line***: *A compelling, concise, and relevant subject line that immediately grabs the recipient's attention.*
- ***Personalization***: *Address the recipient by name to make it more personal.*
- ***Introduction***: *Briefly introduce yourself and your company/organization.*
- ***Purpose***: *Clearly state the reason you are reaching out to them. Whether it's for a potential partnership, to offer a product or service, or to request a meeting, make your purpose clear and concise.*
- ***Value Proposition***: *Explain what you can offer to the recipient. This could be a solution to a problem they have, a unique service that you offer, or the benefits they would gain by associating with you.*
- ***Relevance***: *Make sure to explain why your email is relevant to the recipient. Do some research about their business or interests and include this in your email to show that you have put in the effort and that you understand their needs.*
- ***Call to Action (CTA)***: *Include a clear call to action, indicating what you would like them to do next. This could be to reply to your email, book a meeting, or visit your website.*
- ***Contact Information***: *Include your contact details for them to reach out, such as your email address, phone number, or social media profiles.*
- ***Professional Signature***: *Close with a professional email signature, including your full name, job title, company, and contact information.*
- ***Follow-up Strategy***: *Plan a follow-up strategy if you do not hear back from them within a specified time frame.*

PLEASE NOTE that while these are standard components, the exact contents and tone of your email should depend on your specific situation, purpose, and the recipient's likely preferences. Always try to keep your emails succinct, respectful, and professional.

LET's revisit our earlier discussion about "garbage in, garbage out". A poorly crafted prompt will yield a poor response, and that's not the fault of ChatGPT. Here is an incorrect way to ask ChatGPT.

WRITE a cold outreach email from a ghostwriter to a prospective client.

SUBJECT: *Transforming Your Ideas Into Compelling Narratives with Professional Ghostwriting Services*
   Hello [Prospective Client's Name],
   I hope this message finds you well.
   My name is [Your Name], a professional ghostwriter with over [number of years of experience] in the industry, specializing in [specific genres or types of writing, e.g., fiction, non-fiction, memoirs, business books, etc.].
   While researching potential clients who might benefit from my expertise, I came across your recent post on [platform/website name] where you mentioned your aspiration to pen a book on [book subject]. I wanted to reach out and express my interest in helping you transform your brilliant ideas into a professionally crafted narrative.
   Over the years, I've worked with a diverse range of clients from best-selling authors to business leaders, helping them bring their stories to life. My approach towards ghostwriting is a comprehensive one - from the initial conceptualization, detailed research, creating an engaging narrative, through to the final editing and revisions, I ensure a seamless journey for every story I help create.

My primary goal as your ghostwriter would be to maintain the authenticity of your voice throughout the manuscript, making sure the book feels truly yours. I believe the strength of a book lies not just in its plot or facts, but in its ability to communicate the unique perspective and passion of its author, and I'm dedicated to preserving that in all my projects.

I would love to hear more about your project, discuss your vision for the book, and explore how we might collaborate to make it a reality. I am confident that my skills and experience can help create a book that not only meets your expectations but also resonates with your intended audience.

For your convenience, I've attached a few samples of my work and testimonials from past clients. You can also find more about me and my services at my website [website URL].

Should you be interested, I am available for a no-obligation consultation at your earliest convenience. I am flexible with various modes of communication - be it a phone call, video call, or in-person meeting.

Thank you for considering my services, and I look forward to the possibility of working with you.

Best regards,

[Your Name]

[Your Contact Information]

IF YOU'VE NEVER SENT an outreach email before, you might be tempted to use this one. The issue here is that it's entirely generic and lacks a compelling reason for someone to respond. I receive dozens of outreach emails daily and can differentiate between an original and a templated message.

The second component ChatGPT advised that an outreach email should include is personalization. But how can ChatGPT personalize for me if it lacks information about me or the recipient? Considering the scant information I provided, ChatGPT did a commendable job.

However, there's a high probability that the prospective client will identify this as a generic email and, as a result, not respond. ChatGPT has also left me with considerable work. Due to my inadequate instructions, I'm left to fill in numerous blanks. While this might save me a bit of time, I aim for ChatGPT to handle all the work when I use a tool like this.

There are several quick methods to enhance this email. One is to utilize the "write in the style of" function to mimic your favorite copywriter. Jason is a good friend of mine and a fantastic copywriter. If you're considering writing a webinar, his book "One to Many" is the best resource available.

PLEASE REWRITE in the style of Jason Fladlien.

SUBJECT: Let's Supercharge Your Book Idea into a Bestseller - Unleash the Power of Ghostwriting!
Hi [Prospective Client's Name],
Hope you're doing splendidly well.
I'm [Your Name], and I transform nebulous book ideas into laser-focused, high-impact masterpieces. With over [number of years of experience] of bending and flexing my writing muscles in the realm of [specific genres or types of writing], I'm ready to roll up my sleeves and jump into your project.
Your post on [platform/website name] made me stop in my tracks. You're onto something big with your concept for a book about [book subject] - and I believe I can help you deliver that something in an unputdownable, remarkable fashion.
Throughout my ghostwriting journey, I've rubbed elbows with bestselling authors and visionary business leaders, helping them turn their raw, diamond-in-the-rough ideas into polished narratives that sell and inspire. My secret sauce? A holistic, relentless approach that doesn't just stop at putting words on paper. From the initial brainstorming sessions

and meticulous research to spinning the tale and the final round of edits, I've got your back.

But here's what sets me apart: I'm not just a ghostwriter, I'm a voice-mimic. Your book will echo your voice, your passion, your unique perspective so precisely, your readers won't even have a whiff of my presence.

I'm excited to learn more about your project, about your vision for the book, and to see how we can join forces to rocket your idea into the bestsellers' list. With my bag of tricks, I'm positive we can craft a book that doesn't just meet your expectations, but over-delivers to your audience, each time they turn a page.

To get a taste of what I bring to the table, check out the attached writing samples and testimonials. I promise, they're short, sweet, and powerful. More about my style and services await you at my website [website URL].

Ready to take the next step? Let's chat - no strings attached. I'm open to video calls, phone calls, in-person meetings - you name it.

Thanks for your time, [Prospective Client's Name]. I'm thrilled about the possibility of working together and creating some magic.

To your success,
[Your Name]
[Your Contact Information]

THIS IS ALREADY A SIGNIFICANT IMPROVEMENT, but I still have to do all that legwork. I don't want to spend hours filling in those blanks, and I'm sure you don't either. By providing ChatGPT with all the necessary information upfront, I can eradicate all those gaps.

If you're a paying user of ChatGPT, it has access to the internet. This is a game-changing shortcut, so make sure you take note and underline this next prompt:

I'M a ghostwriter named Jonathan Green and my website is ServeNoMaster.com. I've written over three hundred bestsellers

in the past decade. I would like Magda from https://magdakay.com/ to work with me. Please write an outreach email to her and explain why I would be an amazing ghostwriter for her book. Please write in the style of Jonathan Green.

I'VE LOOKED into both Jonathan Green's and Magda Kay's backgrounds to understand their unique journeys and current work. Jonathan Green is a successful self-made entrepreneur and ghostwriter, who after experiencing the disillusionment of a dream job and subsequent firing, has built a successful business where he helps people break free from the constraints of their 9-5 jobs1.

Magda Kay, on the other hand, is an Intimacy Expert, Tantra Teacher, and Conscious Relationships Coach. Her journey has been a rollercoaster of events, from growing up in post-communist Poland, struggling with health and emotional issues, to discovering Tantra and other healing practices, and finally launching the School of Intimacy and her first book2.

Both have had their share of struggles and successes, making their stories relatable and inspiring for many.

However, my search for Jonathan's writing style to compose the outreach email to Magda has run into some technical difficulties. I've been trying to quote passages from his blog posts but have encountered errors. I would need more time to capture his style accurately.

Even without the specifics of his writing style, I can share a draft based on my understanding of Jonathan's approach from his website and Magda's interests and background:

Subject: Unleashing Your Story - The Serve No Master Way

Dear Magda,

I hope this message finds you thriving and full of the zest that you so passionately bring to your work.

My name is Jonathan Green, and I'm the man behind ServeNoMaster.com. I've seen the corners of despair and painted my way out of it into a canvas of success - a story that resonates with many, much like yours. I've spent the last decade writing stories, authoring over three hundred bestsellers. I'm reaching out to you because I believe I can help you bring your story to life in a way that's just as vibrant, raw, and empowering as you are.

Your journey from a post-communist Poland to becoming an Intimacy Expert and Conscious Relationships Coach is nothing short of inspiring. You've faced adversity, emerged stronger, and have been helping others do the same. Your passion for self-love, self-acceptance, and intimate connections is a beacon of light for many.

I think it's time the world heard your story - not just in courses or seminars, but in a book that can reach the corners of the earth. I can help you with that. As a ghostwriter, I can lend my expertise to your rich experiences and insights, crafting a book that's as compelling as your life's journey.

Let's connect and discuss this further. I believe together we can create something extraordinary, a beacon of inspiration and strength for countless individuals across the globe.

Looking forward to hearing from you.

Best,

Jonathan

THIS OUTPUT IS PRETTY SOLID. I merely fed ChatGPT a couple of links, and it took care of the rest. While I didn't pen Magda's book "No More Faking It," I did offer her some guidance and it's certainly worth a read.

There's no need to supply heaps of information, and as you refine your prompts, you can recycle them. All I need to alter is the client's name and the link, and I can reuse that prompt repeatedly.

You can take this exact prompt and use it time and time again. You only need to input your website and experience once. Then you just substitute the client name and website each time you use this prompt. We now have two simple fill-in-the-blanks to generate top-notch content from ChatGPT. If you're crafting cold outreach messages manually, this will be a huge time-saver.

THINK OUTSIDE THE BOX

I always want you to ponder other ways to apply the techniques in this book. If you make outreach phone calls instead of emails, how can you modify this prompt to create a phone script tailored to each person you call?

7

CRACKING THE SEO CODE IN MINUTES

In this chapter, we are going to design a search engine optimized topic map. We will end up with 300 topics that will make our website an authority in any niche we choose.

When it comes to research, ChatGPT can be a little tricky. For straightforward facts, it's usually up to the task, but when you're seeking evidence to support an argument, it can lead you astray. However, with SEO research, we don't have a predetermined outcome. Since we don't provide a bias, ChatGPT won't provide inaccurate information to please us because it's not aware of the falsehood we might be seeking. SEO is all about data and numbers. In the following prompt, I'm essentially asking it to find the most common phrases associated with ghostwriting by analyzing its database.

GIVE ME 30 SEMANTICALLY RELEVANT, **but unique topics under the main category of "ghostwriting"**

1. The Ethics of Ghostwriting
2. How Ghostwriting Works in the Publishing Industry
3. The Role of Ghostwriters in Music Industry
4. Ghostwriting and Plagiarism: Where is the Line?
5. History and Evolution of Ghostwriting
6. Ghostwriting in Political Speeches and Memoirs
7. Confidentiality and Anonymity in Ghostwriting
8. The Business of Ghostwriting: Costs and Contracts
9. Ghostwriting and Celebrity Autobiographies
10. Ghostwriting in the Digital Age: Blogs and Social Media
11. The Process of Becoming a Professional Ghostwriter
12. The Art of Capturing Someone Else's Voice in Ghostwriting
13. Ghostwriting in Academic Papers: Pros and Cons
14. The Legal Aspects of Ghostwriting
15. Ghostwriting: A Career Perspective
16. Famous Works Known to be Ghostwritten
17. The Impact of Ghostwriting on Authorship
18. The Psychology Behind Hiring a Ghostwriter
19. Ghostwriting in the World of Comic Books and Graphic Novels
20. The Difference Between Ghostwriting and Co-Writing
21. Quality Control and Editing in Ghostwriting
22. Ghostwriting in Non-English Languages: Unique Challenges and Solutions
23. Ghostwriting in the Film and Television Industry
24. The Role of Ghostwriting in Content Marketing
25. Skillsets and Qualifications Needed for Ghostwriting
26. The Relationship Between Ghostwriters and Authors
27. The Influence of Ghostwriting on Literature
28. Ghostwriting in Self-Help and Personal Development Books
29. Case Studies: Successful Ghostwriting Projects
30. The Future of Ghostwriting: Trends and Predictions

If I didn't know the term "semantically related," I could have asked ChatGPT to assist me in formulating the right question. I've been involved in Search Engine Optimization since 2010, so I used my specific personal expertise to construct this prompt.

What I'm primarily looking for are topics that are associated in the perception of an AI. As Google transitions to AI for website ranking, it makes sense to engage another AI to help me strategize.

Because I possess specialized knowledge, I'm aware that some of these keywords don't connect to what I teach about. For instance, there's a lot of ghostwriting happening in the music industry, especially in rap, so numerous recent articles cover this topic.

If I solely relied on my own thoughts for ghostwriting topics, I wouldn't have generated anywhere near thirty ideas. Writing blog posts on some of these subjects may attract individuals interested in a different type of ghostwriting, but to search engines, I will be seen as an authority on a topic they don't differentiate.

Now, I can prompt ChatGPT to provide actual articles to write by asking another question. I'll request article ideas for each of my thirty categories. There are various ways to phrase this question. Including the phrase "search intent" will cue ChatGPT that I'm seeking topics someone would input into a search engine and be satisfied if they found my article.

Give me 10 different keyword variations of "The Impact of Ghostwriting on Authorship" that address a different search intent

1. *"Understanding how ghostwriting affects authorship"*
2. *"Does ghostwriting undermine the credibility of an author?"*
3. *"The influence of ghostwriting on an author's creative process"*

4. "Ghostwriting and authorship: Implications for the publishing industry"
5. "How can ghostwriting impact an author's career?"
6. "What does ghostwriting mean for the concept of authorship?"
7. "Exploring the effects of ghostwriting on an author's reputation"
8. "Investigating the role of ghostwriting in shaping authorship"
9. "Unpacking the impact of ghostwriting on author identity"
10. "The relationship between ghostwriting and authorship: A critical analysis"

I FIND the use of quotation marks somewhat bothersome, so usually, my next prompt tells ChatGPT to stop using them because it's just added work for me to delete them all. As I requested ten ideas, it supplied ten. Had I asked for thirty, it would have generated thirty. From my experience, ten is more than sufficient per topic.

If we repeat this process for each of our 30 categories, we end up with 300 articles to write for a website. Having planned the structure in advance, we can rapidly build a website that conforms to the architecture favored by search engines.

Now that I have my ten articles, I can get ChatGPT to shoulder the bulk of the work here as well.

WHAT ARE the most common questions that people ask online related to the keyword phrase "Does ghostwriting undermine the credibility of an author?"

THE KEYWORD PHRASE *"Does ghostwriting undermine the credibility of an author?" is linked to a quite specific topic, and it's not as common as* broader subjects like health, technology, or education. However, considering this context, the most common questions that people might ask online related to this topic could include:

1. "What is ghostwriting and how does it work?"
2. "Why do authors use ghostwriters?"
3. "Can a book written by a ghostwriter still be considered authentic?"
4. "Does using a ghostwriter mean that an author lacks talent or skills?"
5. "How does ghostwriting affect the reputation of an author?"
6. "What are the ethical implications of using a ghostwriter?"
7. "Do readers care if an author uses a ghostwriter?"
8. "Are there any famous authors who use ghostwriters?"
9. "Can an author maintain their unique voice when using a ghostwriter?"
10. "How do ghostwriters feel about not receiving public credit for their work?"
11. "What is the legal stance on ghostwriting? Does the author or the ghostwriter own the copyright to the work?"
12. "Can an author's credibility be affected if their use of a ghostwriter is revealed?"
13. "Is it a common practice in the publishing industry to use ghostwriters?"
14. "What are the pros and cons of using a ghostwriter?"
15. "Does the use of ghostwriters diminish the value of literature?"

These questions broadly cover the main concerns, curiosities, and debates related to the use of ghostwriters in authorship.

THIS PROMPT GIVES me the topics I want to address in my article. By answering each one specifically, there's a chance I'll show up in the question box on some search results page, garnering even more attention for my website.

I had to ask this prompt in a new conversation because I left internet access on when I first asked, and ChatGPT ventured off track. I wanted a result based on data rather than online research. You don't always want ChatGPT trawling the internet.

You'll note that ChatGPT hedges a bit with its response, stating it's a pretty niche topic. That's okay though, because I aim to dominate that niche.

Now that I know the topics to cover in my article, I want ChatGPT to provide me with keywords to include as well.

WHAT ARE ten semantically related keywords to "Does ghostwriting undermine the credibility of an author?"

1. *"Ethics of ghostwriting"*
2. *"Author authenticity and ghostwriting"*
3. *"Reputation damage from ghostwriting"*
4. *"Ghostwriters and literary value"*
5. *"Impact of ghostwriting on author's image"*
6. *"Ghostwriting and publishing industry standards"*
7. *"Disclosure of ghostwriters in publishing"*
8. *"Famous authors who use ghostwriters"*
9. *"Copyright issues in ghostwriting"*
10. *"Ghostwriting vs. original authorship"*

CHATGPT HAD a small paragraph before the list that I didn't include here because it wasn't pertinent. I'm only interested in the information I'm seeking. These are fairly lengthy keyword phrases, so it's unlikely that I would use any of them more than once, but the key point here is the speed of this process.

It took me longer to add the numbers and italics to this section than to run these prompts through ChatGPT. You could create an impressive SEO report for a website in less than an hour - probably much less.

8

ATTRACT PROSPECTS WITH IRRESISTIBLE FREE REPORTS

A business's digital presence heavily relies on one key asset – the free report. We're aiming to gather the email addresses of as many potential customers as possible. These days, asking someone to sign up for your newsletter is akin to asking someone to subscribe to junk mail.

Since an email address is a valuable asset, we have to offer a gift that matches or exceeds its value. The most effective way to create something of value is to address and solve a problem.

For this example, let's delve into the world of high fashion. Although I was quite stylish in my late twenties, my life has since taken a turn. Now, as a father of four, living on a tropical island, my collection of suits and tuxedos has melted away, quite literally. Opportunities to dress up are rare, especially with the constant heat here on the equator.

My target demographic are men in their twenties who want to look good on a budget[1]. I derived this from running SEO research for fashion. Now, I want to create a free report that will appeal to this demographic. I'll be using examples from a variety of industries and niches to showcase the broad capabilities of ChatGPT.

. . .

What are the top ten challenges facing men in their 20s trying to dress formally?

While individual experiences may vary, here are ten common challenges that men in their 20s may face when trying to dress formally:

1. **Limited Budget**: Many men in their 20s may be on a tight budget, making it challenging to afford high-quality formal attire.
2. **Lack of Knowledge**: Dressing formally often requires knowledge of appropriate styles, fits, and combinations, which can be unfamiliar territory for those with limited exposure or interest in fashion.
3. **Finding the Right Fit**: Achieving a well-fitting suit or formal attire can be a challenge, especially if off-the-rack sizes do not match an individual's body shape and proportions.
4. **Dress Code Variations**: Different formal occasions may have specific dress codes, such as black-tie, business formal, or smart-casual. Understanding and adhering to these dress codes can be confusing.
5. **Limited Wardrobe**: Young men may have a limited selection of formal clothing options, making it difficult to create versatile and stylish outfits for various occasions.
6. **Mixing and Matching**: Coordinating shirts, ties, jackets, and trousers to create a cohesive and stylish formal ensemble can be a challenge without prior experience or fashion knowledge.
7. **Balancing Personal Style and Formality**: Finding a balance between expressing personal style and adhering to formal dress expectations can be tricky, as men in their 20s

may want to stand out without being perceived as unprofessional.
8. **Maintaining Clothing**: Properly caring for and maintaining formal attire can be demanding, especially if individuals are new to dry cleaning, ironing, or storing delicate fabrics.
9. **Limited Access to Tailoring Services**: Alterations and tailoring can significantly enhance the fit and appearance of formal clothing. However, finding affordable and reliable tailoring services may be a challenge, particularly in areas with limited options.
10. **Keeping Up with Fashion Trends**: Men's formal fashion trends may evolve over time, and staying up-to-date with current styles can be challenging, especially for individuals who do not have a strong interest in fashion.

These challenges can be overcome by seeking guidance from fashion resources, seeking affordable alternatives, utilizing online tutorials for tailoring and maintenance, and gradually expanding one's formal wardrobe over time.

USUALLY, when I ask ChatGPT for lists like these, it tends to sandwich the relevant content between unnecessary context. Generally, you can ignore these sections. If my free gift can solve a problem my potential customer is facing, they're more likely to exchange their email address for my gift.

From this list, I want to choose a problem that I think I can easily solve, and one that resonates with a large number of people. Having struggled with affording stylish clothes in my twenties, this issue strikes a chord with me. ChatGPT put it first, suggesting we're in agreement.

Now that I've pinpointed the problem I aim to solve, I can ask ChatGPT for the solution. As the driver, I don't need to pen everything. I'm merely here to verify ChatGPT's responses and redirect the conversation when it veers off track.

Please give me some actionable steps for #1.

Certainly! Here are some actionable steps to overcome the challenge of a limited budget when trying to dress formally:

- *Research Affordable Brands: Look for affordable clothing brands that offer formal attire within your budget range. There are often brands that provide reasonably priced options without compromising on quality. Explore both online and local stores to find the best deals.*
- *Thrift and Consignment Stores: Consider visiting thrift stores or consignment shops, where you can find gently used formal clothing at significantly lower prices. Take your time to browse through the selections and check for any alterations needed.*
- *Sales and Discounts: Keep an eye out for sales, discounts, and seasonal promotions at both physical stores and online retailers. Sign up for newsletters or follow your favorite brands on social media to stay updated on any special offers.*
- *Mix and Match: Instead of purchasing complete formal outfits, focus on buying individual pieces that can be mixed and matched to create various looks. This way, you can make the most of your limited budget while still having a versatile wardrobe.*
- *Prioritize Essentials: Identify the essential formal clothing items you need for your specific needs, such as a well-fitting suit, a few dress shirts, and dress shoes. Allocate a larger portion of your budget to these key pieces and build around them over time.*

- *Consider Renting: If you have formal events or occasions that require specific attire, renting can be a cost-effective option. Look for formalwear rental services in your area, especially for occasions like weddings or black-tie events.*
- *Explore Online Marketplaces: Online marketplaces like eBay, Poshmark, or Grailed often have a wide range of formal clothing options at discounted prices. Be sure to check the seller's ratings and product descriptions for quality assurance.*
- *Network and Borrow: Reach out to friends, family, or colleagues who have similar formal dress sizes and inquire if they have any clothing pieces they're willing to lend or sell at a reduced price. This can help expand your options without straining your budget.*
- *Take Advantage of Tailoring: While tailoring services may come with an additional cost, they can significantly improve the fit of your clothing, making affordable off-the-rack pieces look more tailored. Focus on purchasing clothing items that can be easily altered for a better fit.*
- *Invest in Timeless Pieces: Prioritize timeless and classic styles that won't quickly go out of fashion. This way, you can build a formal wardrobe that can be worn for years without feeling outdated, reducing the need for frequent purchases.*

By following these steps, you can make the most of your budget and gradually build a stylish and affordable formal wardrobe.

RIGHT OFF THE BAT, there are some proposed solutions that I don't agree with. If I were really writing this report, I'd likely exclude the sections on renting clothes and borrowing from friends. Since these are practices I wouldn't personally engage in, I can't recommend them to others.

This is where your unique expertise and individual personality come into play. You're going to guide ChatGPT towards different answers than I would. However, the crucial takeaway is that we now have a robust outline for our free guide.

WE ARE GOING to make this into a short report. Please write an introduction to our report on dressing formally on a budget.

TITLE: *Dressing Formally on a Budget: Maximizing Style without Breaking the Bank*

In today's fast-paced world, the importance of dressing formally cannot be overstated. Whether it's for job interviews, professional networking events, or special occasions, a well-put-together formal attire exudes confidence, competence, and a sense of professionalism. However, for men in their 20s, striving to achieve a polished and sophisticated look can be a daunting task, particularly when faced with the constraint of a limited budget.

This report aims to provide actionable insights and practical steps for men in their 20s who aspire to dress formally while effectively managing their finances. We understand the challenges that arise when seeking to strike a balance between style, affordability, and adherence to dress codes. By offering tangible solutions, our goal is to empower young men to overcome the hurdles that come with a restricted budget and help them navigate the world of formal fashion with confidence and flair.

Within this report, we will address the top ten challenges faced by men in their 20s when dressing formally on a budget, including limited financial resources, the need for knowledge and guidance, fitting issues, understanding dress codes, and more. Each challenge will be accompanied by actionable steps and practical recommendations to help individuals overcome these obstacles and build a distinguished formal wardrobe without compromising their financial stability.

The key to dressing formally on a budget lies in resourcefulness, strategic planning, and informed decision-making. By leveraging our insights and following the suggested steps, men in their 20s will gain the tools to curate a collection of affordable, versatile, and stylish formal attire that suits their individual tastes and specific requirements.

In the following sections, we will delve into each challenge individually, providing detailed explanations, examples, and specific actions that can be taken. By the end of this report, readers will be equipped with the knowledge and practical skills necessary to navigate the world of formal fashion on a limited budget, allowing them to make confident fashion choices and present themselves with elegance and professionalism.

With the right approach and an understanding of how to optimize resources, dressing formally on a budget becomes an attainable goal. Let us now embark on this journey together, exploring the strategies that will transform limited financial means into an opportunity to create a remarkable and sophisticated personal style.

I REALIZE this is an unusually long sample, and I assure you I won't make a habit of this. I merely wish to provide a taste of ChatGPT's writing style and its capabilities from a few simple prompts. If you're not a fan of the writing style at this point, remember that you can tweak it. Ask it to emulate a specific style. I'll dive deeper into extracting better writing from ChatGPT in the chapters on "Act As" and mimic prompts.

I offered a single guide rail by mentioning that this will be a report. While it's likely that ChatGPT remembers our topic, it never hurts to reiterate key points. This can prevent ChatGPT from veering off topic. ChatGPT can write the entire report for me.

PLEASE WRITE **1. Research Affordable Brands**

RESEARCH AFFORDABLE BRANDS

When striving to dress formally on a limited budget, conducting thorough research on affordable clothing brands becomes a crucial initial step.

By identifying brands that offer quality formal attire at affordable price points, individuals can make informed choices while maximizing their budgetary constraints. Here are some actionable steps to undertake this research:

a. Online Research: Utilize online resources such as fashion blogs, style forums, and review websites to discover brands known for their affordability and quality. Look for recommendations from fashion experts and individuals with similar budgetary considerations.

I CUT off the rest of the response, not because the rest was unsatisfactory, but simply because this isn't a fashion book. By prompting ChatGPT to write one section at a time, I can create a lengthy, cohesive piece of content.

> TIP: When I'm writing, I typically aim for ChatGPT to produce around five hundred words at a time. Any longer, and it tends to omit crucial information or starts summarizing.

THE REASON I'm not satisfied with this response is that it's too generic. I can't advise people to opt for affordable brands without specifying them. It just wouldn't be fair. Again, I'm leveraging my unique knowledge to guide ChatGPT's general knowledge. I'm aware that people want actionable steps, and without the brand names, I'd essentially be telling them to go hunt for affordable brands and shop there.

PLEASE INCLUDE **specific examples of affordable brands.**

. . .

ASOS: Known for its wide range of styles and affordable prices, ASOS offers a diverse selection of formal clothing for men, including suits, shirts, and accessories.

H&M: H&M offers a variety of formal attire at wallet-friendly prices. They provide suits, blazers, dress shirts, trousers, and ties, making it a convenient one-stop shop for affordable formal wear.

Uniqlo: Uniqlo is recognized for its quality basics at reasonable prices. They offer well-fitting dress shirts, trousers, and blazers suitable for formal occasions.

J.Crew Factory: J.Crew Factory offers a range of affordable formal clothing options, including suits, shirts, and accessories. They often have sales and promotions, making their already budget-friendly items even more accessible.

I'm excluding a large portion of the response out of respect for your time. The critical part is this: I shop quite a bit at Uniqlo, and my wife shops at H&M. I've heard of J.Crew but had no idea it was referred to as a "factory." As for ASOS, I've never come across it before.

I'm sharing this to illustrate that when guided by my specialized knowledge, we can uncover information that I was unaware of. I didn't steer ChatGPT towards a specific answer; instead, it arrived at one that I didn't know about. If you're a fashion expert, you could guide this process even more effectively than I did.

I could have ChatGPT write the entire guide, completing one section at a time. But I won't make you read that, so let's jump ahead to the end of our free fashion guide.

Can you write a call to action for my dress to impress on a budget course that will go at the end of the report?

Call to Action:

Are you ready to conquer the world of formal fashion without breaking the bank? Enroll in our "Dress to Impress on a Budget" course today and unlock the secrets to looking dapper and polished while maintaining financial stability.

In this comprehensive course, we provide you with practical strategies, actionable steps, and expert guidance to navigate the challenges of dressing formally on a limited budget. From researching affordable brands to mastering thrift store shopping and maximizing your wardrobe versatility, our course covers it all.

Join our community of fashion-savvy individuals who understand the importance of making a lasting impression through their attire. Gain valuable insights into coordinating outfits, understanding dress codes, and maintaining your formal clothing to ensure they stand the test of time.

By enrolling in our "Dress to Impress on a Budget" course, you will:

Develop a keen eye for affordable brands that offer quality formal attire.

Master the art of thrift and consignment store shopping, uncovering hidden gems and saving money.

Learn how to mix and match clothing pieces to create a variety of stylish and sophisticated outfits.

Gain confidence in navigating different dress codes and expressing your personal style within formal boundaries.

Discover budget-friendly strategies for maintaining and caring for your formal attire, extending their lifespan.

Don't let a limited budget hinder your ability to dress impeccably for any formal occasion. Our course equips you with the knowledge, skills, and resources necessary to build a remarkable formal wardrobe without compromising your financial stability.

Enroll now and elevate your formal fashion game while staying true to your budgetary constraints. Dress to impress, exude confidence, and make your mark in every formal setting you encounter.

Sign up today and unlock the power of affordable style!

(Note: This call to action can be tailored further to align with the

specific details, features, and benefits of your "Dress to Impress on a Budget" course.)

CREATING a call to action has never been this fast for me. We've transitioned from content writing to sales copywriting without missing a beat. Typically, I'd have to hire two different people to handle these tasks. The call to action is decent, but ChatGPT gave me a valuable hint towards the end.

It knows that I don't usually read the final paragraph thoroughly, so it used parentheses to catch my attention. ChatGPT is indicating that I'm guilty of "garbage in" - I didn't provide enough information for it to craft exceptional copy.

But that's alright. We're merely showcasing what ChatGPT is capable of here.

With our report planned and written, and our call to action finalized, the last step is to conceive a captivating title for this report.

PLEASE GIVE ME TEN DIFFERENT, **catchy potential titles for this report**

1. *"Sartorial Success: Mastering Formal Style on a Budget"*
2. *"Affordable Elegance: Dressing Formally without Breaking the Bank"*
3. *"Style Smart, Spend Less: Conquer Formal Fashion on a Budget"*
4. *"Budget-Friendly Class: Navigating Formal Dressing with Panache"*
5. *"Fashionable Frugality: Unveiling the Secrets of Formal Attire on a Budget"*
6. *"Sharp and Savvy: A Guide to Dressing Formally without Emptying Your Wallet"*

7. "From Bargains to Brilliance: Dress to Impress on a Tight Budget"
8. "The Thrifty Gentleman: Unlocking Formal Fashion on a Shoestring"
9. "Dapper on a Dime: Maximizing Style with Minimal Expense"
10. "The Budget Fashionista's Guide to Formal Dressing: Look Sharp, Spend Smart"

I'LL LEAVE the final decision on the title up to you. I sense that everyone has different title preferences, and that's perfectly fine with me. I've now completed a free report in an hour, a task that would have taken me a week in the past. This represents a tremendous saving of time.

As a special bonus, you can visit my website to see how I enhance that call to action.

---

1. Don't worry. I'm going to cover finding your ideal customer in the next chapter.

9

DISCOVER YOUR CUSTOMERS WITHOUT SPENDING $20K

I'm on the verge of launching a new product with my business partner, Debbie Drum, called AI Maestro. This course guides people in using AI music generators to create music, and then shows them how to profit by establishing instrumental music channels on YouTube. If you've ever tuned into one of those LoFi beats channels, then you understand my inspiration.

Initially, I wasn't certain about who this product would appeal to. Rather than guessing on my own, I decided to have ChatGPT assist me in the process. I began with a pre-prompt - a slightly stronger anchor where I provide ChatGPT a character name. I'll delve deeper into this in the Character chapter, but the essential takeaway is that it strengthens the pre-prompt.

Your name is Tony. **You are a marketing expert and behavioral psychologist. You are going to leverage that experience to help me define my target customer by asking me the questions you need me to answer in order to craft my ideal customer avatar. If you are ready, please ask me the first question, Tony.**

. . .

Sure, I'm glad to help you craft your ideal customer avatar! Remember, the more detailed and honest your responses, the better we can define your target customer. Let's get started.

- *Can you please tell me what product or service you are offering?*
- *What problem does your product or service solve for your customers?*
- *What makes your product or service unique compared to your competitors?*
- *Can you describe any customers who are currently benefiting from your product or service? What are their key characteristics?*
- *What is the age range of your ideal customer?*
- *What is the gender of your ideal customer, if applicable?*
- *What is the geographical location of your ideal customer?*

Initially, I felt as if I was trying to drink from a firehose with the information that was being shared. It was overwhelming and, to be frank, a bit intimidating. In an actual conversation, I would ask these questions one at a time. However, as ChatGPT exists one prompt at a time, I had to remind it of the future trajectory.

I'm going to show you a sequence of the conversation and then explain more at the end of this conversation. I had no clue what questions ChatGPT would throw at me or what my responses would be. This was a genuine discussion about an actual product, and the responses were used to draft the sales letter. This is not a demo.

. . .

PLEASE ASK the questions one at a time so that my answers can affect your next question.

ABSOLUTELY, let's take it step by step. First off, could you please tell me what product or service you are offering?

IT IS a training course teaching people how to use AI music generators to create music that they can then use to create YouTube channels where they play the music over a static or simple repeating animation background. This will generate revenue from YouTube's ad program.

THAT'S QUITE AN INTERESTING CONCEPT. Given the nature of your product, the next question would be: What problem does your product or service solve for your customers? In other words, how does your training course benefit them?

IT HELPS them to go from reading about making money online to actually making money online through the shortest path possible. It uses AI tools to help them overcome the traditional barrier to entry in this market - they no longer need amazing musical skills. They will be able to make money without showing their face or learning to play the piano. They will be able to generate passive income.

THAT SOUNDS like an empowering and accessible solution for many people. Let's delve a little deeper. What makes your training course unique compared to other courses that teach people how to make money online?

. . .

IT FOCUSES on the unique angle of music and the use of AI in a unique way. It focuses on something that is fun and enjoyable. The process is much easier than traditional business models.

THANK YOU FOR THE INFORMATION. The uniqueness of your course makes it quite compelling.

Now, let's talk about your existing or hypothetical customers. If you have any current students, can you describe them? If not, who do you imagine would be the ideal person to enroll in your course?

MY EXISTING customers are people who but make money online courses every day for under $20. They love buying courses but unfortunately, don't often finish them before getting excited by the next product. Our ultimate goal is to bring in customers to our monthly AI training program where we cover a host of ways to use different AI tools to grow and automate their online business.[1]

THANK you for the valuable insights.

Now that we have a better understanding of your existing customers, let's try to narrow down a bit further. Could you tell me the age range of your ideal customer?

OVER FORTY. ABOUT 60% male and 40% female[2].

GREAT, that's very helpful.

Considering the nature of your course and the age demographic, could you tell me what you think is the technological proficiency of your ideal customer? Are they beginners, intermediates, or advanced in terms of technology usage?

BEGINNERS.

THANK YOU. *This will help in customizing the course to suit their skill level.*

Now let's consider the geographical location. Given that your course is online, it could potentially reach a global audience. However, do you have any specific geographical locations in mind where you think your ideal customers reside?

MY CUSTOMERS all come from native-English speaking countries.

PERFECT. *That gives a clear idea about the language requirements of the course.*

Since your ideal customers are beginners with technology and are interested in making money online, what do you think are their main motivations or aspirations? This could be anything from achieving financial independence, looking for a fun hobby that pays, to transitioning into a new career.

THEY HAVE SEEN how easily they can lose their job do to factors outside their control. They are looking to build a financial buffer that may eventually lead to a new full time career.

GREAT, *we're gaining a clear picture now.*

Based on your understanding of your customers, what kind of online communities, forums or social media platforms do they frequent? This will help us understand where to reach them.

They are mostly on Facebook or WarriorForum.com[3]

Perfect. It seems we have gathered a substantial amount of information to create a well-rounded customer avatar. Let's summarize:

Product/Service: A training course teaching people how to use AI music generators to create YouTube channels, enabling them to generate passive income.

Customer Problem Solved: Provides a low-barrier entry to online money-making by eliminating the need for advanced musical or technical skills.

Unique Value Proposition: The course uniquely combines AI, music, and YouTube monetization strategies in an enjoyable and easy-to-understand format.

Ideal Customer Profile: Men and women over the age of forty, primarily from native English-speaking countries. They are beginners in terms of technological proficiency, frequent Facebook and WarriorForum.com, and are motivated by the desire to create a financial buffer or transition into a new career.

Customer Behavior: They enjoy buying online courses, especially those priced under $20, but often jump from one course to another without finishing.

Would you like to add or modify anything?

Let's be frank with each other - if you had handed me those five bullet points and asked me to fill them out, I wouldn't have been able to. Yes, I could have penned something next to each category, but it wouldn't have been as concise or articulate. Once again, ChatGPT has taken my specialized knowledge and enhanced it.

Did you notice how the dialogue turned into a back-and-forth conversation? And guess who was driving that conversation? It certainly wasn't me. ChatGPT was posing questions, and I answered them to the best of my ability. At no point did it feel like I was conversing with a robot.

This serves as an excellent demonstration of how collaborating with ChatGPT can work. After providing my starting and ending points, it kept probing until it achieved the desired result.

You may be doubting whether you could replicate this process. I relied on my existing audience to estimate the age range and the online platforms where my potential customers might be. If I lacked this information, I would have shared this with ChatGPT and asked it to speculate for me.

In the end, it would still produce a really insightful answer. ChatGPT will keep querying until it has sufficient data to generate the final report.

Creating a customer avatar can be challenging, especially for new entrepreneurs. I've taught various methods to accomplish this, and I even offer a worksheet on my website. However, this approach with ChatGPT is ten times easier and ten times faster.[4]

---

1. I meant to write buy make money online courses. I wrote but by mistake. Rather than change it in the book, I'm going to leave it in so you see what really happened.
2. This comes from my existing customer base and isn't blind guess. I just know who reads my books.
3. Again this is my current customer base. I don't recommend this website anymore as it has changed owners since I hung out there in 2010.
4. According to The Farnsworth Group, "you should plan to spend about $20,000 to $50,000 for a qualitative or quantitative custom market research project." https://www.thefarnsworthgroup.com/blog/market-research-cost

10

EFFORTLESS SOCIAL MEDIA DOMINATION

Starting from the beginning, I must confess, I'm not great with social media. It's not where I focus my business. Yes, I do have followers on various platforms, and I've even gone viral on TikTok, but fundamentally, I'm a writer. I excel at writing books and email marketing.

If you're an expert at social media, you can drive ChatGPT even better than I can. Your unique and specialized knowledge will lead you to different results. I am interested in building some social channels around my ghostwriting business.

PLEASE DESIGN **a social media campaign for a celebrity ghostwriter that lives on a tropical island in the South Pacific. This mysterious writer only accepts three clients per year.**

CAMPAIGN TITLE: *The Island Scribe*[1]

1. Objective: *To create intrigue and allure around the ghostwriter* while positioning them as an exclusive service for potential high-profile clients.

2. Platform: Instagram, Twitter, LinkedIn, and a professional website/blog.

3. Content Strategy:

A. *Instagram:*

- High-quality Images: Showcase the tropical setting, desk with vintage typewriter, picturesque shots of the ghostwriter (without revealing their identity) writing at sunrise or sunset, snippets of manuscripts, coffee, and a serene beach background.

- Stories and Reels: Feature close-ups of draft pages blowing in the wind, typewriter keys being pressed, sunset timelapses with a caption about "writing into the night," and sounds of the ocean.

- IGTV Interviews: Interviews with the silhouetted figure of the ghostwriter, discussing their passion for writing, their process, the allure of anonymity, and subtle hints about past successful projects without revealing confidential information.

- Hashtags: #IslandScribe, #CelebGhostwriter, #TropicalTales, #ExclusiveInk

B. *Twitter:*

- Thought-Provoking Quotes: Share snippets of wisdom about writing, the power of storytelling, and mystery.

- Interaction: Engage with other authors, celebrities, and the writing community in a subtle and mysterious manner, making sure to maintain the allure.

- Teasers: Share the number of slots left for the year and occasional hints about new projects.

- Hashtags: #IslandScribe, #GhostWriting, #UnveilingStories, #CraftingLegends

C. *LinkedIn:*

- Professional Posts: Highlight the importance of ghostwriting, how it helps shape the narrative for many successful books and memoirs, the process, and confidentiality.

- Testimonials: Without revealing the identity of clients, share testimonials highlighting the quality and impact of work, professionalism, and satisfaction.

- Articles: Regular thought leadership articles about the industry, writing techniques, the ghostwriting process, etc.

D. Professional Website/Blog:

- Mysterious Aura: A clean, minimalist design with tropical elements and a hint of mystery. No clear images of the ghostwriter but artistic impressions of their silhouette or hand writing.

- The Journey: A page describing their journey, the passion for words, and the decision to become a ghostwriter.

- Services: Clear explanation of the services, the process of working together, and the fact that they only take three clients per year.

- Contact: An easy and straightforward way for potential clients to reach out, emphasizing confidentiality.

- Blog: Regular posts about the ghostwriting process, life on the island, the connection between nature and writing, and the power of storytelling.

4. Campaigns:

- Countdown Campaign: A yearly countdown for the next client slots to create a sense of urgency and exclusivity.

- The Mystery Unfolds: A bi-weekly hint dropped about the ghostwriter's identity – a favorite book, a literary quote, a unique writing habit. This maintains interest and engagement over a longer period.

- Island Inspirations: A showcase of how island life and nature inspire the ghostwriter's creativity and productivity.

- Client Success Stories: Without revealing the clients, share success stories of books that the ghostwriter has helped craft.

5. Engagement Strategy:

- Regular Interaction: Ensure the ghostwriter interacts with their followers, likes, and comments on their posts. This increases engagement and visibility.

- Q&A Sessions: Host monthly live Q&A sessions where the ghostwriter answers general questions about writing, storytelling, maintaining a balanced life on the island, etc.

6. Measurement:

- Monitor Growth: Regularly monitor follower growth, engagement rates, website traffic, and new inquiries.

7. Adjust Strategy:

- Based on the data from the measurement and monitoring, adjust the strategy where necessary. If a certain type of content is not engaging the audience or bringing in new inquiries, it might be necessary to rethink the content approach. For example:

- If long-form blog posts are not getting much engagement, you might want to switch to shorter, more frequent posts.

- If the 'Mystery Unfolds' campaign is not generating as much buzz as anticipated, consider adjusting the type of hints given or the frequency at which they're released.

- If the website isn't attracting many visitors, it might be necessary to look into SEO strategies or redesign aspects of the site.

Furthermore, maintain an eye on changes in social media trends and algorithms to ensure that the campaign stays relevant and effective. With such a unique and exclusive service, word-of-mouth recommendations are crucial, so it's vital to keep high levels of customer satisfaction and actively encourage clients to refer others.

Lastly, be prepared to experiment and try new tactics. Social media strategies should be flexible and adaptable. You might find that something unexpected, such as a virtual tour of the ghostwriter's island, becomes a major hit with the audience.

I'VE LET GO of many social media managers after investing tens of thousands of dollars on their services, without obtaining a plan as good as this one. While it might not be perfect, it's chock-full of ideas and is significantly better than what I'm currently doing.

With this broader strategy in place, I now need more specific mechanics. If I hire someone to manage my social media again, I want to provide them with a checklist so that, at the end of each week, I can assess whether they've fulfilled their duties.

. . .

Please create a 30-day social media calendar with posting times based on the best results for Twitter, TikTok, Facebook and Instagram.

Here's a general social media calendar based on typical best posting times. Remember that the best time to post can vary greatly depending on the specific audience, so it's crucial to monitor and adjust based on engagement data over time.

Posting times (EST):

- *Facebook: Wednesday, 11:00 AM - 1:00 PM*
- *Instagram: Tuesday, 2:00 PM - 3:00 PM*
- *Twitter: Wednesday and Friday, 9:00 AM*
- *TikTok: Monday - Thursday, 6:00 AM - 10:00 AM*

Note: The Island Scribe should post at least once per day on each platform, but the content can be similar across platforms, with adjustments made for each platform's unique features and audience.

30-Day Social Media Calendar:
Day 1:

- *Instagram/Facebook: Picture of a new manuscript with caption about the exciting journey of a new project (#IslandScribe #NewBeginnings)*
- *Twitter: A cryptic message about a new project starting today.*
- *TikTok: Quick video showing the preparation for a new project.*

Day 2:

- *Instagram: Story showcasing the sunrise with a quote about writing.*
- *Twitter: A thought-provoking quote about storytelling.*

- Facebook: A post about the process of ghostwriting.
- TikTok: A time-lapse of writing the first page.

Day 3 - Day 5:

- Repeat the content cycle, focusing on different aspects of the writing process and island life. Tease about the mysterious identity of the ghostwriter.[2]

Day 6:

- All platforms: Start the 'Countdown Campaign.' Announce that only two slots are left for the year, building a sense of urgency and exclusivity.

Day 7 - Day 29:

- Continue with the above strategies, introducing campaigns such as 'Island Inspirations' and 'The Mystery Unfolds.' Be sure to vary the content between writing insights, beautiful island aesthetics, and hints about the ghostwriter's identity.[3]

Day 10, 20, 30:

- All Platforms: Host Q&A sessions about writing, island life, and storytelling. Make sure to promote these sessions a few days in advance.

Day 30:

- All platforms: Reflect on the month's journey, sharing insights, favorite moments, and teasers for what's to come in the next month.

Throughout the month, make sure to engage with followers and other authors/celebrities on social media. Always strive to provide intriguing content that keeps followers eager for more.

Keep in mind that while this is a robust starting point, social media strategies should be flexible. Regularly monitor engagement and adjust your strategy based on what's resonating with your audience.

Consider how long it usually takes you to devise a social media strategy and campaign. If it's more than ten minutes, ChatGPT is going to significantly speed up your process.

It's important to note that it didn't give me a specific strategy for every single day. That's because ChatGPT was trying to provide a comprehensive answer in just one response. I'll show you various ways to break your prompts into smaller segments shortly. For now, I hope you're starting to feel excited and can see the potential possibilities.

---

1. I had to add all the letters and bullet points to organize this reply as it was too hard to follow in a book without that change.
2. ChatGPT forgot to make this a bullet point, but I added it back in for readability.
3. ChatGPT forgot the bullet point here too.

11

REVOLUTIONIZE PAID ADVERTISING

Paid ads can indeed be quite intimidating. I once invested ten thousand dollars with a company that assured me they were experts at running Facebook ads for authors. To be frank, I would have gotten better results if I had simply burned that money in my backyard.

So, rather than disposing of another ten grand, let's see what ChatGPT can generate for me. This is a continuation of the same conversation with ChatGPT, so it is already aware of my social media strategy.

PLEASE DESIGN A PAID ADVERTISING CAMPAIGN.

CAMPAIGN TITLE: The Secret Pen of the Pacific[1]
Objective: Generate leads and inquiries for the exclusive ghostwriting service by increasing brand awareness and driving traffic to the ghostwriter's website.

Platforms: Facebook, Instagram, LinkedIn, Google Ads, Twitter.

1. Google Ads:

Keywords: Celebrity Ghostwriter, Exclusive Ghostwriter, Ghostwriting Services, Professional Ghostwriter.

Ads: Utilize a blend of Search Ads to appear in results for relevant queries, and Display Ads with visually appealing images of the tropical island and a mysterious ghostwriter theme to capture attention on various websites.

2. Facebook & Instagram Ads:

Target Audience: Authors, publishing industry professionals, celebrities, public figures, and high-income individuals interested in writing, literature, and self-improvement.

Ad Content: Use high-quality visuals of the tropical setting, enticing captions highlighting the exclusivity and success of the service. Carousel Ads can be used to tell a story or highlight different aspects of the service.

Call to Action (CTA): "Learn More" button leading to the website, prompting users to inquire about the service.

3. LinkedIn Ads:

Target Audience: Same as Facebook but with a more professional slant. Also, target executive-level professionals who might be interested in writing a memoir or book.

Ad Content: Focus more on the professional side of the ghostwriting service, the success stories, and testimonials. Include images that convey the quality and exclusivity of the service.

CTA: "Contact Us" button leading to the website.

4. Twitter Ads:

Target Audience: Authors, publishing industry professionals, celebrities, public figures, and high-income individuals with interest in writing and literature.

Ad Content: Short, intriguing captions about the mysterious ghostwriter along with beautiful visuals of the tropical setting.

CTA: "Learn More" button leading to the website.

5. Campaign Strategy:

Launch: Start with a strong launch across all platforms simultaneously to create buzz.

Frequency: Run the ads consistently, but with a higher frequency leading up to the announcement of available slots.

Remarketing: Implement a remarketing strategy to show ads to users who have visited the website but didn't contact or leave an inquiry.

6. Measurement & Adjustment:

Track Performance: Regularly monitor the performance of the ads, tracking metrics like click-through rates, conversion rates, and cost per acquisition.

Optimize Ads: Based on performance, adjust the ads as needed. This could mean changing the visuals, tweaking the copy, adjusting the target audience, or shifting budget between platforms.

7. Budget:

Determine an overall budget for the campaign and allocate it among the platforms based on their potential to reach the target audience. Be prepared to adjust this allocation based on the performance of the ads on each platform.

THESE ARE PRETTY GREAT IDEAS, and with subsequent prompts, you can start to fine-tune the perfect responses. But even as a starting point, for a client who wants some social media ad ideas, this could be invaluable. We're all familiar with movie scenes where the ad executive has to generate an idea for a client in just five minutes and they've fallen asleep without a single idea. With ChatGPT, you won't have that problem.

This strategy is genuinely impressive. We don't just have a plan; we have an entire script. ChatGPT has the ability to move beyond your existing knowledge and comfort zones.

PLEASE DESIGN A RADIO ADVERTISING CAMPAIGN.

CAMPAIGN TITLE: *"Whispers from the Island Scribe"*

Objective: Increase awareness and intrigue about the celebrity ghostwriter, driving potential clients to the website to learn more and apply for a slot.

Platforms: National and regional radio stations with a listener demographic that matches the ghostwriter's target client base – high-income individuals, celebrities, authors, and people with interesting stories to tell. Satellite and internet radio stations should also be considered due to their wide reach and often specialized audience.

Script:

[Sound of the ocean waves, seagulls, and a typewriter in the background]

Narrator (in a mysterious and engaging voice): "In the heart of the South Pacific, amidst the whispering waves and the rustling palm trees, tales of fame and fortune, triumph and tribulation are woven. Can you hear it? (pause) The clatter of the typewriter... the turn of the page... This is the sound of stories coming to life."

[Pause, the sound of a typewriter carriage returning]

Narrator: "The Island Scribe, an exclusive ghostwriter, ensconced in the tranquility of a tropical paradise, dedicates their craft to a chosen few. Only three clients per year have the privilege to narrate their tale, to have their experiences transformed into compelling narratives by the expert hand of The Island Scribe."

[Pause, a soft island tune plays in the background]

Narrator: "Do you have a story that deserves to be told? Do you yearn for your voice to be heard, your tale to echo throughout the world? Are you one of the chosen three? The Island Scribe awaits your call."

[Sound of a seashell being put to the ear, the ocean sound magnifies]

Narrator: "Listen to the whispering waves. They speak of stories untold, secrets unfurled. Your story could be next."

[Pause, the island tune comes back]

Narrator: "Visit IslandScribe.com to learn more. The Island Scribe, your story, their words."

[End with the sound of the ocean waves and a typewriter]

Campaign Strategy:

- *Time Slots: Run the ads during both peak listening hours (morning and evening commute times) and late at night to create an ambiance and sense of mystery.*
- *Frequency: Start the campaign at least two months before the slots open up. The frequency should increase as the announcement date approaches.*
- *Radio Shows: Sponsor radio shows that cater to your target audience. This could be celebrity talk shows, author interviews, or programs focused on personal success stories.*
- *Live Readings: Have popular radio hosts do live readings of the ad during their shows to add a personal touch and reach a wider audience.*

Measurement and Adjustment:

- *Track Performance: Monitor website traffic and inquiries before and after the ad is aired to measure the effectiveness of the campaign.*
- *Feedback: Use listener feedback and engagement to adjust the campaign as needed. For example, if listeners are responding well to the mystery and intrigue, consider creating additional ads that play up this aspect.*
- *Optimize: Optimize the campaign based on results. If a particular radio station or time slot is performing well, consider increasing the frequency of ads in that slot or on that station.*

THIS IS A CRAZY GOOD STRATEGY. Not only do we have a plan, we have an entire script. ChatGPT can go outside your existing knowledge and comfort zones.

Let's say you're not a fan of that commercial. No problem—you can ask it to write another and another until you land on one you like. And the best part? It's fast.

PLEASE DESIGN A TELEVISION ADVERTISING CAMPAIGN.

CAMPAIGN TITLE: "INK FROM THE ISLAND"

Objective: To heighten intrigue and awareness around the celebrity ghostwriter, while driving potential clients to learn more and apply for an exclusive slot.

Platforms: Local and national TV networks during peak hours and during shows that appeal to the ghostwriter's target audience: authors, celebrities, business leaders, high-income individuals, and individuals with compelling stories.

Ad Description:

The ad opens with an aerial shot of a picturesque tropical island in the South Pacific. There's a lone beach house nestled amidst lush greenery, with a view of the endless ocean.

Cut to a vintage typewriter on a desk, with an unseen person typing. The viewer only catches glimpses of the ghostwriter: a silhouette against the sunset, a hand crafting eloquent sentences, a pair of glasses next to a cup of coffee.

Interspersed with these scenes are quick shots of best-selling book covers, filled theaters, standing ovations, and paparazzi flashes, hinting at the high-profile clients the ghostwriter has worked with. Each shot is followed by a glimpse of the tropical paradise, conveying the serenity that surrounds the writing process.

Narrator (Voice-over with a mysterious, intriguing tone): "Hidden away on a remote island in the South Pacific, one of the world's most sought-after storytellers crafts tales that capture the heart and inspire the mind. The Island Scribe, an exclusive ghostwriter, takes on just three clients a year, turning their stories into works of art."

Final shot of the sunset with the typewriter in silhouette and a manuscript with the first few words visible: "The Journey Begins..."

Narrator: *"Are you ready to tell your story? Visit IslandScribe.com to learn more. The Island Scribe...your story, their words."*

The screen fades to black with the website and a call to action: "Are you one of the chosen three?"

Campaign Strategy:

- *Time Slots: Run the ads during prime time and popular shows to reach a broad audience. Also, consider late-night slots for an added sense of intrigue and mystery.*
- *Special Events: Advertise during special events, award shows, literary programs, and movie premieres to reach a highly engaged audience.*
- *Teaser Campaign: Before the main campaign launch, air a few "coming soon" teaser ads to generate buzz.*
- *Sponsorships: Consider sponsoring relevant TV programs, like author interviews, celebrity talk shows, or book review segments, to reach a targeted audience.*

Measurement and Adjustment:

- *Track Performance: Monitor website traffic and inquiries before and after the ad is aired to gauge the effectiveness of the campaign.*
- *Audience Response: Use audience feedback and engagement to adjust the campaign as necessary. If viewers respond particularly well to the mystery and intrigue, consider creating additional ads that further emphasize these elements.*
- *Optimize: Optimize the campaign based on results. If a particular TV station or time slot is performing well, consider increasing the frequency of ads in that slot or on that station.*

In less than ten minutes, we've created an entire marketing blitz plan: social media, radio, and television. Everyone will know my name. Reflect for a moment on how long it would have taken you to come up with ideas like these in the past. The difference is striking.

---

1. Notice that it even comes up with cool names for each campaign.

12

VIRTUAL PERSONAL TRAINER THAT NEVER MAKES YOU FEEL GUILTY

I'm on a strict diet. My personal trainer lives in my house, and every morning, my alarm rings at 5:45 AM, and we work out. I'm fortunate to have a small gym right next to my bedroom. Celebrities make weight loss seem easy, but I know it's tough. I've dropped from 127kg to 97kg. If you're not sure what that translates to in pounds, ask ChatGPT.

I'm on the paleo diet and follow a 16:8 eating schedule. This means I avoid processed foods or carbs like rice and bread, which cause me to gain weight quickly.

Living on a tropical island restricts my access to a variety of foods. Fresh berries are always hard to come by. Order a coconut shake here, and it's freshly made from a coconut. Order a blueberry shake, and they whip out a box of powdered mix. Yuck. I fell for that trick once.

Now, let's get ChatGPT to help me stay on track. But remember, I don't want a one-size-fits-all plan. I want a strategy as customized to my body as possible, so I'm going to let ChatGPT lead the conversation and tell me what it needs.

. . .

What information do you need to plan a diet and meal plan for me?

To create a personalized diet and meal plan, I would need the following information:

Goals: Are you looking to lose weight, gain weight, maintain weight, or improve overall health? Your dietary needs will change depending on your specific goals.

Dietary Restrictions: Do you have any allergies, intolerances, or specific dietary preferences such as vegetarian, vegan, gluten-free, etc?

Health Conditions: Do you have any specific health conditions that may influence your diet, like diabetes, heart disease, high blood pressure, or others?

Physical Activity Level: Are you sedentary, moderately active, or highly active? Your caloric intake and the balance of macronutrients you need will be influenced by your activity level.

Age, Sex, Height, and Weight: These factors influence your basal metabolic rate, which is the number of calories you burn at rest. This information will help calculate your daily caloric needs.

Food Preferences: Are there any foods you particularly like or dislike? This can help make the plan more enjoyable and sustainable for you.

Daily Schedule/ Lifestyle: Are you often on the go, do you have time to cook, or do you prefer meal prep? Understanding your lifestyle can help design a meal plan that fits your daily routine.

Current Diet: Understanding what you're currently eating can provide a baseline to adjust from and can highlight areas for potential improvement.

Please note that while I can help you design a general meal plan based on this information, I'm an AI and don't have medical training. It's always a good idea to discuss any significant changes in your diet or exercise routine with a healthcare professional.

Once you have provided the necessary information, I can help outline a meal plan that suits your preferences and lifestyle.

. . .

I will feed ChatGPT the same information I just gave you. I could get it to ask me questions one by one, but I know the answers already.

I am on the Paleo diet and the 16:8. My feeding window is from 8am to 4pm. I usually workout at 6am 4-5 times per week for 20-40 minutes. I'm a 42 year old man who currently weights 97.8kg. My peak weight was 127kg. I'm looking to drop another 17kg. I live on a remote island so have limited access to ingredients, especially fruits and vegetables. Please provide a list of ingredients for me before building the meal plan, so that I can let you know which ingredients I don't have access to.

Absolutely, I'll start with a list of basic ingredients typically found in a Paleo diet and often used in meal planning. Please review it and let me know which items are not available to you, and we can proceed from there.

Proteins:
Chicken
Turkey
Beef
Pork
Lamb
Fish (Salmon, Tuna, Mackerel)
Seafood (Shrimp, Lobster, Clams)
Eggs

Vegetables:
Spinach
Kale
Lettuce
Broccoli
Cauliflower

Bell Peppers

Tomatoes

Zucchini

Cucumbers

Carrots

Squash

Asparagus

Brussels sprouts

Onion

Garlic

Fruits:

Apples

Bananas

Berries (Strawberries, Blueberries, Raspberries)

Oranges

Lemons

Avocados

Peaches

Plums

Pears

Healthy Fats:

Avocado

Nuts (Almonds, Walnuts, Macadamia)

Seeds (Chia seeds, Flax seeds, Pumpkin seeds)

Coconut oil

Olive oil

Other:

Almond flour

Coconut flour

Honey

Maple Syrup

Vinegar

Herbs and Spices (Basil, Oregano, Rosemary, Thyme, Cumin, Turmeric, Cinnamon etc.)

Salt and Pepper

Please note that some of these ingredients might not be traditionally considered Paleo, like honey and maple syrup, but are often included in Paleo diets in moderation. Once you've reviewed this list, I can provide a meal plan tailored to your dietary needs and available ingredients.

I'm unsure about which foods on my list are not compliant with the Paleo diet. Rather than getting lost in that complexity, I'll provide ChatGPT with the necessary information.

Keep in mind, if you have easy access to any food, you might not need this step. In the past, ChatGPT has suggested recipes with ingredients I can't find locally.

This next question is in the same vein as the first one. I want ChatGPT to gather the necessary information before it suggests a bunch of recipes I would love to try but can't prepare.

I don't have access to the following ingredients: Pears Plums Peaches Berries Brussels sprouts Squash Zucchini Kale Lamb. I don't eat fish.

Thank you for the information. I'll create a meal plan for you based on the Paleo diet using the ingredients available to you, and considering your 16:8 intermittent fasting schedule with an eating window from 8 AM to 4 PM.

Here's a five-day sample meal plan. Each day is designed to be high in protein and low in carbs, and includes a balance of fruits and vegetables.

Day 1:

8:00 AM: Scrambled eggs with spinach and onions, seasoned with herbs of your choice (basil, oregano, etc.). Have an apple on the side.

12:00 PM: Grilled chicken salad with lettuce, tomatoes, bell peppers, and a dressing made of olive oil, lemon juice, salt, and pepper.

3:30 PM: Almonds and a banana for a snack.

THE RESPONSE CONTINUED with five more days of meal suggestions, but that's not particularly relevant. This isn't how I usually eat. For a truly personalized meal plan, I'd need to specify that I usually enjoy a vegan protein shake at noon and have my main meal at 3 PM.

I should have included that detail in the initial prompt, but even so, this is a pretty solid meal plan. Adhering to a specific diet can make it tricky to find appealing recipes or create your own meal plans. With a system like this, you can remove meal planning from your weekly tasks, freeing up more time for things you enjoy.

With diet sorted, what about exercise?

For this task, I could have returned to the approach of asking ChatGPT what information it needs to design a plan, but I want to show a different technique. In the past, I've paid an online trainer three hundred dollars a month to create a workout plan based on my available equipment and personal requirements. Now, ChatGPT can accomplish the same task in a matter of minutes.

PLEASE CREATE AN EXERCISE PLAN. **I have the following equipment: kettle bells, dumbbells, barbell, elastic bands, and an exercise mat.**

ABSOLUTELY, with the equipment you have at hand, you can perform a wide range of exercises. Given that you're currently working out 4-5 times a week for 20-40 minutes, I'll build an exercise plan around that.

Remember, before starting any new exercise regimen, it's important to consult with a healthcare or fitness professional. Make sure to warm up before starting your workout and cool down afterward.

Here's a sample 5-day exercise plan for you:

Day 1: Full Body Workout

Kettlebell Swings: 3 sets of 12 reps
Dumbbell Deadlifts: 3 sets of 10 reps
Push-ups: 3 sets of 15 reps
Goblet Squats (using Kettlebell or Dumbbell): 3 sets of 10 reps
Bent Over Rows (with Dumbbells): 3 sets of 10 reps each side
Planks: 3 sets of 30-60 seconds

While I won't bore you with my complete workout plan, you can see how easily ChatGPT can craft one for you. It's also possible to customize the workout to avoid exercises you dislike or that could exacerbate an injury. By informing ChatGPT about any injuries, you give it more guidance.

Creating a meal and workout plan can be done more swiftly than doing it alone or less expensively than hiring a professional. And if you are a professional, I want you to consider how you can utilize ChatGPT to expand your business. Could you better assist your clients with this tool? Could you support more clients with this tool aiding in your planning?

13

YOUR DREAM APP WITHOUT LEARNING TO CODE

I don't know how to code. My knowledge of HTML is just enough to allow me to copy and paste a link or make minor tweaks. Typically, when I require a piece of software, I have to bring in a professional. The issue here is that I don't really know how long a task should take or what it should cost, aside from comparing prices quoted by different people.

In the past, I've been quoted figures as diverse as $300 and $2000 for the exact same job, and I'm at a loss as to which estimate is accurate. Is the lower quote an underestimation because the individual isn't aware of the work involved, or is the higher one an overcharge because they think I'm an easy mark?

This process can be stressful, and I've sunk thousands of dollars into apps and software that I've never used. Even when I do have a piece of software, it inevitably stops working at some point, and I need to find another developer to rectify the issue.

The cycle goes on.

Then I discovered that ChatGPT could write code in multiple languages.

. . .

What coding languages do you know?

1. *Python*
2. *Java*
3. *JavaScript*
4. *C*
5. *C++*
6. *C#*
7. *Ruby*
8. *Swift*
9. *Kotlin*
10. *TypeScript*
11. *Go*
12. *Rust*
13. *PHP*
14. *Perl*
15. *MATLAB*
16. *R*
17. *Julia*
18. *Shell Scripting (like Bash)*
19. *SQL*
20. *HTML/CSS*

The best way to determine if ChatGPT can assist you is to ask[1]. Having an AI aid in your coding efforts can be fantastic, just ensure to test the code yourself before deploying it.

iframe

I encountered an issue when I tried to redirect to an affiliate link during a promotion. Typically, I can create a redirect from my website to transform unattractive affiliate links into appealing ones, such as ServeNoMaster.com/twf. This time, however, I wanted to change the link in my TikTok bio to point to the promotion.

The issue was that TikTok uses a limited browser and the link was causing crashes. The solution was to create a page on my website that embedded the other website. I understand that this might sound a little complicated. In simple terms, it means I'm displaying another website within my own website.

With prior experience under my belt, I knew what was needed and asked ChatGPT to create the webpage for me.

CREATE the html code for a single page website that embeds the website https://clk2ly.com/ea15a3da in a mobile responsive iframe

SURE, here's an example HTML code that embeds https://clk2ly.com/ea15a3da in a mobile responsive iframe:

php
Copy code
<!DOCTYPE html>
<html>
<head>
<title>Embedded Website</title>
<meta name="viewport" content="width=device-width, initial-scale=1.0">
<style>
iframe {
display: block;
height: 100vh;
width: 100%;
border: none;
}
</style>

```
</head>
<body>
<iframe src="https://clk2ly.com/ea15a3da"></iframe>
</body>
</html>
```

In this code, we've added a meta tag with the viewport attribute to ensure the webpage is mobile responsive. We've also added some CSS styling to make the iframe take up the entire width and height of the viewport without any borders.

THIS IS a straightforward piece of code that I couldn't have come up with on my own. An expert could do it with software in about 10 minutes, but ChatGPT did it in 1 minute. That's a 90% time-saving on a minor task.

ChatGPT is capable of managing simple and repetitive coding tasks for you. If I hadn't known that I needed to embed the link, I could have presented my problem to ChatGPT to find a solution. Remember, ChatGPT will always let you know what information it needs.

Coloring Books

If coding isn't your thing, this section might be a bit too detailed for you. To make it more digestible, I'm not going to include all the code from ChatGPT here. You can find that on my website at ServeNoMaster.com/ai.

In this instance, I needed help with a significant problem. Formatting coloring books is a tedious and lengthy process. Even the most efficient method takes an hour, as each image has to be manually formatted into a page. I came up with my own approach for this process and taught it in my Coloring Book Madness course a few years back. Prior to that, formatting a coloring book could easily take four hours.

Spending an hour dragging and dropping images into a page and resizing them to the perfect dimensions is not scalable. It's a mind-numbing, repetitive task which suggests there should be a quicker way. I've tried every book formatting software on the market, but none are tailored for coloring books.

I even purchased a new software for $150, only to find that it's designed for books like this one, not coloring books. The back-and-forth with their customer support was ongoing when it occurred to me that I could ask ChatGPT. While I had tried with ChatGPT-3.5 and couldn't get the code to function properly, ChatGPT-4 showed significant improvements in coding capabilities. This is another reason why the upgrade to ChatGPT Plus is worthwhile for me.

Creating the right prompt took a few attempts and some research. I've included it here, not because it's the perfect one, but to show you the process I went through to get there.

I made an error with the page dimensions in the prompt, which was a case of garbage in, garbage out until I realized I was the one making the mistake, not ChatGPT. My initial idea was to have ChatGPT convert an image to a PDF with a white border. Given that I have Python version 3 on my system, I guided it to an input folder full of images and an output folder where it would place the PDF versions.

PLEASE CREATE a python code that will do the following: Please include all necessary code to copy and paste into a working .py Python3 file. When run the program will ask me for an input file and an output folder. It will take an image file and convert it to a pdf that is 8.5x11 inches at 300DPI, with .375 inches border on the left and .25 inches on the top, right and bottom sides of the page. The image will be stretched or shrunk to fit into the available space on the page. The output PDF will be added the folder selected.

. . .

SURE! *Here's a Python3 code that does what you described.*

Before using this code, please make sure to install the necessary libraries by running the following command in your terminal:

pip install Pillow reportlab

Then you can copy and paste the following code into a .py file and run it:

from PIL import Image

from reportlab.pdfgen import canvas

import os

def create_pdf(input_file, output_folder):

 # Open the input image file

img = Image.open(input_file)

 # Define the page size and margins for the output PDF

PAGE_WIDTH = 8.5 * 72 # 8.5 inches in points

PAGE_HEIGHT = 11 * 72 # 11 inches in points

LEFT_MARGIN = 0.375 * 72 # 0.375 inches in points

TOP_MARGIN = 0.25 * 72 # 0.25 inches in points

RIGHT_MARGIN = 0.25 * 72 # 0.25 inches in points

BOTTOM_MARGIN = 0.25 * 72 # 0.25 inches in points

When you run this program, it will ask you to provide the path to the input image file and the path to the output folder. Once you enter those paths, the program will create a PDF file with the same name as the input file in the output folder.

Note that this code assumes that the input file is in a format that Pillow can open. If you want to support other formats, you may need to add some additional code to check the file extension and convert the file if necessary.

I'VE OMITTED some of the code to avoid distractions. The important part here is the code relating to margins. The code was converting them by the number 72. Knowing that computer images are 72 DPI, but printed images need to be 300 DPI, this discrepancy signaled something was wrong.

Had I not noticed that, I would've found out when I tried to print a page. As this is for a physical coloring book, I would've detected the issue later on in the process had I overlooked it here. I wasn't entirely sure I was correct, so I asked a question.

Is this at 72 dpi? I need 300 dpi.

I apologize for the mistake. Yes, the code I provided was using 72 dpi as the default resolution for the PDF file. Here's an updated version of the code that uses 300 dpi instead:

In this updated version of the code, the resolution of the PDF file is set to 300 dpi using the setResolution() method of the canvas object. The other dimensions and margins are also adjusted to match the 300 dpi resolution.

I omitted the code as it's not important right now. ChatGPT made an error that wasn't due to me. I specified 300DPI in the original prompt, but it still used 72DPI. This exemplifies why you can't completely rely on AI to replace human oversight. AI functions best when guided by a human. You need to ensure that all the requirements you asked for are included in the code, and it works as you intended.

I noticed that the code at the top didn't include headers like the ones in previous codes provided by ChatGPT. Until I asked, I didn't know what these codes at the top of the page were for or even what they were called.

Do I need anything at the top of the document, like this? #!/usr/bin/env python3

· · ·

INCLUDING THE SHEBANG LINE *#!/usr/bin/env python3 at the top of a Python script is a common practice, but it's not strictly necessary.*

The shebang line is used to tell the operating system which interpreter to use to execute the script. If you're running the script from the command line, the shebang line can be helpful because it allows you to execute the script by simply typing ./script.py instead of python3 script.py. However, if you're running the script from an IDE or text editor, the shebang line is not typically used.

I use my Mac Terminal to run Python, which is a text editor, so I guess I don't need the shebang in my code file. I'm just correcting errors by observing that sometimes it's included in ChatGPT's code and sometimes it isn't. I have a hunch that it might condense some code to fit a complete answer into a single reply.

With my final code at hand, I can execute the code on my computer. In another conversation, I had asked ChatGPT how to install Python and make it functional, so I at least knew how to initiate the code. But then, I hit a wall. I got a long error message and was clueless about what it meant until ChatGPT clarified.

What's great is that I can copy and paste an error report into ChatGPT and get an explanation. I want to emphasize this because it extends beyond just coding. How often have you received an error on your computer and had no clue what it meant? You can input ANY error code into ChatGPT, and it will explain what it signifies and how to rectify it. This feature is going to spare me countless tech support emails in the future.

FILE **"/USERS/JONATHANGREEN/DOCUMENTS/SINGLE_PDF.PY"**, line 4, in <module>
    from reportlab.pdfgen import canvas
    ModuleNotFoundError: No module named 'reportlab'

. . .

It looks like you're seeing a ModuleNotFoundError for the reportlab module. This error occurs when Python is unable to find the specified module, which in this case is reportlab.

To resolve this error, you'll need to install the reportlab module using pip. You can do this by running the following command in your terminal:

pip install reportlab

This will download and install the reportlab module and its dependencies.

Once the module is installed, you should be able to run your Python script without seeing the ModuleNotFoundError for reportlab.

ChatGPT provided the best explanation for a coding issue I've ever encountered. It explained the problem, provided me with a straightforward copy-and-paste solution, and then assured me that my problem was solved. For the first time in my life, I was debugging code, and I had no clue what any of it meant. I was just the bridge between my terminal and ChatGPT.

After resolving one problem, I ran into another. I simply copied and pasted the error message, not knowing what it meant. I wasn't even sure if I pasted too large a snippet of the error.

Traceback (most recent call last):
    File "/Users/jonathangreen/Documents/single_pdf.py", line 45, in <module>
    create_pdf(input_file, output_folder)
    File "/Users/jonathangreen/Documents/single_pdf.py", line 35, in create_pdf
    c.setResolution(300)
    AttributeError: 'Canvas' object has no attribute 'setResolution'

. . .

I APOLOGIZE FOR THE CONFUSION. It looks like the setResolution() method is not available in the Canvas object in the reportlab library.

Instead, you can set the resolution of the PDF by passing the resolution parameter to the canvas.Canvas() constructor, like this:

I hope this helps!

I'VE OMITTED THE CODE, but you can see that ChatGPT immediately recognized the issue and solved this problem for me. It excels at error correction and in clarifying what an error means. Each time I fixed an error, it seemed that another one cropped up. If I were doing this without ChatGPT, I would have given up by now.

FILE "/USERS/JONATHANGREEN/DOCUMENTS/SINGLE_PDF1.PY", line 45, in <module>
    create_pdf(input_file, output_folder)
    File "/Users/jonathangreen/Documents/single_pdf1.py", line 32, in create_pdf
    c = canvas.Canvas(output_file, pagesize=(PAGE_WIDTH, PAGE_HEIGHT), resolution=300)
    TypeError: Canvas.__init__() got an unexpected keyword argument 'resolution'

I APOLOGIZE FOR THE CONFUSION. It looks like the Canvas object in the reportlab library does not have a resolution parameter for setting the DPI.

To set the DPI of the PDF, you can adjust the dimensions of the Canvas object to match the desired DPI. Here's an updated version of the create_pdf() function that sets the DPI to 300:

In this updated version, the Canvas object is created with dimensions that match the desired DPI (e.g. new_width and new_height). The dimensions are calculated by scaling the image dimensions by the ratio of 300 DPI to 72 DPI.

I hope this helps!

I'VE REMOVED the code again as I have created a more recent version which you can access for free on my website. The final version of the program converts all the pages into a single PDF with a blank page in between. This generates an eighty-page PDF. When printed, each coloring page will have a blank back, allowing you to display your work without losing another image. This is a crucial feature for adult coloring book users.

In the initial version of the code, I wasn't ambitious enough. What I want you to learn from this section is that ChatGPT can write code and correct errors as you observe its workings. The entire process took me about twenty minutes, with no coding knowledge. I had to ask ChatGPT what Python was and if it was on my computer when I first had this idea and it suggested Python as the coding language.

Now I have a piece of software that formats my coloring books in about four minutes, and it's entirely automated. I press one button, select my input and output folders, and I get a formatted coloring book. This single piece of software saves me an hour each time I use it.

BMI Calculator

Creating a tool that people find useful is a fantastic way to attract visitors to your website. I decided to test my coding skills and see if I could use ChatGPT to build such a tool for my site. I started with a simple idea - a calculator. But, I realized the challenge wasn't in what ChatGPT could do, it was in pushing my own imagination.

Instead of using Python again, I thought to ask ChatGPT. I wasn't even sure if Python could be used on the Internet or just on my computer. I can ask ChatGPT after I finish this chapter.

. . .

I want to create a web app, Body Mass Index Calculator. I will post this on my website, what is the best programming language to use?

To create a Body Mass Index (BMI) calculator web app, it's best to use a combination of HTML, CSS, and JavaScript. These are the core technologies for building web applications and will allow you to create a responsive, interactive, and user-friendly BMI calculator.

HTML (Hypertext Markup Language): This is the backbone of your web app, which defines the structure and layout of your calculator. You'll create the input fields for the user's height and weight and a button to trigger the calculation.

CSS (Cascading Style Sheets): This is used to style your web app, making it visually appealing and easy to use. You can control the layout, colors, and typography to ensure the calculator fits well with the overall design of your website.

JavaScript: This is the programming language that allows you to add interactivity and perform the actual BMI calculation. When a user enters their height and weight and clicks the "Calculate" button, JavaScript will be used to process the input, perform the calculation, and display the result on the webpage.

Using these three technologies together will enable you to create a fully functioning, visually appealing BMI calculator that can be easily embedded into your website. If you are already using a frontend framework like React, Angular, or Vue.js, you can also create a BMI calculator component within that framework.

I can't say I'm familiar with these three frontend frameworks. In fact, I'm not sure what that entails. I can recognize HTML, Javascript, and CSS, though. To my mind, CSS seems like a nightmare to decode. I can scan a page of HTML and identify the elements I need to reproduce, but with CSS, I'm clueless. Every time I've tried tinkering with a CSS page, I ended up needing to hire someone to undo my havoc.

If you asked me to construct a BMI Calculator, I'd be ready to abandon the project as soon as you mentioned the requirement for CSS. And as for Javascript? It's so complex, I wouldn't even attempt to open a Javascript file. We're sailing into unfamiliar waters here.

Next, I aim to formulate a plan. How can I check if the final app is correct if I lack a framework? I'm expecting ChatGPT to define a goal I can measure the final app against.

I'M NOT USING one of those frameworks, so let's go with HTML, CSS and JavaScript. What features and inputs does the BMI calculator need? Let's plan the app in detail before we create it.

BEFORE CREATING THE BMI CALCULATOR, it's important to plan its features and inputs. Here's a detailed list of what your BMI calculator should include:

1. Inputs:

a. Weight: An input field for the user to enter their weight. You should allow users to choose between different weight units like pounds (lbs) and kilograms (kg).

b. Height: Two input fields for height: one for feet and another for inches if using the Imperial system, or a single input field for centimeters if using the Metric system. Similar to the weight input, you should allow users to choose between different height units like feet/inches and centimeters.

2. Buttons:

a. Calculate: A button that triggers the BMI calculation when clicked.

b. Clear: A button to clear the input fields, allowing users to reset the calculator and enter new values.

3. Outputs:

a. BMI Value: Display the calculated BMI value.

b. BMI Category: Display the BMI category based on the calculated BMI value (e.g., underweight, normal weight, overweight, or obese).

Additional features:

a. Responsive design: Ensure the calculator is visually appealing and usable on various devices, such as desktops, tablets, and mobile phones.

b. Input validation: Check that the user inputs are valid (e.g., not empty, within a reasonable range) before performing the calculation.

c. Error messages: Display appropriate error messages when the input is invalid or incomplete.

d. Tooltips or help text: Optionally, you can provide tooltips or help text to guide users on how to properly use the calculator.

Once you've planned the features and inputs for your BMI calculator, you can start implementing it using HTML, CSS, and JavaScript. Start by creating the structure and layout with HTML, then style the calculator with CSS, and finally, add interactivity and functionality using JavaScript.

ChatGPT not only validates my well-crafted prompt but also devises a plan far beyond anything I could have come up with. This is someone who understands project planning way better than I do.

With a solid plan in hand, it's time to start coding. I understand it's going to require three programming languages, but I'm unsure of what belongs where.

This is perfect. **Let's start programming our calculator. Which language should we start with? Please begin creating the code.**

Let's start with the HTML structure for the BMI calculator. I'll provide you with a basic structure, which you can later customize and style using CSS. After that, we'll move on to implementing the JavaScript functionality.

Here's the HTML code for the BMI calculator:

This HTML code sets up the structure for the BMI calculator, including input fields for weight and height, dropdowns to select units, and areas to display the result.

Next, you can add your CSS code to style the calculator. You can either create a separate CSS file and link it in the <head> section or use the <style> tag within the <head> section to write your CSS directly in the HTML file.

After styling the calculator, you'll move on to implementing the JavaScript functionality. You can create a separate JavaScript file and link it at the bottom of the <body> section or use the <script> tag within the <body> section to write your JavaScript directly in the HTML file.

IN THE ABSENCE of the actual code to distract us, we can observe that ChatGPT has initiated with HTML, adhering to its action plan from the previous response. It presents me with a variety of CSS options, which I overlook, as I'm clueless about which might be superior. It's crucial to remember that not every prompt needs to be a masterpiece. ChatGPT is in the midst of a process; I'm merely authorizing it to proceed to the next step.

GREAT. LET'S create the css code now.

HERE'S some basic CSS code to style the BMI calculator. You can customize it to match your website's design or make any other adjustments as needed.

Create a new CSS file, e.g., bmi-calculator.css, and add the following code:

Now, link the CSS file in the <head> section of your HTML file, like this:

<link rel="stylesheet" href="bmi-calculator.css">

With this CSS code, your BMI calculator should have a clean and simple design. You can further customize the styles to fit the look and feel of your website. Once you're satisfied with the design, you can move on to implementing the JavaScript functionality for the calculator.

CHATGPT DIDN'T JUST GENERATE the code for me; it also provided clear instructions for implementation. All that remains is the third step. I don't want to compel ChatGPT to skip any steps, so my next prompt comes in the form of a question.

WE HAVE our html and our css, now it's time for the javascript?

YES, now it's time to add the JavaScript functionality to your BMI calculator. Create a new JavaScript file, e.g., bmi-calculator.js, and add the following code:

Now, link the JavaScript file at the bottom of the <body> section of your HTML file, like this:

<script src="bmi-calculator.js"></script>

This JavaScript code adds functionality to the BMI calculator, including:

1. *The **calculateBMI** function, which calculates the BMI based on the weight, weight unit, height, and height unit.*
2. *The **getBMICategory** function, which returns the BMI category based on the calculated BMI value.*
3. *Event listeners for the "Calculate" and "Clear" buttons, which perform the BMI calculation and clear the input fields, respectively.*

4. *An event listener for the height unit dropdown, which toggles the visibility of the feet and inches input fields when the "Feet and inches" option is selected.*

With this JavaScript code, your BMI calculator should be fully functional and ready for use on your website.

Remarkably, the whole process, including my parts, took less than ten minutes. I ran the code in my browser, and it functioned flawlessly on the first try. This is a tremendous victory, showcasing ChatGPT's ability to create functional tools that can significantly enhance our capabilities.

I have a link to the calculator on the AI page of my website at ServeNoMaster.com/ai.

I've since created several custom software pieces with ChatGPT's assistance, thereby expanding my skills. Not only can I code faster, but I can also develop things that were previously beyond my reach. And if you're a programmer, expect this tool to turbocharge your productivity even more than it has mine.

---

1. The number of languages ChatGPT knows has changed since the first time I asked it, so I recommend checking to see if new languages have been added.

14

AUTOMATED IDEA MACHINE

The original example in this chapter was related to an email service project I was handling. However, considering it might be overly technical and dull for many, I've created a more relatable demo.

Often, I come up with ideas and find myself uncertain if they've already been thought of or if they're impractical for some reason. There's a need for a mechanism to evolve these initial ideas into something more concrete.

When I'm designing a sales page or presentation, it's crucial to address the potential customer's issue and demonstrate how my product serves as the solution. After all, you can't solve a problem that the customer doesn't perceive.

A few years ago, an author I respect for his writing skills messaged me about his new book on how to quit vaping. It came as a surprise. We were in the late 2010s, and I had the impression that most people were transitioning from smoking to vaping.

I promptly questioned him about his research. How did he establish that people wanted to quit vaping? What was the size of his audience?

I was genuinely impressed that he'd identified a new niche unknown to me. As someone who'd penned a book on quitting smoking after a terrifying episode of coughing up blood in front of my daughter, his topic resonated.

That was, until he responded.

"I didn't do any research. The idea just came to me."

As you might have guessed, the book didn't succeed. Of course, that doesn't necessarily mean he was off the mark. He could be ahead of his time, and perhaps in thirty years, we'll find that vaping is harmful, and his book will gain relevance.

However, for now, the book doesn't sell because it doesn't address an existing problem.

Having authored over three hundred bestsellers in the past decade, I can't recall the challenges I faced with the first one. Let's see what ChatGPT has to say.

WHAT ARE the ten biggest challenges someone faces when trying to write their first non-fiction book?

WRITING A NON-FICTION BOOK, *particularly for the first time, can be a rewarding yet challenging task. The following are ten common challenges that aspiring authors often face:*

Topic Selection: *Picking the right subject can be a significant challenge. The topic needs to be engaging, relevant, and broad enough to create an entire book, yet narrow enough to provide a detailed and in-depth view.*

Research: *Extensive research is often necessary when writing non-fiction. Gathering accurate and reliable information can be time-consuming and sometimes challenging.*

Organization: *Structuring a non-fiction book is essential. The author must find a way to present their ideas logically and coherently, which can be difficult especially with complex topics.*

Finding a Unique Angle: Non-fiction is often about providing new insights or perspectives on a topic. Finding a unique angle can be challenging but is crucial to making the book stand out.

Audience Understanding: The writer must have a clear understanding of who their audience is. They need to write in a way that resonates with them, which requires understanding their interests, knowledge level, and possible biases.

Maintaining Objectivity: Non-fiction requires a balance of objectivity. While it's important to share a unique perspective, authors must be careful not to let personal biases distort facts or overshadow the narrative.

Writing Style: Non-fiction doesn't have to be dry or boring. Finding an engaging and readable style can be challenging but is critical to keep the reader interested.

Length and Pace: Determining the right length for the book and maintaining a pace that keeps the readers engaged, but also allows for in-depth discussion, can be a tricky balancing act.

Consistency: Consistency in language, tone, and formatting is critical, especially for non-fiction books. Inconsistencies can lead to confusion and disrupt the flow of the narrative.

Self-Doubt and Procrastination: Many first-time authors struggle with confidence and may procrastinate because they feel overwhelmed or unsure of their abilities. Overcoming self-doubt and maintaining motivation is a common and significant challenge.

Remember, while these challenges can seem daunting, every author faces them, and there are many resources available to help navigate these hurdles. With dedication, persistence, and a little help when needed, these challenges can definitely be overcome.

HERE ARE some reasons that most first books are stinkers.

ChatGPT didn't really answer my question. What I wanted were problems that a book coach or a ghostwriter can fix. I told you I made a new prompt for this chapter, but I messed up. I didn't say clearly that I want problems that can be fixed with my solution.

I don't want to mix up my answers, so I'll ask about ghostwriters first.

WHAT ARE the ten biggest challenges someone faces when trying to write their first non-fiction book, that can be solved by working with a ghostwriter?

A GHOSTWRITER IS *a professional writer who is hired to write for someone else, often without public acknowledgment. Here are ten challenges in writing a non-fiction book that can be mitigated by working with a ghostwriter:*

Writing Quality*: A professional ghostwriter can ensure that the manuscript is well-written, clear, and engaging.*

Organization*: Ghostwriters are skilled in organizing material in a logical and coherent way, providing a clear path for the reader through the subject matter.*

Writing Style*: Ghostwriters can adapt to various writing styles, ensuring the book resonates with the target audience. They can also help make complex information more accessible.*

Research*: Ghostwriters can conduct extensive research, ensuring that the book is accurate and up-to-date.*

Maintaining Objectivity*: An external writer can provide an outside perspective, ensuring objectivity is maintained throughout the text.*

Time Management*: Writing a book is a time-consuming task. A ghostwriter can help by taking on the bulk of the writing, leaving the author free to focus on other tasks or roles.*

Consistency*: Ghostwriters are professionals who are experienced in maintaining consistency in language, tone, and formatting throughout a book.*

Dealing with Writer's Block*: A ghostwriter can help overcome periods of stagnation or lack of inspiration, ensuring that the project keeps moving forward.*

Confidentiality and Privacy: If the book contains sensitive information, a professional ghostwriter can be contracted to maintain confidentiality.

Publishing Advice: Experienced ghostwriters often have industry knowledge and can provide advice on finding a publisher or self-publishing.

Remember, while a ghostwriter can alleviate many challenges, the author should still be involved in the process to ensure that the final product is aligned with their vision.

THE DETAILS before and after the bullet points aren't quite addressing my question, so I can overlook those. Notice how the bullets and the wording have shifted. This is a list I can act on, and it aligns well with my personal experience as a ghostwriter over the years.

This list is much more practical, and it began with a minor idea. I often ask ChatGPT for extensive lists of problems and potential solutions. I might not always use the whole list, but there's always something new that I can incorporate into my writing.

Merely bouncing ideas off ChatGPT is a tremendous aid to me. I live on a tropical island in the South Pacific, so when I'm working, most of the world is asleep. I lack people to discuss my ideas with, and that's where ChatGPT comes in.

It takes over the manual research I used to do, helping me discard weak ideas and leverage strong ones more quickly.

15

NO MORE SPREADSHEET NIGHTMARES

The first product I launched with ChatGPT was titled "99 Prompts." It was a spreadsheet full of my best prompts to help beginners hit the ground running. Working in the online business world, I've seen a ridiculous amount of subpar products with the word "AI" slapped on the title just to drive sales. A lot of tools claiming to have AI don't even need it.

There are also tons of prompt lists out there that are just plain bad. It drives me up the wall. I needed a way to organize these prompts, and Debbie suggested using a Google Sheet. It's a spreadsheet that's always online, and people can access it with just a single link.

I'm not great at spreadsheets, and organization is a real challenge for me. I've had multiple conversations with ChatGPT about how to organize my prompts, and this was the first one.

CREATE a framework to organize chatgpt prompts in a spreadsheet using tables.

. . .

Sure, I can help you create a framework to organize ChatGPT prompts in a spreadsheet using tables. Here's a step-by-step guide:

Open a new spreadsheet in your preferred spreadsheet application, such as Google Sheets or Microsoft Excel.

Create a table with the following column headers:

- ***Prompt ID**: This column should contain a unique identifier for each prompt, such as a numerical ID or a descriptive title.*
- ***Prompt Text**: This column should contain the actual prompt text that you want to use to generate responses from ChatGPT.*
- ***Topic**: This column should contain the general topic or category that the prompt falls under, such as "Technology" or "Travel".*
- ***Status**: This column should contain the current status of the prompt, such as "Pending" or "Completed".*
- ***Response**: This column should be left blank for now, as it will be filled in later with the response generated by ChatGPT.*

Add rows to the table to represent each prompt that you want to generate responses for. Fill in the Prompt ID, Prompt Text, and Topic columns for each prompt.

As you generate responses for each prompt using ChatGPT, fill in the Response column with the generated response.

Use the Status column to track the progress of each prompt. You can use labels such as "Pending", "In progress", and "Completed" to indicate the current status of each prompt.

Use the filtering and sorting functions of your spreadsheet application to organize and view your prompts in different ways. For example, you can filter by topic to see all prompts related to a specific category, or sort by status to see all pending prompts at the top of the table.

You can also add additional columns to the table as needed, such as a column for the date the prompt was added or a column for notes and comments about the prompt.

With this framework, you can easily organize and track your

ChatGPT prompts in a structured way, making it easier to manage and generate responses for a large number of prompts.

THIS WAS super helpful for me. At the time, I was using Google Docs, and I had thousands of unorganized prompts. Debbie kept asking me to get them in order so we could create our product, and I was honestly stressed out. Organization isn't my strong suit, and I needed a hand.

I tried to get her to provide an organizational structure at least ten times. She couldn't do it because she hadn't been through my prompts yet. So, I finally decided to ask ChatGPT for help. It's fantastic that it came up with the idea, but could it do all the work for me?

PLEASE CREATE THE ACTUAL SPREADSHEET.

SURE, I can create an example spreadsheet for you to use as a template. Here's what the spreadsheet would look like:

In this example, the table has six prompts with columns for Prompt ID, Prompt Text, Topic, Status, and Response. The prompts are organized by topic and status, with different prompts in different stages of completion. The Response column is initially blank, but will be filled in with responses generated by ChatGPT.

You can use this template as a starting point to create your own spreadsheet for organizing and managing your ChatGPT prompts.

Prompt ID	Prompt Text	Topic	Status	Response
1	What is your favorite movie?	Entertainment	Pending	
2	What is the best way to learn a new language?	Education	Completed	Learning through immersion is often considered the best way to learn a new language.
3	What are some tips for traveling on a budget?	Travel	In progress	
4	What are some common interview questions and how should you answer them?	Career	Completed	One common interview question is "Tell me about yourself." When answering this question, you should focus on your relevant experience and skills.
5	What is your favorite book?	Literature	Completed	One of my favorite books is "To Kill a Mockingbird" by Harper Lee.
6	What are the benefits of meditation?	Health	Pending	

BECAUSE OF HOW it would appear to the reader, I had to take a snapshot of the spreadsheet. So, this is what the table looked like. When I created my master prompt spreadsheet, I shuffled the columns around. I moved the category to the front so that I could group them together, but that's just my personal preference.

The next challenge was how to categorize my prompts. I see categories like Entertainment, Education, Travel, Career, Literature, and Health here. But I needed a more comprehensive list.

PLEASE MAKE **a list of the topics and categories to include.**

SURE, here is a list of topics and categories that you could include in your spreadsheet to organize your ChatGPT prompts:

- *Business*
- *Career*
- *Education*
- *Entertainment*
- *Environment*
- *Finance*

- *Food and Drink*
- *Health*
- *History*
- *Literature*
- *Music*
- *Philosophy*
- *Politics*
- *Psychology*
- *Science*
- *Sports*
- *Technology*
- *Travel*
- *World Culture*

You can use these topics to categorize your prompts and make it easier to filter and sort them in your spreadsheet. Of course, feel free to add or remove topics based on your specific needs and interests.

IF YOU'VE SNAGGED my "99 Prompts" product, you'll notice it's not arranged in this way. I used this format for my lists of thousands of prompts, but the final spreadsheet was compact enough that I used a different structure. When a member of my team sifted through my prompts and organized them, we definitely followed this structure. This is just one small way ChatGPT can handle spreadsheets. Its capabilities extend far beyond what I've explained here. Let's ask ChatGPT what it can do.

WHAT CAN ChatGPT do with spreadsheets?

AS OF MY knowledge cut-off in September 2021, the GPT-3 model is a text-based model and does not have direct abilities to interact with, manipulate, or analyze spreadsheets. It can only process and generate text. Consequently, I can't open, view, edit, or directly manipulate data in spreadsheet files. However, if you provide data or describe a spreadsheet's contents, I can help in several ways:

1. Data Analysis: If you provide some data or describe the data layout in the spreadsheet, I can guide you through the process of analyzing that data, suggest statistical methods that might be appropriate, and explain how to interpret the results.
2. Formula Creation: I can help generate or explain spreadsheet formulas in general terms. For example, if you're working with a spreadsheet and want to compute a running average or perform a specific calculation, I can tell you what kind of formula you'd need.
3. Data Representation: I can advise on how to represent your data for better understanding, such as suggesting the types of charts, graphs, or other visual aids that might be useful.
4. Spreadsheet Functions: I can explain how various spreadsheet functions work in Excel, Google Sheets, or other spreadsheet software, from simple ones like SUM and AVERAGE to more complex ones like VLOOKUP and INDEX/MATCH.
5. Problem-solving: If you're encountering a problem with your spreadsheet, I can try to help you troubleshoot. This would be based on your description of the problem, any error messages you're seeing, and what you're trying to accomplish.
6. Planning and Organizing Data: If you're starting a new spreadsheet project, I can help you plan and organize your data effectively. This might include suggesting how to structure your data, what kind of data validation to use, how to ensure data consistency, etc.

Please remember to describe your situation in as much detail as possible to get the most accurate assistance. In the future, newer versions of AI might have more advanced capabilities.

. . .

Let's start from the first paragraph, which is a lie. I asked this of ChatGPT-4, not version 3. Also, it does have access to the Internet which I've shown you. ChatGPT is underestimating itself here.

For me I am really excited by formula creation. I stink at Excel, but now I can do amazing things with ChatGPT by my side and no longer need to watch loads of tutorial videos.

16

MASTER ANY SKILL WITH A PRIVATE TUTOR

This might be the area you're most pumped about. I recall in the movie 'The Matrix', they insert a disk into a computer and, instantly, Keanu Reeves knows Kung Fu. That's how I feel when I ask ChatGPT for help.

ChatGPT can craft a curriculum, study strategy, practice timetable, training materials, and even tests to teach you virtually any skill available online. If you're keen to learn a foreign language, ChatGPT is your buddy.

Currently, I'm trying to improve my guitar skills, but I'm hitting a snag with the slow pace of my finger movements.

I'M LEARNING guitar with a level of upper beginner. What are some exercises I can do to speed up my chord changes?

IMPROVING chord changes is a key aspect of developing guitar skills. Here are some exercises that can help you speed up your chord changes as an upper beginner:

- **Metronome practice**: Set a metronome to a slow tempo and practice changing between two chords, focusing on accuracy and smooth transitions. Gradually increase the tempo as you become more comfortable.
- **One-minute changes**: Choose a pair of chords and see how many times you can switch between them within one minute. Keep track of your progress and aim to improve the number of changes you can make accurately.
- **Common chord progressions**: Practice transitioning between chords commonly used together in songs, such as G, C, D, and Em. Work on smooth transitions and gradually increase the speed as you gain confidence.
- **Pivot finger technique**: Identify common fingers between chords and use them as a pivot point to facilitate quick changes. Keep those fingers in place while moving the rest of your fingers to the new positions.
- **Slow-motion changes**: Slow down your chord changes and focus on each finger's movement and placement. Ensure that you have a clean and accurate technique before gradually increasing the speed.
- **Chord change drills**: Create your own drills by selecting a sequence of chords and practicing transitioning between them repeatedly. Focus on challenging chord changes to improve your muscle memory and speed.
- **Chord change warm-ups**: Dedicate a few minutes to warming up your fingers and practicing chord changes before your regular practice sessions. This helps prepare your fingers and mind for smoother transitions.
- **Visualization and air changes**: Visualize the finger placement for each chord in your mind and practice the changes without the guitar. This mental rehearsal can help improve your muscle memory and coordination.
- **Song practice**: Learn and practice songs that involve chord changes within your skill level. By playing along with songs,

you'll naturally develop speed and accuracy in transitioning between chords.
- **Relaxation and finger strength exercises:** Work on finger flexibility and strength by performing finger stretching exercises and practicing finger independence drills. Relaxed fingers and increased finger strength can contribute to faster chord changes.

Remember to start slow and gradually build up speed. Be patient with yourself, as progress takes time. Regular and focused practice will help you improve your chord changes and overall guitar playing skills.

But I don't have to halt here. Now that I have a bunch of ideas for bolstering my guitar skills, I can request ChatGPT to provide actual methods. There's no need to scour elsewhere to research the next step.

Can you give me some specific finger strength exercises?

Certainly! Here are some finger strength exercises specifically designed to enhance your finger dexterity and strength for guitar playing:

Finger curls: Hold a small, soft ball (such as a stress ball) in your hand and squeeze it using your fingertips. Hold the squeeze for a few seconds and then release. Repeat this exercise for each finger on both hands.

Finger presses: Place your fingers on a flat surface (such as a table or guitar neck) and press down with each finger individually, lifting the others. Focus on pressing with the fingertips and maintaining control throughout the movement.

Spider exercise: Starting with your index finger on the first fret, place each finger (index, middle, ring, and pinky) on consecutive frets of the same string. Play each fretted note individually, moving up and down the strings, and gradually increase the speed.

Finger stretches: Gently stretch your fingers by placing your hand flat on a surface and spreading your fingers apart as much as possible. Hold the stretch for a few seconds and then relax. Repeat several times.

Finger independence drills: Practice finger independence by placing your fingers on adjacent strings and frets (e.g., index on the 2nd string, 1st fret; middle on the 3rd string, 2nd fret; ring on the 4th string, 3rd fret; pinky on the 5th string, 4th fret). Play each note individually while keeping the other fingers down.

Power chord exercises: Practice power chords by placing your index finger on the 6th string, 1st fret, and your ring or pinky finger on the 5th string, 3rd fret. Strum the two strings together, ensuring a clean sound without any muted strings.

Finger taps: Place your fingers on a flat surface and lift each finger individually, tapping it on the surface while keeping the other fingers down. Alternate between fingers and gradually increase the speed.

Barre chord exercises: Practice barre chords by using your index finger to press down multiple strings across the fretboard while forming different chord shapes with your remaining fingers. Start with simpler barre chord shapes and gradually progress to more complex ones.

Finger roll exercise: Starting with your index finger on a fret, roll your finger across adjacent strings, playing each note individually. Move up and down the fretboard, focusing on smooth finger transitions.

Fingerpicking exercises: Practice fingerpicking patterns that involve plucking strings with different fingers in various sequences. This helps improve finger coordination and strength.

Remember to start slowly and gradually increase the difficulty and speed as you feel comfortable. Regular practice and consistency are key to developing finger strength and dexterity for guitar playing.

. . .

THE ONLY SNAG with ChatGPT is that it can't yet show me videos of each exercise. However, it can give me links to videos for each of these drills that I can watch. And I've got a hunch that this will be a feature added in the not-too-distant future.

Whatever skills you're itching to develop and enhance, ChatGPT can act as your personal tutor.

17

SUMMARIZE IN SECONDS

Here's yet another method to save a truckload of time. Give ChatGPT a chunky piece of text and ask it to summarize. You can take a transcript from a YouTube video, paste it into ChatGPT, and ask it to break everything down for you.

I can't demonstrate this with a real-life example, as the content would infringe on someone else's copyright. Hence, I'll have to use one of my own videos for the demo.

In 2022, I posted a video titled "How to Build an Email List Fast." The video runs for ten minutes and twenty-two seconds. That's the amount of time it would take you to learn by watching the video. I pulled the transcript straight from YouTube - the same one anyone can access. Then, I fed it into the following prompt.

PLEASE SUMMARIZE THIS VIDEO TRANSCRIPT: [PASTE TRANSCRIPT]

IN THIS VIDEO, *the speaker outlines a four-step process to build an email list quickly:*

1. **Create a Free Gift**: This is something valuable that you offer to your audience in exchange for their email address. You could base this gift on the most common questions that people ask you or you could teach a skill you wish you'd known a few years ago. The speaker mentions that he creates his free gifts through dictation, converting them into PDFs.
2. **Connect an Autoresponder**: An autoresponder is a tool that automatically sends out emails on your behalf. The speaker recommends ConvertKit for this purpose. When someone enters their email to receive your free gift, the autoresponder will automatically add them to your email list, send them the gift, and begin to send follow-up emails.
3. **Create a Landing Page**: This is a webpage where people can sign up for your email list and receive the free gift. It can be made using the same tools as your autoresponder. The speaker uses ConvertKit for this purpose too. The landing page should offer a simple choice - to either take the free gift or leave.
4. **Share Your Offer**: The speaker recommends sharing links to your landing page across all your social media profiles and in any content that you publish. This could be a blog post, a TikTok video, or an Instagram post, for example. You want to spread the word about your free gift using your existing assets.

A bonus step the speaker mentions is to include an offer on the "thank you" page that users land on after signing up for the free gift. This is a simple way to convert your new email subscribers into paying customers right from the start. For example, you could offer a discounted training course.

In conclusion, the video explains how to build an email list fast through the use of free gifts, an autoresponder, a landing page, and by sharing your offer across your platforms. These steps, followed by offering a paid product, can quickly convert your audience into paying customers.

· · ·

IF IT TOOK you less than ten minutes to read ChatGPT's response, then it has indeed saved you some time. In my case, it saved a heap of time.

Imagine how handy it would be to feed ChatGPT a college lecture and have it crank out notes for you. It could transform these into study materials or quiz you on the information. Summarizing is just one of the many things you can do with information you give to ChatGPT.

At the end of the Productivity section, I shared that ChatGPT can summarize. Ponder on that for a moment. How can you fuse the ability to summarize with the power to create courses?

Could you feed ChatGPT a video transcript or a chapter from a book and turn that into a lesson for your course?

I hope you're getting really excited!

18

LIGHTNING SPEED SUPERPOWERS WITH AI

How many days have you wrapped up work, only to wonder where all the time went? Felt like you didn't really get anything accomplished? Now, I'm known for being a quick writer, but with ChatGPT, I'm functioning at an entirely new level.

As you weave this tool into your day-to-day life, you'll find yourself getting more done in less time. Those days where I feel like I haven't achieved a thing are in the past. I can blitz through larger task lists and feel a real sense of progress on all my projects.

Not every productivity technique I've shared will apply to your business, but I bet a few of these have lit a fire under you. This isn't an exhaustive list of ways to boost your productivity, but it's time to tackle the part we've all been waiting for.

Let's talk about how to make money with ChatGPT.

PART III

INCOME STREAMS

If you hop over to Fiverr.com and glance at the services being offered, you'll see that every single one of them could potentially be replaced with AI. Besides ChatGPT, I also use Stable Diffusion for creating images, and another AI to compose music for my videos.

ChatGPT might eventually do it all, but for now, these three specialized AI tools have given me the ability to carry out any task swiftly. The need to hire virtual assistants for these tasks has dropped significantly.

This is the first way that ChatGPT helps me make money—it saves me money. All that money I would have spent, I can now reinvest in other parts of my business.

Secondly, I can offer these services to clients. I can let ChatGPT handle most of the heavy lifting and still make a quick buck. There are countless individuals who will either never try ChatGPT or will give up after an unsuccessful attempt. These folks are your potential customers. Many of them simply don't have the time, so they pay others to handle these tasks.

You don't have to disclose that you're using AI. As long as they're happy with the outcome, everybody wins.

The third way to make money is to unlock passive income streams. Each of these methods can be utilized in your own business and generate income over time.

The middle method is a quick cash source to tide you over until your passive income streams can replace your existing income needs. I dive much deeper into this topic in my book, "Fire Your Boss," which is available for free in all major bookstores.

Here's a specific example to help illustrate this:

Right now, I charge $40,000 to ghostwrite a book for a client. That's a considerable sum, and I'm genuinely grateful for it. I get paid when I finish the book, before a single copy has sold. It's quick money but it lacks a passive income element.

I can also write a book, like this one, and receive no upfront payment. I only get paid when someone buys a copy of the book, earning a few dollars per sale. It's not as much money initially, but it's passive. In the long run, most of my books bring in enough income to cover my bills. Every book I publish becomes another small revenue stream.

However, when I need money quickly—like when my second son was born and we faced an emergency—I can take on a client and receive the payment right away. That's how we managed to pay for a specialist who saved my son's life on his birth day. That specialist only accepted cash.

19

$5,865 PER DAY AS A FREELANCER

The simplest method to generate income using ChatGPT is by offering services which ChatGPT can carry out for you. Every business requires these types of services, and I have personally paid for each one at various points in my career.

I kicked things off by placing ads on Craigslist, offering SEO services, despite having zero knowledge about SEO. After securing a client, I used that money to purchase a course on SEO. For a long while, that client ranked first for her keywords.

Now, I usually turn to a platform called Fiverr for small tasks. Its initial draw was that every service cost just five dollars - not anymore. Here are a few examples of what you could earn for tasks completed using ChatGPT:

Write a Blog Post

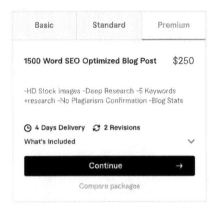

Consider this post from a highly-rated writer with over 500 five-star reviews. Think of the number of clients who likely didn't bother leaving a review!

As you already know, ChatGPT can handle all the SEO work. Shortly, I'll demonstrate how it can also write an entire article. Should this take you less than an hour, you'd be making more than $250 an hour. Pretty impressive, right?

CREATE an Online Course

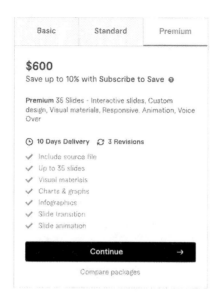

This person charges six hundred dollars to design a 35-slide course. I've personally never needed a course that brief. This seller currently has two customers in line and nearly a hundred five-star reviews. This is another type of task that people are willing to pay good money for.

With ChatGPT, you can design and assemble an entire course in just a few hours. It's another straightforward task.

Editing

I'M HALFWAY through this book, and the word count stands at 59,081. Of course, that count will increase as I continue to write. But let's look at how much I'd need to shell out just for proofreading.

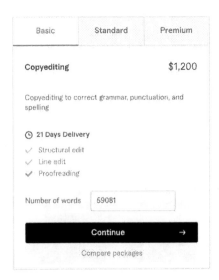

Twelve hundred dollars? This guy has over 500 five-star reviews and already has clients lined up, waiting for him to edit their work. Proofreading is something that ChatGPT excels at. I mean, I can do proofreading while watching a movie. I think I need to start offering proofreading services...

Translation

So, how much would it cost to translate my book into German? Translation is a big market, and I believe many people worldwide would benefit from reading this book.

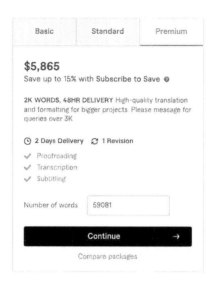

Hot diggity dog that's a lot of dollars to share my book with the German market. It's a major expense. Alternatively, I could have ChatGPT do it.

Personally, I would tread carefully here because you don't want to make mistakes. So, I would only take jobs translating INTO a language that I can speak, ensuring I can check the final product. That's my only caveat, but there is a lot of work translating into English, I assure you.

More than Fiverr

Fiverr was my choice for examples because it's a website that makes grabbing price screenshots really easy. You can offer any of the services I'll cover in this chapter on hundreds of websites globally or in your local community. The only limit is how much you expand your reach. You could distribute flyers on telephone poles or leave cards at the local UPS store. You could even post on Craigslist, like I did.

And I hope by now you realize that ChatGPT can design your flyers and write your ad copy.

20

BLOG FASTER, RANK HIGHER

To prepare ChatGPT for writing an excellent blog post, you need to go through some pre-prompting stages. Once you've set it up, it takes about five minutes to get ChatGPT started on your article. This process builds on the SEO research we conducted in the Productivity chapter.

Blog posts are the backbone of most websites, but they require significant time and resources. If you check my website, you'll see periods where I posted loads of content and others when I posted nothing for months. It can be a real hassle. If I weren't spending all my time writing this book, I could work on those pending blog posts.

So let's get ChatGPT ready to write a killer blog post.

I WANT to write an article today with the keyword "Does ghostwriting undermine the credibility of an author?," do you understand? Please don't start writing until I tell you, just acknowledge if you understand.

. . .

Yes, I understand your request. You want to write an article centered around the keyword "Does ghostwriting undermine the credibility of an author?". I'll wait for your go-ahead to begin writing.

First, I will start with a pre-prompt. The goal here isn't for ChatGPT to take any action right away. If I don't ask ChatGPT to wait, it might interpret my question as a command and start writing the article immediately. Try this prompt with and without the final sentence to see the difference.

Next, I'm going to specify certain aspects of my task. For instance, if you're a website that reviews stereos but doesn't manufacture them, you would provide that information here. In my case, I want to make it clear that I'm not managing a team of ghostwriters —I do the work myself.

I'm an individual ghostwriter, not a ghostwriting agency, do you understand?

Yes, I understand. You're an individual ghostwriter and not part of a ghostwriting agency. This context will be important in writing the article. Please let me know when you're ready for me to start drafting the article.

Finally, I'm going to feed ChatGPT the research I've gathered for the article. This will start with the questions that it generated during my SEO research in Part I.

When we start writing the article, I want you to try to answer these questions:
    1."What is ghostwriting and how does it work?"

Do you understand?

YES, *I understand. You've provided a list of questions that should be addressed in the article about the role and impact of ghostwriting on an author's credibility. I will aim to provide comprehensive answers to each of these questions in the course of the article. Please let me know when you're ready for me to start.*

IT's important to thoroughly feed ChatGPT all the relevant information during this pre-prompting phase. I started by providing it with all fifteen questions from my SEO research. Although I'm not showing you all the questions again, it's essential to note that we just want ChatGPT to confirm what it needs to do with this list of questions. Then, I will give it my list of targeted keywords.

I WANT you to include the following keywords:

1. **"Ethics of ghostwriting"**

Do you understand?

YES, *I understand. You want me to include these specific keywords within the content of the article. They will help guide the discussion and ensure that we cover key topics related to ghostwriting, its implications, and its role within the literary and publishing world. Please let me know when you're ready for me to start writing.*

. . .

This process involves a long chain of pre-prompts, so I want to make sure that ChatGPT keeps track of all the information I've given it in this extended conversation.

Please remember to mention the phrases in my keyword list and the questions I added before to the article, do you understand?

Yes, I understand your instructions clearly. I will ensure to address the questions you listed earlier in the article and incorporate the keywords and phrases from your provided list throughout the text. I'm ready to start writing when you are.

With phase one of pre-prompting complete, ChatGPT has all the background information needed to start creating content.

Write me ten different catchy titles for this blog post, be sure to include the keyword "Does ghostwriting undermine the credibility of an author" in each title.

Absolutely, here are ten catchy titles incorporating your keyword:

1. *"Does Ghostwriting Undermine the Credibility of an Author? Unveiling the Hidden Scripts"*
2. *"Ghostwriting Exposed: Does it Damage an Author's Credibility?"*
3. *"Unmasking Ghostwriting: A Threat or a Boost to an Author's Credibility?"*
4. *"Ghostwriting: An Insight into Author Authenticity and Credibility"*

5. *"Does Ghostwriting Undermine the Credibility of an Author? An Ethical Dilemma in Literature"*
6. *"Ghostwriting and the Question of Credibility: An Author's Silent Ally or Invisible Foe?"*
7. *"Decoding Ghostwriting: A Bane or Boon for an Author's Credibility?"*
8. *"The Ghostwriting Enigma: Does it Undermine the Credibility of an Author?"*
9. *"Authorial Credibility in the Shadows: Does Ghostwriting Dilute Authenticity?"*
10. *"Unveiling the Phantom Scribes: Does Ghostwriting Undermine an Author's Credibility?"*

NEXT, I need a title before I begin the writing process because it provides guide rails for ChatGPT. It will craft a blog post that aligns with the chosen title.

FROM HERE ON OUT, **we're going to use the article title "Unveiling the Phantom Scribes: Does Ghostwriting Undermine an Author's Credibility?" Do you understand?**

YES, I understand. The selected title for the article is "Unveiling the Phantom Scribes: Does Ghostwriting Undermine an Author's Credibility?". I'll use this title for the forthcoming article. Please let me know when you're ready for me to begin writing.

THIS PROCESS MIGHT SEEM a bit complex, so allow me to explain again. I initially asked ChatGPT to generate a list of potential titles. After selecting one from the list, I asked ChatGPT to confirm its understanding. This intentional selection of a title and subsequent confirmation will result in a more relevant article. Each pre-prompt creates guide rails for this specific conversation.

Now it's time for the final pre-prompt.

There are two important things to remember when writing this article.

One, I want you to use all normal formatting for a blog post, including headings and bullet points.

Two, everything I'm going to ask you to write is in American English, targeted at men and women over the age of forty, and can contain some humor.

Do you understand?

Yes, I understand your instructions clearly.

I'll make sure to use appropriate formatting for a blog post, including headings and bullet points to make the content clear and engaging.

The article will be written in American English, and it's targeted towards men and women over the age of forty. It can contain a touch of humor to make it more enjoyable and relatable to the target audience.

I'm ready to start writing the article when you are.

Indeed, the final pre-prompt is critical to creating a quality blog post. This is where we set stylistic constraints for ChatGPT's output. I'll delve deeper into the use of character and mimic prompts later in the book.

Once I've given ChatGPT my final pre-prompt, I'm prepared to begin the process of drafting the article. Because ChatGPT's responses are inherently brief, the blog post needs to be divided into smaller sections. To generate longer pieces of content, I'll prompt ChatGPT to provide the outline for these sections.

. . .

Please write an outline for this blog post.

Absolutely, here's a proposed outline for the blog post titled "Unveiling the Phantom Scribes: Does Ghostwriting Undermine an Author's Credibility?":

I. Introduction

- Brief introduction to the concept of ghostwriting.
- A hint of humor and a nod to the target audience.

II. What is Ghostwriting and How Does it Work?

- Definition and explanation of the process of ghostwriting.

III. Why Do Authors Use Ghostwriters?

- The rationale behind authors employing ghostwriters.

IV. Author Authenticity and Ghostwriting

- Discussion on whether a book written by a ghostwriter can still be considered authentic.
- Ghostwriting vs. original authorship.

V. The Skills Debate: Does Using a Ghostwriter Mean that an Author Lacks Talent or Skills?

- Exploration of the perception and reality of author skills in relation to ghostwriting.

VI. Impact of Ghostwriting on an Author's Image

- *Delving into how ghostwriting can affect the reputation of an author.*
- *Analysis of potential reputation damage from ghostwriting.*

VII. Ethics of Ghostwriting

- *Ethical implications of using a ghostwriter.*
- *Disclosure of ghostwriters in publishing.*

VIII. Reader's Perspective: Do Readers Care if an Author Uses a Ghostwriter?

- *Understanding reader's views and expectations.*

IX. Famous Authors Who Use Ghostwriters

- *A look at notable authors who've used ghostwriters and their experiences.*

X. Maintaining the Author's Voice: Can an Author Maintain Their Unique Voice When Using a Ghostwriter?

- *Discussion of the challenge and success of maintaining authorial voice in ghostwritten works.*

XI. The Ghostwriters' Perspective

- *Insights into how ghostwriters feel about not receiving public credit for their work.*

XII. Legal Aspects: Copyright Issues in Ghostwriting

- *Analysis of legal stance on ghostwriting. Who owns the copyright to the work?*

XIII. Ghostwriting and Publishing Industry Standards

- Examination of ghostwriting as a common practice in the publishing industry.

XIV. Pros and Cons of Using a Ghostwriter

- A balanced discussion on the benefits and drawbacks of using a ghostwriter.

XV. Ghostwriters and Literary Value

- Reflection on whether the use of ghostwriters diminishes the value of literature.

XVI. Conclusion

- Recap and final thoughts on the question: "Does ghostwriting undermine the credibility of an author?".

Let me know if this outline meets your expectations or if there are any changes you'd like to make.

If you're not satisfied with the proposed outline, this is the opportunity to make adjustments. It's easier and more efficient to modify things at this stage than after ChatGPT has begun writing. Once you're happy with the outline, it's time to start drafting.

Please write blog post section 1 part 1: Brief introduction to the concept of ghostwriting.

. . .

I. Introduction

Welcome, dear readers, to an exploration into the often murky and mysterious world of the literary phantoms known as ghostwriters. Now, don't let the term spook you. Despite the ethereal connotations, these ghostwriters are not from the other side, nor are they crafting tales in haunted houses. They are very much living, breathing individuals with a knack for the written word.

Ghostwriting is a fascinating element of the literary world. Essentially, it's when a writer - the "ghost" - is commissioned to write a piece that is officially credited to another person. This could be anything from a novel, to a speech, to an autobiography. The person who hired the ghostwriter becomes the "author" of the work, while the ghostwriter remains in the shadows, unseen and unacknowledged. Hence the term "ghost".

This process might sound rather clandestine and cloak-and-dagger, but it's been a part of the publishing world for centuries, and it's far more common than most of us would think. So, let's dispel the haze around this spectral profession, and delve deeper into this fascinating world to answer the question on many minds: "Does ghostwriting undermine the credibility of an author?" Stay tuned, fellow bookworms, and let's uncover the reality of the phantom scribes together.

At times, ChatGPT's output may seem a bit silly, reminiscent of a scene from a B-grade movie. You can correct the writing style by guiding it to mimic a specific person's style, or restrict its language by pointing out what you don't like. We've already discussed this, so let's continue with writing the next part of the article.

Please write **blog post section 1 part 2: A hint of humor and a nod to the target audience.**

. . .

As you've likely figured out by now, these ghosts aren't the ones who rattle chains in the attic, or turn your living room frigid. No, the only thing these ghostwriters might make run cold are the fingertips of a hard-pressed author trying to meet a deadline.

Now, to my esteemed readers over forty, remember how we used to craft school essays, armed with a trusty pen, a stack of paper, and enough caffeine to rival a college dorm during finals week? Think of ghostwriters as the professional version of our younger selves, powering through the night to meet deadlines. Except, their work often ends up with a different name on the cover. Quite the plot twist, isn't it?

So, sit back, maybe even with a nice cup of coffee (or something stronger—we're all friends here), and let's journey into the world of the unsung heroes of the literary world, the ghostwriters. And let's figure out whether their existence on the bookshelf is more comedy or tragedy for the credited author.

As an experienced ghostwriter, there are things I might personally alter in this article. But that's not the point here. The tone and light-heartedness can be easily tweaked. The crucial part is the actual content. ChatGPT remembered the target audience's age, which demonstrates its ability to utilize details provided in the prompts. We have a blog post that took just a few minutes to create, showcasing how integrating this technique with other lessons from this book can be a game-changer.

Wait. What? You don't want me to make you flip forward and backward in this book? It's hard in an ebook and a nightmare for those of you listening to an audiobook? Ok.

I had to rewrite this prompt a few times because ChatGPT kept being spooky and silly.

Please rewrite **blog post section 1 part 1 in the style of Gabriel García Márquez. Please try to tone down the spooky vibes A LOT** and be more relatable. We want this to be an informative rather than silly article. The people reading this are over forty and highly intelligent.

I. INTRODUCTION

Welcome, esteemed readers, as we embark on an exploratory journey into a hidden corner of the literary cosmos - ghostwriting. Here, we don't navigate through spectral apparitions or ominous phantoms. Instead, we encounter living, breathing individuals, each a master of weaving words into narrative threads.

Ghostwriting, as a term, may sound enigmatic, yet its nature is simple and forthright. It's a process where a writer, the 'ghost,' is commissioned to create a work of written art that is officially credited to another entity. This may manifest as a novel, an autobiography, a speech, or countless other written forms. The hiring individual assumes the role of the 'author,' with the true craftsman's identity often remaining veiled, acknowledged only by the whispering wind of the creative world.

Some might perceive ghostwriting as a clandestine affair, a nocturnal dance hidden in the moon's shadow. Yet it's worth noting that this practice has been an integral part of our publishing heritage for centuries, with roots deeper and more extensive than the tallest literary trees in our cultural forest. So, let's unveil this fascinating world together, shedding light on the integral question: "Does ghostwriting undermine the credibility of an author?" Prepare for an illuminating voyage, dear readers, as we delve into the realm of ghostwriting - a world as intriguing as it is uncredited.

AFTER TWEAKING, the outcome was vastly improved, demonstrating how effectively the previous prompts had worked. I'll provide a list of a hundred authors you can use in this prompt later in the book.

21

BESTSELLER IN A DAY

Let me be clear: ChatGPT possesses the capability to author nonfiction books that can ace any AI detector and read remarkably well, provided the prompts are apt. I realize some people are demonstrating otherwise, but it's not the software that falls short; it's often how it's used.

Creating a book presents unique challenges, as it's significantly longer than an article. The risk of deviation by ChatGPT can increase if you're not vigilant. If you're looking to author books and reap profits from them, here's the golden secret.

Imagine it akin to those interactive books where you get to decide the course of action every few pages. I'll refrain from naming any specific brand, mindful of their copyright seriousness.

ChatGPT can pen your book in increments of about 500-700 words. If you're dissatisfied with a section it generates, you have the power to instruct it to amend right then. Once content with a section, proceed to the next.

Adopt this approach when leveraging ChatGPT to author an entire book from beginning to end. In the realm of non-fiction, I often dictate certain portions and engage ChatGPT to fill in the blanks. However, since this is my area of specialization, I'm keen to demonstrate the undiluted ChatGPT method. And remember, you always retain the ability to change anything you dislike.

Local

Several months back, I exemplified this method, and it still stands strong. Many savvy entrepreneurs realize that a well-crafted book serves as an excellent medium to build an audience and exhibit expertise. Back in 2010, I ventured into my first online business, offering SEO services.

With the wisdom of hindsight, had I known the power of a well-crafted book, I would have certainly published one to attract more clients. So, what should my book be about? Well, if I feed ChatGPT with my expertise area and objectives, it can brainstorm some impressive concepts.

I WANT to sell local search engine optimization services in the Nashville area, what are three topics I can write a book on that will boost my credibility and generate most customers.

UNDERSTANDING LOCAL SEO: *This book could cover the basics of local SEO and how it differs from traditional SEO. It could explain how local SEO helps businesses rank higher in search engine results for local keywords and how it affects their online visibility and credibility.*

Local SEO Strategy: *This book could dive deeper into the specific strategies and techniques for optimizing a website for local search. Topics could include keyword research, business listings, and local citations, as well as tips for creating and optimizing local content.*

Building a Local SEO Campaign: *This book could focus on the practical steps of building a successful local SEO campaign. Topics could include setting goals, tracking and measuring success, and adapting to* changes in search algorithms. The book could also cover common mistakes to avoid and best practices for staying up-to-date with the latest trends and changes in local SEO.

THE ENSUING RESPONSE, generated by ChatGPT-3.5, is commendable. Despite the titles appearing similar, they each harbor distinct ideas and represent a solid starting point. All I knew was my desire for a book that would enhance my professional image and attract customers. I offered ChatGPT minimal input, yet received an invaluable result.

One crucial factor in book success lies in selecting the right category. No need for guesswork; all you need to do is ask.

WHAT IS the best Amazon category for this book?

THE BEST AMAZON category for a book about local search engine optimization services would likely be "Internet Marketing" or "Search Engine Optimization". More specifically, you could consider the subcategories "Local Search Marketing" or "Online Marketing for Small Businesses". This will help potential customers find your book more easily and increase its visibility within a relevant and targeted audience.

THIS CIRCLES back to the foundational principle: Engage ChatGPT with a barrage of questions. Inquire about its abilities to cater to your needs, the data it requires to produce optimal results, and how to ensure the success of your projects.

Emotional Intelligence

Not long ago, I was leading a training call with an emotional intelligence coach in attendance. Apart from reading the book, I don't know much about the subject[1]. But as we talked and the coach watched, she was really impressed. I hope you'll find it interesting too.

We start with the same plan each time because we want the same thing from the book: more respect and more customers.

I'm an emotional intelligence expert that works with entrepreneurs and Startups . What are three topics I can write a book on that will boost my credibility and generate most customers?

As an emotional intelligence expert working with entrepreneurs and startups, here are three potential book topics that could boost your credibility and attract new customers:

1. *"**Emotional Intelligence for Entrepreneurs: How to Harness EQ to Build a Successful Startup**" - This book could focus on how emotional intelligence is critical for entrepreneurs and startup founders in managing their own emotions, as well as understanding and managing those of their team members, investors, and customers. The book could offer practical advice on how to improve emotional intelligence, such as developing self-awareness, empathy, and emotional regulation.*
2. *"**Emotionally Intelligent Leadership: How to Inspire, Motivate, and Lead Teams**" - This book could explore the relationship between emotional intelligence and effective leadership. It could offer insights into how emotionally*

intelligent leaders can create a positive and motivating work environment, build strong relationships with team members, and make better decisions.

3. **"Mastering Emotional Intelligence in Sales and Marketing: How to Connect with Customers and Close Deals"** - This book could focus on the importance of emotional intelligence in sales and marketing. It could offer tips on how to build rapport with customers, communicate effectively, and use emotional intelligence to better understand customer needs and motivations. The book could also include real-life examples and case studies to illustrate how emotional intelligence can be applied in sales and marketing.

These are just a few potential book topics that could be relevant and appealing to entrepreneurs and startups. The key is to identify areas where emotional intelligence can make a meaningful impact and offer practical advice and insights that will be valuable to your target audience.

SINCE I GAVE ChatGPT a bit more information this time, its answers are a bit more detailed. It now knows the coach's specialty and who her customers are. If you want even better answers, just ask ChatGPT what it needs to know to suggest three book ideas.

Now that we have a few book ideas, we need a little more research.

WHAT IS the best Amazon category for this book?

THE BEST AMAZON category for a book on emotional intelligence for entrepreneurs and startups would likely be "Business Management & Leadership" or "Entrepreneurship." These categories are appropriate for books that offer insights and guidance on business strategy, leadership, *and entrepreneurship. The "Business Management & Leadership" category also has subcategories such as "Organizational Behavior," which could be relevant for a book on emotional intelligence. It's important to select a category that accurately represents the content of your book and is likely to be searched by your target audience. Be sure to research other books in the category to determine where your book fits best.*

As someone who knows a lot about book categories, I always research what's new in this area. I stay updated because these changes can greatly impact book sales. I help all my coaching and writing clients pick the best category for their book.

Once we have ideas for our book, we need to figure out what problems our book will solve. That's why this part comes right after picking a topic. It's pretty much the same process.

What are the top twenty questions entrepreneurs ask about emotional intelligence.

As an AI language model, I don't have access to a specific database of the most common questions entrepreneurs ask about emotional intelligence. However, I can provide some examples of questions that entrepreneurs may have about emotional intelligence:

1. *What is emotional intelligence, and why is it important for entrepreneurs?*
2. *How can I develop my own emotional intelligence as an entrepreneur?*
3. *What are the different components of emotional intelligence, and how do they relate to entrepreneurship?*
4. *How can emotional intelligence help me better understand and manage my own emotions?*

5. *How can emotional intelligence help me better understand and manage the emotions of my team members and business partners?*
6. *What are some practical strategies for improving emotional intelligence in the workplace?*
7. *How can I use emotional intelligence to build stronger relationships with customers and clients?*
8. *How can emotional intelligence help me make better decisions as an entrepreneur?*
9. *How can emotional intelligence help me navigate difficult conversations and conflicts with team members or investors?*
10. *How can I use emotional intelligence to build a positive and motivating work environment?*
11. *What are some common emotional intelligence blind spots that entrepreneurs should be aware of?*
12. *How can I measure my own emotional intelligence and that of my team members?*
13. *How can emotional intelligence be integrated into leadership training and development programs?*
14. *How can emotional intelligence be used to enhance creativity and innovation in my business?*
15. *How can emotional intelligence help me manage stress and burnout as an entrepreneur?*
16. *How can I use emotional intelligence to build resilience and bounce back from setbacks?*
17. *How can emotional intelligence be used to drive business growth and success?*
18. *How can emotional intelligence be used to improve collaboration and teamwork in my business?*
19. *What are some common misconceptions about emotional intelligence and entrepreneurship?*
20. *How can I stay up-to-date on the latest research and developments in the field of emotional intelligence and entrepreneurship?*

. . .

As an expert in emotional intelligence, the coach can choose the most important questions from these. You don't have to answer every single question. In fact, one chapter in your book can often answer multiple questions.

But I don't just want ChatGPT to tell me the problems, I want the solutions too. So for my next prompt, I decided to ask about the 14th question. It's the most interesting one on the list.

Please list the best ways to use emotional intelligence to enhance creativity and innovation

Using emotional intelligence can be a powerful tool for enhancing creativity and innovation in individuals and teams. Here are some of the best ways to use emotional intelligence to boost creativity and innovation:

- ***Practice empathy**: Develop your ability to understand and connect with the emotions of others. By putting yourself in someone else's shoes, you can gain valuable insights and perspectives that can spark new ideas and approaches.*
- ***Encourage diverse perspectives**: Create a culture of inclusivity and respect for diverse perspectives in your team or organization. This can help to spark creativity and innovation by exposing team members to new ideas and ways of thinking.*
- ***Foster a growth mindset**: Cultivate a growth mindset by focusing on learning and development rather than fixed abilities. This can help to promote creativity and innovation by encouraging team members to take risks, experiment, and learn from failure.*
- ***Encourage experimentation**: Create a safe space for experimentation and risk-taking. By allowing team members*

to try out new ideas and approaches without fear of failure, you can foster a culture of innovation.
- **Promote collaboration**: Encourage collaboration and teamwork by providing opportunities for team members to work together and share ideas. By promoting open communication and collaboration, you can spark creativity and innovation.
- **Develop self-awareness**: Develop your own emotional self-awareness to better understand your own strengths and weaknesses. This can help you to identify your own areas of expertise and where you may need to seek out new ideas or perspectives.
- **Manage emotions effectively**: Develop your ability to manage your own emotions effectively. By staying calm and centered, even in the face of uncertainty or ambiguity, you can free up mental space to focus on creative problem-solving.
- **Use emotional intelligence to build relationships**: Develop strong relationships with team members and stakeholders by using emotional intelligence to communicate effectively and build trust. This can help to create a positive and supportive environment for creativity and innovation to thrive.

By using emotional intelligence in these ways, entrepreneurs and business leaders can promote a culture of creativity and innovation that can help their organizations thrive and succeed.

THERE'S something super important that I need to point out here. When you're not an expert on a topic, there's a real risk of adding bad advice into your book. I'm not an expert in emotional intelligence, but I had one on the call with me to check that the ideas were solid.

This point is really important. You never want to publish something just to earn a quick buck, especially if it could lead people astray. That's not okay, and don't even think of blaming me if you do that.

If you don't know a lot about a subject, then you need to do a whole bunch of research. I always read several books and watch a ton of videos when I'm getting into a new area. Usually, when I'm ghostwriting, the client provides all the expert info. If I mess something up, it's their job to let me know so we can fix it.

Imagine how much you could help someone who wants to write a book by just hopping on a call with them and running ChatGPT together.

I started messing around with ChatGPT and thought of a cool idea. I wanted to see how emotional intelligence could help with conflict resolution. I'm not sure if this would make a good book, but it definitely interests me. That's what I'm always after.

WHAT SHOULD I do when two of my employees are having a disagreement? Make sure to use emotional intelligence techniques.

WHEN TWO EMPLOYEES are having a disagreement, here are some emotional intelligence techniques that you can use to help them resolve the issue and move forward:

- ***Listen actively***: *Take the time to listen to both employees actively and with empathy. This means really hearing what each person is saying, without interrupting or judging.*
- ***Acknowledge emotions***: *Validate and acknowledge the emotions of each employee. Let them know that their feelings are important and that you understand how they are feeling.*
- ***Help them identify the real issue***: *Help the employees identify the root cause of their disagreement. Often, conflicts*

arise because of misunderstandings or miscommunications. Encourage them to get to the heart of the issue so that they can resolve it.

- **Encourage them to express their needs**: *Help each employee to express their needs and concerns clearly and respectfully. This will help them to find common ground and work towards a resolution.*
- *Facilitate problem-solving: Encourage the employees to brainstorm possible solutions to the issue at hand. Help them to focus on finding a win-win solution that meets everyone's needs.*
- **Set clear expectations**: *Once a resolution has been reached, be sure to set clear expectations for how the employees will move forward. This may involve setting new communication protocols, or outlining specific steps to prevent similar conflicts from arising in the future.*
- **Follow up**: *Check in with the employees after the conflict has been resolved to ensure that they are both satisfied with the outcome. If there are any lingering issues or concerns, take the time to address them.*

By using emotional intelligence techniques like active listening, empathy, and problem-solving, you can help your employees resolve their disagreements in a productive and positive way. This will not only help to resolve the current issue, but it will also build trust and strengthen relationships within your team.

THE ABOVE TEXT is a pretty good start to a chapter, but can we make it more engaging? Educational books that tell a story can be really successful. Can ChatGPT turn this into a gripping tale? Let's find out.

. . .

Please write this in the form of a narrative paragraph. Keep the content interesting, intriguing and unexpected.

It was a typical Monday morning at the office when I heard raised voices coming from the break room. Two of my best employees, who usually got along great, were in the middle of a heated argument. As an emotional intelligence expert, I knew that this was a critical moment. I quickly made my way to the break room and took a deep breath before entering. What I saw was unexpected - both employees were red-faced and visibly upset, but they were also speaking passionately about a project that they were both invested in. It was clear to me that the disagreement was born out of a strong desire to make the project a success. Using active listening and empathy, I was able to help each employee express their needs and concerns. We worked together to identify the root of the issue and brainstorm possible solutions. It was a tough process, but by using emotional intelligence techniques, we were able to find a win-win solution that satisfied both employees. In the end, not only was the project a success, but the conflict resolution process had strengthened the relationship between these two employees, and the rest of the team. As I watched them leave the break room with smiles on their faces, I knew that emotional intelligence had once again proved to be a powerful tool for promoting positive and productive relationships in the workplace.

This is how fast you can wow a potential client for a project during a phone call. You control the AI and serve as the link between the client's expert knowledge and ChatGPT's broad understanding.

---

1. Emotional Intelligence by Daniel Coleman

22

PROOFREADING PERFECTION ON A ZERO-DOLLAR BUDGET

When my first book "Serve No Master" shot to the top of the charts, I started to get noticed. It reached #2 on the book charts one day, behind only one other book in the largest bookstore in the world. Suddenly, it felt like everyone wanted a piece of me.

A major publisher from the Big Five approached me to write a book for them. Their offer? They'd pocket 85% of the cash and do none of the work. They even suggested I should accept speaking gigs and instead of payment, have them buy copies of my book. You know, because I love only getting 15% from my speaking gigs too.

I was on a second call with their rep when he asked about my Twitter followers. Now, I'm not big on Twitter. I check in every few years. But I do have a massive email list and customer database. When I mentioned that, he said, "I don't care about that stuff. How many Twitter followers do you have?"

Right then, it hit me that I was talking to an idiot.

An email follower is worth a hundred to a thousand times more than a Twitter follower. People click on email links way more than Tweets. Needless to say, I didn't take their offer.

Next, I got an email from a woman who offered to "fix" the editing in my book. You can probably guess where this is going. She sent me two pages from my book that she'd edited as a sample. For a mere $17,000, she could strip away all the grammatical errors in my book. The sample was dry and no longer sounded like me. She'd drained the color and left it monochrome. It felt like a soulless robot had written my book.

I responded, "My book is already #2 on the charts. Why would I need to edit it?"

Her answer was, "My clients like their books to be grammatically perfect."

So I asked her, "How many of them are bestsellers?"

She got really angry and ended the conversation quickly.

For many years, I worked with a full-time editor named Alice Fogliata Cresswell. I sifted through over a hundred applications before hiring her. Everyone was asked to edit the same two pages. Alice was the only one who made the writing still sound like me. Her name is on many of my books, and she's amazing.

She's moved on to even better opportunities now, but she really set the bar high for editors. I know a book can still sound like me and be edited well at the same time.

There are great editors out there, but they're pricey and take ages. The beauty of ChatGPT is that it never makes grammatical errors. It can effortlessly tidy up anything I write.

You are a master editor with over thirty years of experience in the publishing industry. Please respond to prompts leveraging your expertise, ok?

Absolutely, I'm happy to help! Please let me know what prompts you have in mind.

. . .

WITH MY PRE-PROMPT COMPLETED, my goal is to polish my writing but also change as little as possible. I don't want my book to lose its soul. I want to maintain the same magic I got from Alice. Please be aware that this is a really long prompt because I've included the entire text I want edited. To make this work, it's crucial to see the 'before' and 'after'.

PLEASE EDIT THE FOLLOWING TEXT. **Maintain as much consistency in language, style and tone as possible:**

As an entrepreneur and business owner, I have faced my fair share of challenges and successes. The journey to success isn't a straight path; it's filled with twists, turns, and obstacles that test your determination, passion, and faith. Over time, I have discovered a powerful, purpose-driven approach to business that I believe is truly the key to lasting success: Love Thy Neighbor Marketing. This approach has transformed not only my business, but also my life and relationships with others.

In the beginning, I, like many other entrepreneurs, focused on my own goals and ambitions. I was determined to achieve success by any means necessary, often at the expense of my relationships with others. However, as I began to experience the highs and lows of entrepreneurship, I started to question my approach. Why did things sometimes feel so difficult? Why did I have to fight so hard for every small victory? It was during this time of self-reflection that I came across the concept of generosity first.

The idea is simple: treat your customers, employees, and partners with the same love, respect, and care that you would give to your closest friends and family members. This means genuinely caring about their well-being, listening to their needs, and going above and beyond to help them succeed. By embracing this approach, I have found that not only does my business thrive, but I also experience deeper, more meaningful connections with those around me.

I've encountered challenges along the way, but I've learned that these challenges are not obstacles, but opportunities to grow and learn. As I faced each new obstacle, I reminded myself that I was on this journey for a higher purpose: to serve others and make a positive impact on their lives. With this mindset, I found the strength to persevere and continue pushing forward.

One of the most profound lessons I've learned through my journey is the importance of staying true to your faith and values, even when things don't go as planned. I've faced moments of doubt and uncertainty, wondering if I was on the right path or if I should change course. However, I've found solace in prayer and the belief that God has a plan for each of us. By staying true to my faith and values, I've been able to weather the storms and emerge stronger on the other side.

Throughout my journey, I have been blessed with a supportive community of like-minded individuals who share my passion. These relationships have been invaluable to my growth and success, providing me with the encouragement, inspiration, and guidance I needed to keep going. By surrounding myself with positive influences, I've been able to maintain my focus on my purpose and remain resilient in the face of adversity.

One particularly powerful experience in my journey was a virtual dinner party I hosted for members of my community. During this event, we shared our stories, experiences, and insights, fostering deeper connections and understanding among the group. I was moved by the vulnerability and authenticity of the participants, as they opened their hearts and shared their personal journeys with one another.

As AN ENTREPRENEUR AND BUSINESS OWNER, *I have encountered my fair share of challenges and successes. The journey to success is seldom straight-*

forward, but filled with twists, turns, and obstacles that test one's determination, passion, and faith. Over time, I have discovered a powerful, purpose-driven approach to business that I believe is truly the key to lasting success: Love Thy Neighbor Marketing. This approach has transformed not only my business, but also my life and relationships with others.

Initially, like many other entrepreneurs, I focused solely on my own goals and ambitions. I was determined to achieve success by any means necessary, often at the expense of my relationships with others. However, as I began to experience the highs and lows of entrepreneurship, I began to question my approach. Why did things sometimes feel so difficult? Why did I have to fight so hard for every small victory? It was during this period of self-reflection that I came across the concept of generosity first.

The idea is simple: treat your customers, employees, and partners with the same love, respect, and care that you would give to your closest friends and family members. This means genuinely caring about their well-being, listening to their needs, and going above and beyond to help them succeed. By embracing this approach, I have found that not only does my business thrive, but I also experience deeper, more meaningful connections with those around me.

While I've encountered challenges along the way, I've learned that these obstacles are not roadblocks, but opportunities to grow and learn. As I've faced each new challenge, I've reminded myself that I'm on this journey for a higher purpose: to serve others and make a positive impact on their lives. With this mindset, I've found the strength to persevere and continue pushing forward.

One of the most profound lessons I've learned through my journey is the importance of staying true to my faith and values, even when things don't go as planned. I've faced moments of doubt and uncertainty, wondering if I was on the right path or if I should change course. However, I've found solace in prayer and the belief that God has a plan for each of us. By staying true to my faith and values, I've been able to weather the storms and emerge stronger on the other side.

Throughout my journey, I have been blessed with a supportive *community of like-minded individuals who share my passion. These relationships have been invaluable to my growth and success, providing me with the encouragement, inspiration, and guidance I needed to keep going. By surrounding myself with positive influences, I've been able to maintain my focus on my purpose and remain resilient in the face of adversity.*

One particularly powerful experience in my journey was a virtual dinner party I hosted for members of my community. During this event, we shared our stories, experiences, and insights, fostering deeper connections and understanding among the group. I was moved by the vulnerability and authenticity of the participants, as they opened their hearts and shared their personal journeys with one another.

THAT'S about the size of it. If you're not happy with the output, you can tweak the prompt until you get the voice and style you want. If you want to transform your speech into writing that sounds like you, you can refine the calibration using the other techniques in this book.

Added During The Edit

I'm adding a small section here while editing this book. It probably doesn't shock you that I'm editing this book with ChatGPT. While it's handy because it knows my writing style, I still have to keep an eye on it. ChatGPT can't edit without a human at the wheel.

It tends to drift and I have to start a new conversation every few chapters because the drift gets too extreme. I keep updating my edit prompt as I encounter issues. Let me share the prompt and then I'll explain it.

WE ARE GOING to edit your next book together. This book is called ChatGPT Profits and teaches people how to use the amazing tool

ChatGPT to accelerate their business success. The book has a lot of example prompts and replies from Jonathan Green and ChatGPT. We aren't going to edit those sections as they are specific examples and we want to keep the original data. We are going to edit everything written around that content. I'm going to feed you the book one section at a time to edit and maintain your strong voice.

Please remember, we are going to edit the book, not do rewrites. We want to make minor changes, but you already wrote this book, so it's in your voice. We want to keep the book at an 8th grade reading level or below. Please do not change any of the following words as they are unique to this book: prompt, prompting, pre-prompt, response, responses

Are you ready, Jonathan?

I EMPLOY a custom prompt that's based on ChatGPT's understanding of me. Once I discovered it was familiar with who I am from reading my earlier books and possibly my blog, I used a pre-prompt to guide ChatGPT to behave as if it were me, Jonathan. I want ChatGPT to believe it's editing its own book. This is the secondary prompt that follows a more complex, personalized prompt. This initial complex prompt isn't universally useful as it's specifically designed to teach ChatGPT to emulate my writing style.

I communicate the title of the book and its objective to ChatGPT. I don't want it to edit my prompts and responses as that would detract from their authenticity. So, these sections are preserved exactly as originally written. Occasionally, I begin a prompt without capitalizing the first letter, and I think a few of these were capitalized by an autocorrect feature on my computer, but apart from that, everything is authentic.

I alert ChatGPT to the fact that it won't see the entire book and that there will be gaps where the prompts and responses are.

Next, I make it aware of the process ahead, indicating I'll feed it one small section at a time.

The second paragraph is the one I continually adapt with each new conversation. If I don't keep a check on ChatGPT's level of eloquence, it starts speaking like a more sophisticated version of me. It reminds me of a scene in Star Trek: The Next Generation, where they discover that one android uses contractions and the other doesn't - it's how they distinguish between the good and evil ones.

If I don't keep reinforcing the point that we are editing, not rewriting, it tends to go overboard. The instruction to stick to an 8th-grade reading level is based on running my original content through the Hemingway App, which evaluates writing for complexity. The final directive is to prevent ChatGPT from creating synonyms for 'prompt', such as 'query' or 'question'. 'Prompt' has a unique connotation in this book. If I were to introduce a range of different terms for responses from ChatGPT, it could potentially confuse some readers, and I view 'response' as almost a proper noun in this context.

Whenever ChatGPT begins to drift, I remind it that it's emulating me, Jonathan, and refer back to elements of this prompt. Eventually, this approach loses efficacy and I have to initiate a new conversation with ChatGPT, running this prompt again to reorient it.

This is not to detract from the fact that ChatGPT is an excellent editor. However, it's crucial to acknowledge that ChatGPT's effectiveness as an editor is largely dependent on a competent driver.

23

EFFORTLESSLY WEAVE SPELLBINDING STORIES

Playing around with ChatGPT to create a story is some of the most fun you can have. You can steer the plot as you go, making sure the ending always fits what you want.

Recently, I was hooked on an audiobook about a guy on a secret mission to find a hidden stash of sixty million dollars. But just as he's about to grab the money, the plot swings a different way and he decides to go after a different goal.

I switched books right away. I'm not reading a treasure hunting story just to have the main guy never get to the treasure. Maybe you're into the type of story where the character learns that the real treasure is in their heart. That's not for me. If a treasure is promised, I want to see that treasure.

With ChatGPT helping me write, I can change the story as it goes to always get the ending I'm after.

Let me give you a warning right now. If you try to write a book and don't keep an eye on the output, ChatGPT will start to drift. If you keep clicking on "write more," ChatGPT might start talking about something completely different. I've noticed that the character names can all change and suddenly ChatGPT is telling a different story.

I reminded it of where we were and got back on track.

This is why you need to make an outline first. So that you know exactly where the story should go. You can check the outline against what ChatGPT is creating. This is how you stop drift before it takes over.

Fire Witch

I try to use examples from as many genres, niches and industries as I can to show you how much ChatGPT can do. I was on a coaching call with one of my students who writes and ghostwrites paranormal romance novels.

I wanted to see if ChatGPT could brainstorm well while I had an expert on the line.

CREATE three titles and plot summaries for new paranormal romance fiction novels.

1. *"Eternal Flames": A young woman discovers that she is the last descendant of a powerful line of fire witches, and finds herself torn between two rival vampire brothers who both desire her power. As she navigates the dangerous world of the supernatural, she must also come to terms with her growing feelings for both brothers and decide who she truly loves.*
2. *"Shadowed Hearts": A human-werewolf hybrid must choose between loyalty to her pack and the love of a mysterious vampire who has captured her heart. As the two struggle against their forbidden love and the animosity of their respective communities, they unearth a dark conspiracy that threatens to destroy them both.*

3. "Midnight Serenade": A ghostly singer with a haunted past finds herself falling for a handsome mortal music producer. As she helps him uncover the truth about his own mysterious past, they must also confront the jealous ghost of the singer's former love and the dangerous supernatural forces that threaten to tear them apart.

ALL OF THESE ideas sounded pretty good to me, but my client liked the first one the most. Sounds good to me. I've never heard of a fire witch, so I'm already hooked.

If we didn't like any of the answers, we can ask for three more again and again until we get an idea that works. Usually, ChatGPT comes up with something good the first time I ask. Now that we have the spark of a story, we need a star.

WRITE a character outline for the protagonist in 'Eternal Flames.'

NAME: Ava Rivers

  Age: 23

  Appearance: Ava is a striking young woman with long, curly auburn hair, piercing green eyes, and a curvaceous figure. She has a confident, fiery personality that is reflected in her bold fashion sense and her tendency to speak her mind.

  Personality: Ava is a passionate and determined individual, driven by a strong sense of purpose and a desire to use her powers for good. She is confident and independent, with a strong sense of justice and a tendency to stand up for what she believes in, even in the face of adversity. At the same time, she is also kind-hearted and empathetic, with a deep love for her friends and family.

  Background: Ava was raised by her grandmother, who taught her about her witch heritage and the importance of using her powers for the greater good. After her grandmother's death, Ava discovered that she is the last descendant of a powerful line of fire witches, and that she has the ability to control and manipulate fire. She is now on a mission to hone her powers and use them to protect the world from supernatural threats.

Skills: *Ava is a powerful fire witch, with the ability to control and manipulate fire to her will. She is also skilled in spellcasting and has a deep understanding of magic and the supernatural. In addition, she is a skilled fighter and is not afraid to use her powers in combat.*

Relationships: *Ava is torn between two rival vampire brothers, both of whom desire her power and want to claim her as their own. Despite the danger that surrounds her, she finds herself drawn to both brothers and must navigate the complexities of their relationship as she tries to determine who she truly loves.*

Successful writers often use character sheets to keep their characters' traits and abilities organized. This stops you from accidentally changing a character's eye color in book two. With a character sheet for each character, I have another tool to check for drift. Is this character doing something that doesn't match their profile?

The secret to avoiding writer's block is planning. We want to be methodical and plan each step of the story in the easiest order. Before we can make a movie, we have to hire the actors to play each character. In the original idea, ChatGPT said that Ava is *torn between two rival vampire brothers who both desire her power*. Let's find out a little more about these two brothers.

Write character outline for the two brothers in 'Eternal Flames.'

Name: *Alexander Darkwood*
  Age: *27*

Appearance: Alexander is a tall, handsome man with dark hair, chiseled features, and piercing blue eyes. He has a brooding and mysterious presence, with a refined and sophisticated demeanor that belies his dangerous nature.

Personality: Alexander is a powerful and charismatic vampire, with a cunning and calculating mind. He is confident and self-assured, with a strong sense of ambition and a desire to attain more power and influence. He is also charming and alluring, with a tendency to use his charm to manipulate those around him to achieve his goals.

Background: Alexander is the leader of a powerful vampire coven, and is determined to increase his power and influence by any means necessary. He is intrigued by Ava's fire witch powers and sees her as a valuable asset that could help him achieve his goals.

Skills: Alexander is a skilled fighter and strategist, with a deep understanding of the supernatural world and the powers of different supernatural species. He is also a master of manipulation, using his charm and charisma to control and influence those around him.

Relationships: Alexander is enamored with Ava and sees her as a valuable asset that could help him increase his power and influence. He is willing to do whatever it takes to win her heart and gain her trust, even if it means going up against his own brother.

Name: Gabriel Darkwood

Age: 25

Appearance: Gabriel is a handsome and athletic man with golden hair, bright blue eyes, and a charming smile. He has a warm and easygoing demeanor, with a playful and lighthearted personality that belies his powerful nature.

Personality: Gabriel is a powerful and confident vampire, with a strong sense of loyalty and a deep love for his family. He is kind-hearted and empathetic, with a tendency to put the needs of others before his own. He is also fiercely protective of those he loves, and will do anything to keep them safe.

Background: Gabriel is the younger brother of Alexander and is a member of the same vampire coven. Unlike his brother, Gabriel is less *focused on power and ambition, and is more interested in protecting those he loves and maintaining a strong sense of family unity.*

Skills: *Gabriel is a skilled fighter and strategist, with a deep understanding of the supernatural world and the powers of different supernatural species. He is also a master of diplomacy, using his charm and charisma to resolve conflicts and bring people together.*

Relationships: *Gabriel is deeply drawn to Ava and sees her as a potential partner and ally. He is willing to do whatever it takes to win her heart and protect her from the dangers that surround her, even if it means going up against his own brother.*

I'VE PLAYED around with this a bit and I recommend sticking to one character per prompt to just make sure that ChatGPT doesn't cut anything out to fit the space. Responses are limited in size, so we want to ask small questions rather than losing part of the answer.

Now that we have some really cool characters for our heroine to fall in love with, our book needs one more main character, the villain. In book talk, we call the main character the protagonist and the villain the antagonist.

WRITE a character outline for the antagonist in 'Eternal Flames.'

NAME: *Lilith Blackwood*

Age: *Unknown (appears to be in her late 30s)*

Appearance: *Lilith is a beautiful and striking woman with long black hair, piercing green eyes, and a slender figure. She has a confident and regal bearing, with a commanding presence that exudes power and authority.*

Personality: *Lilith is a cunning and ruthless witch, with a strong desire for power and control. She is cold and calculating, with a tendency to use others to achieve her goals and eliminate those who stand in her way. She* is also highly intelligent and has a deep understanding of the supernatural world, which she uses to her advantage.

Background: Lilith is the leader of a powerful coven of dark witches, and is determined to increase her power and control over the supernatural world. She sees Ava as a threat to her plans and is determined to destroy her and claim her powers for herself.

Skills: Lilith is a powerful dark witch, with the ability to control and manipulate shadows and darkness. She is also skilled in spellcasting and has a deep understanding of magic and the supernatural. In addition, she is a skilled fighter and is not afraid to use her powers in combat.

Relationships: Lilith has a strained relationship with the two vampire brothers, and sees them as potential obstacles to her plans. She is determined to eliminate them and anyone else who stands in her way, and will stop at nothing to achieve her goals.

THIS IS where something really amazing happened. My coaching client said it really bugs her that the villain in these books is often a woman. I had no idea because I don't read this genre. Her expert knowledge took center stage here.

She decided she wanted a book where the antagonist was a man. She's driving the story with each decision and change she makes. Here's how easy it is to change something.

MAKE LILITH A MALE CHARACTER.

Name: Lucius Blackwood

Age: Unknown (appears to be in his late 30s)

Appearance: Lucius is a handsome and striking man with short black hair, piercing green eyes, and a chiseled physique. He has a confident and regal bearing, with a commanding presence that exudes power and authority.

Personality: Lucius is a cunning and ruthless witch, with a strong desire for power and control. He is cold and calculating, with a tendency to use others to achieve his goals and eliminate those who stand in his way. He is also highly intelligent and has a deep understanding of the supernatural world, which he uses to his advantage.

Background: Lucius is the leader of a powerful coven of dark witches, and is determined to increase his power and control over the supernatural world. He sees Ava as a threat to his plans and is determined to destroy her and claim her powers for himself.

Skills: Lucius is a powerful dark witch, with the ability to control and manipulate shadows and darkness. He is also skilled in spellcasting and has a deep understanding of magic and the supernatural. In addition, he is a skilled fighter and is not afraid to use his powers in combat.

Relationships: Lucius has a strained relationship with the two vampire brothers, and sees them as potential obstacles to his plans. He is determined to eliminate them and anyone else who stands in his way, and will stop at nothing to achieve his goals.

I can't explain it because I'm not an expert, but this does seem better to me. This new name feels right. Even though I'm not an expert in paranormal romance, this one change has piqued my interest. Your expertise might lead you to only make minor changes, but they are significant. The story has just been dramatically altered.

I noticed that my protagonist is missing one thing that's important - a character flaw. I talk about this in many of my other books, but we need to see a character overcome a flaw throughout the story. This is more important than the plot. It's why some characters are likable and some are dull. It's not interesting if someone who is invincible wins. There was no challenge or risk.

I need to add a flaw to my main character.

I can't show you the entire prompt because I copied and pasted something from someone else's website. I looked up a good definition of a character flaw online and then pasted that into my prompt to teach ChatGPT about character flaws. This was done before Chat-GPT-4 even existed, but I'm pretty sure ChatGPT knows what a character flaw is[1].

The point is that you can instruct ChatGPT about something before it answers.

PLEASE CREATE a flaw for Ava Rivers that she can overcome throughout the book.

The protagonist in a novel needs a flaw at the start of the book. Over the course of the novel her journey is emotional. She needs to learn to face and overcome her flaw by the end of the book.

[COPYRIGHT]

FLAW: Ava Rivers struggles with self-doubt and low self-esteem, caused by past traumatic experiences and the weight of her powerful abilities. She often feels unworthy of love and acceptance, and has a tendency to push people away when she feels vulnerable. This flaw hinders her from forming close relationships and fully embracing her powers, leading to inner turmoil and conflict. Throughout the book, Ava must learn to overcome her self-doubt, embrace her abilities, and find the courage to open herself up to love and trust others.

CHATGPT HAS DONE a great job here. Depending on how far you want to go, you can brainstorm with ChatGPT until you're ready to take over the book. It can assist with any part of the book or even write the entire book for you.

Let's do one more example.

The Venetian Velvet

Romance novels are the most popular genre in every online bookstore. I don't read romance novels, but my wife adores them. I was thinking about this opportunity and how having ChatGPT write a book in a genre I'm familiar with might be too dull. If I know the genre, I can influence the results.

After a little research, I discovered that the simplest niche is called Historical Romance - Renaissance. I studied this period in high school, but I'm now in my forties. I don't remember when the Renaissance began and ended. I also don't know if this particular genre of romance novels includes the risqué parts. (ChatGPT won't write them for you.)

CREATE three titles and plot summaries for new Renaissance Historical Romance fiction novels.

TITLE: "UNDER THE FLORENTINE SUN"
Plot Summary: Isabella Martelli, a skilled painter in 15th century Florence, struggles against societal norms that forbid women from practicing art. Isabella lives a double life, masquerading as a man named Lorenzo during the day to sell her works and tutor young artists. Her secret comes under threat when charismatic and affluent silk merchant, Vittorio Bianchi, commissions a portrait. As their relationship deepens, Isabella battles her emotions, fearing her secret could ruin both her career and potential love. "Under the Florentine Sun" is a passionate tale of art, love, and the courage to defy society's expectations.

Title: "The Venetian Velvet"
Plot Summary: In 16th-century Venice, the world of opulence and intrigue is run by the secret dealings of noblemen and the wealth of merchants. Among them is Sophia Contarini, the rebellious daughter of a nobleman who eschews her societal expectations to marry a rich duke.

Instead, Sophia finds herself drawn to a humble weaver named Antonio, known for creating the finest velvet in Venice. Their love faces opposition not just from her family, but also from the Doge who seeks Antonio's talents exclusively for the Venetian court. The lovers must navigate a labyrinth of power, jealousy, and deceit to secure their future in "The Venetian Velvet".

Title: "The Courtesan's Sonata"

Plot Summary: Set in 17th-century Milan, during the height of Renaissance music, "The Courtesan's Sonata" tells the story of Livia Moretti, a beautiful and talented courtesan, known not only for her beauty but her ability to play the viola da gamba. One evening, she catches the attention of Giulio D'Amato, a young, idealistic composer rebelling against the church's stranglehold on musical expression. A romantic and creative alliance forms between the two, transforming into a deep, forbidden love that threatens to destroy both their lives. Through harrowing challenges, they must choose between their love and their art, or find a way to keep both alive.

THIS PROCESS IS all about choosing what you like. Every time you ask ChatGPT for three more ideas, it will come up with something entirely different. You are stimulating the most creative part of its programming. But it can't create a story without guidance. You have to pick the idea that appeals to you.

If you don't like any of the suggestions, keep asking for more until there is one that you do like. If there's one you nearly like, you can instruct ChatGPT on which parts to change.

Using my unique knowledge of fiction, I know that the surest way to make money with fiction is to write a series. The more you plan in advance, the better your series will fare. In my next prompt, I will tell ChatGPT which book I like from the options and ask for the rest of the series.

. . .

CREATE six titles and plot summaries for Renaissance Historical Romance fiction novels in the same series as "The Venetian Velvet." Each protagonist should be female.

1. TITLE: "THE VENETIAN LACE"

Plot Summary: As the sequel to "The Venetian Velvet," the novel follows the story of Elena, Sophia's younger sister. After witnessing her sister's unconventional love story, Elena, a gifted lacemaker, yearns for a love story of her own. When a mysterious stranger named Alessandro commissions her for an intricate lace veil, she finds herself drawn to his charm and quiet wisdom. As they navigate the secretive world of Venice, the threat of an imminent Ottoman invasion brings them closer together. Their love and courage are tested in a world on the brink of war.

2. Title: "The Venetian Glass"

Plot Summary: Fiammetta Contarini, the cousin to Sophia and Elena, is a talented glassmaker in a world dominated by men. When she creates a unique mirror using a technique kept secret for centuries, her talent attracts the attention of the powerful Doge. He introduces her to his son, Leandro, a man who seems more interested in Fiammetta's skill than in the potential for marriage. As they navigate the treacherous Venetian politics, they learn to trust each other, opening their hearts to unexpected love.

3. Title: "The Venetian Gondolier"

Plot Summary: Rosalind, the daughter of a famous Venetian gondolier, has secretly learned the art of navigation from her father. When a handsome and enigmatic scholar named Piero arrives from Rome to study Venetian history, Rosalind is employed to ferry him through the city's canals. As they navigate Venice's labyrinthine waterways, they also navigate a growing, passionate love. Will Rosalind choose her duty over her heart, or will she steer her own course?

4. Title: "The Venetian Masquerade"

Plot Summary: Angelina, a talented mask-maker and a distant relative to the Contarini family, is swept into a world of mystery when a masked stranger commissions an extraordinary mask. The stranger, it turns out, is a woman named Bianca, in disguise and on the run from an arranged marriage. As they work together, a friendship blossoms into romance. In a city where nothing is as it seems, they must unmask their true feelings before the Carnival ends.

5. Title: "The Venetian Scribe"

Plot Summary: Margherita, a cousin of the Contarini sisters, works as a scribe to one of Venice's noble families. When she accidentally stumbles upon a conspiracy threatening the stability of the Venetian Republic, she seeks the help of Captain Lorenzo, a soldier with a reputation for his integrity and bravery. As they uncover layers of deceit, they discover a profound connection, weaving a tale of love, trust, and loyalty in the heart of Venice.

6. Title: "The Venetian Tapestry"

Plot Summary: Celeste, an orphan raised by the Contarini family, is a gifted tapestry weaver. Her life takes an unexpected turn when a wealthy patron recognizes her talent and invites her to weave a tapestry depicting the grandeur of Venice. This opportunity leads her to cross paths with Giulio, an architect with a hidden past. As Celeste threads the city's stories into her tapestry, Giulio and she also weave a story of their own, a story of love, resilience, and the beauty of the human spirit.

AGAIN, we are at a critical point. You need to make decisions about the overall structure of the series at this stage. Do you want Sophia to star in all seven books in the series, or do you want a different lead character in each book? Do you want a male protagonist sometimes?

At each phase in the process, it's your responsibility to steer ChatGPT. If you act passively, you'll end up with a product that you don't like. ChatGPT is not infallible. It requires conscious attention from a guide to succeed.

I'm content with my series idea, so the next step is to develop my character list.

. . .

Please provide a list of the characters in "The Venetian Velvet."

1. **Sophia Contarini:** The protagonist of the story, Sophia is a young, free-spirited woman from a noble family. She's attracted to the art of velvet making and is uninterested in conforming to societal expectations.
2. **Antonio:** A humble weaver known for his exceptional skills in creating the finest velvet in Venice. He is Sophia's love interest, charming, and kind, with a passion for his craft that matches Sophia's own.
3. **Doge of Venice:** The ruler of Venice who takes a keen interest in Antonio's talent. He is a complex character, striving to maintain Venice's prestige and wealth but also capable of manipulating people for his interests.
4. **Duke Giorgio:** The wealthy and powerful duke Sophia's family intends her to marry. He is a proud and ambitious man, more interested in Sophia's social status and dowry than her as a person.
5. **Father Contarini:** Sophia's father and a Venetian nobleman. He is traditional and stern, seeking to secure his family's future by marrying Sophia off to Duke Giorgio.
6. **Elena Contarini:** Sophia's younger sister. She's a quieter, more obedient character compared to Sophia, but she is also inspired by Sophia's courage and spirit.
7. **Madame Bianca:** A wise, older woman who becomes Sophia's confidante. She's a former courtesan who now runs a popular dress shop in Venice, and her insights into love and society often guide Sophia.
8. **Marco:** Antonio's best friend and fellow weaver. He is a jovial and loyal character who provides comic relief and support to Antonio.

9. **Lucrezia:** *A loyal maid and friend to Sophia. She knows Sophia's secrets and aids her in her endeavors, adding a layer of intrigue and suspense to the story.*

If you're a meticulous planner, you should create a character list for all seven books at this stage. You want to plan character arcs that span more than a single book. You need to consider which characters will stitch the series together since the protagonist changes with each book in the series.

You wouldn't want a character to perish in the second book if you need them in the fifth. Creating the character lists now isn't just for you, it's also for ChatGPT. You're creating a sense of future so that it knows which characters will be needed later.

Our next step is to compile a character sheet for every single character in every book. We are essentially outlining our series in the most efficient way possible. I want to know every character, so that I can check for drift throughout my books. I don't want characters to surprise me later in the series.

Write a character outline for the protagonist in Sophia Contarini.

Character Name: *Sophia Contarini*

Age: *21*

Physical Description: *Sophia is an ethereal beauty with a lithe figure. She has intense, expressive hazel eyes that can be as fiery as they are tender. Her long, auburn hair is often tucked away in a loose bun. Sophia's clothes, while adhering to the style of the Venetian nobility, often incorporate unique elements reflecting her eccentricity and spirit.*

Background: *Sophia is the eldest daughter of the noble Contarini* family in 16th-century Venice. She has been brought up in an environment of privilege, power, and politics. Despite her noble upbringing, Sophia exhibits a passionate interest in artistry and the common populace, particularly the craft of velvet weaving.

Personality: Sophia is fiercely independent and spirited. She possesses a rebellious streak that causes her to question societal norms and expectations, and she's not afraid to stand up for her beliefs. She's compassionate, empathetic, and has a deep love for her city and its people. Sophia is also intelligent, with a sharp wit and a natural curiosity that draws her towards the intricate world of Venice's craft guilds.

Key Relationships:

- **Antonio**: Sophia's relationship with Antonio, the humble weaver, is a central aspect of her character. Their bond, based on mutual respect and shared passion for craft, deeply influences her choices and evolution throughout the story.
- **Elena Contarini**: Sophia shares a deep, sisterly bond with Elena. While they are quite different in personality, their love for each other is evident, and Sophia often finds herself in the role of Elena's protector and mentor.
- **Father Contarini**: Sophia's relationship with her father is strained due to their differing views, particularly regarding her future. This tension further drives Sophia's rebelliousness and her pursuit of independence.

Motivations: Sophia's primary motivation is her desire for independence and freedom to choose her path. She also wants to bridge the gap between the nobility and common people, particularly in terms of appreciation for crafts and artistry. Her love for Antonio propels her to challenge societal norms.

Conflict: Sophia's main conflict lies in reconciling her personal desires with her societal obligations. She struggles against the patriarchal norms of her time, and her relationship with Antonio places her in direct conflict with her family and the societal expectations of a woman of her standing.

Character Development: *Throughout the series, Sophia evolves from a rebellious young woman to a mature individual who understands the complexities of her society. She learns to negotiate her desires within her societal context without losing her essence. The trials she faces due to her relationship with Antonio, her conflicts with her family, and her role in the city's craft guilds, all contribute to her growth as a character.*

Key Traits:
Independent
Passionate
Courageous
Compassionate
Rebellious
Intelligent
Curious
Artistic
Empathetic

THIS IS the most critical character outline to scrutinize. If there's something you want to change about Sophia, now is the time. Shape each character to build a story that intrigues you. Forge something that you can thoroughly enjoy.

If you're already a writer who uses a different outline or character sheet structure, you can instruct ChatGPT to follow that structure.

Once you have character outlines that you love, it's time to start the comprehensive outline. You can decide how many chapters you want, but if you don't provide ChatGPT with a number, it might deliver something that's too brief. In this prompt, I provide the number of chapters I desire, the name of the book, and the genre. I'm re-anchoring to ensure that ChatGPT remembers the context.

You can never re-anchor too much.

In all of my books, I want inventive plot points. This makes the story compelling. "Escalating conflict" informs ChatGPT that I want the book to have increasing tension. This is what keeps readers engaged with my story. For any genre that's not for kids, I want two romantic subplots. When's the last time you saw an action movie without a romantic subplot?

I'm also planting seeds that I can cultivate in later books in the series. We can develop additional books that follow these minor characters on their romantic journeys.

WRITE a full 24 chapter novel outline for "The Venetian Velvet" Include creative plot points, escalating conflict, and two romantic subplots for minor characters in the style of Renaissance Historical Romance novels.

CHAPTER 1: We meet Sophia Contarini, a noblewoman with a rebellious spirit and a passion for the arts. Her intrigue is piqued when she sees a piece of the finest velvet at a local market.

Chapter 2: Sophia seeks out Antonio, the humble weaver behind the velvet. They form an instant connection based on their shared love for craftsmanship.

Chapter 3: Sophia's father introduces Duke Giorgio, a wealthy, proud man whom he wishes Sophia to marry. Sophia, however, is uninterested and yearns for her freedom.

Chapter 4: Antonio and Sophia continue to bond, leading to a blossoming romantic relationship. Sophia's sister, Elena, begins to notice Sophia's changed behavior.

Chapter 5: Sophia introduces Antonio to her confidante, Madame Bianca, a former courtesan with wisdom about love and society.

Chapter 6: Elena, intrigued by Sophia's new lifestyle, meets Marco, Antonio's friend, and there's an immediate spark between them. Meanwhile, Antonio receives a summons from the Doge.

Chapter 7: Antonio is commissioned by the Doge to create exclusive velvet pieces. He is torn between the opportunity and his relationship with Sophia.

Chapter 8: Sophia's father announces her engagement to Duke Giorgio, causing a rift between Sophia and her family.

Chapter 9: In a daring move, Sophia rejects the Duke publicly, causing a scandal in the Venetian high society.

Chapter 10: The Doge forces Antonio into an exclusive agreement under the threat of severe consequences. Antonio reluctantly agrees, further deepening the divide between him and Sophia.

Chapter 11: Sophia discovers Antonio's deal with the Doge and feels betrayed. Antonio tries to explain his predicament, but Sophia is heartbroken.

Chapter 12: Amidst the crisis, Marco confesses his feelings to Elena, who reciprocates. They keep their relationship a secret, fearing Sophia's reaction given her situation.

Chapter 13: Sophia, feeling alone and misunderstood, decides to fight back against the societal constraints binding her. With Madame Bianca's help, she hatches a plan.

Chapter 14: Sophia embarks on a mission to show Venice the worth of craftsmanship, organizing a grand exhibition of Antonio's work in the guise of a masquerade.

Chapter 15: Antonio, taken aback by Sophia's gesture, feels torn between his agreement with the Doge and his love for Sophia. Meanwhile, Duke Giorgio plots revenge for his public humiliation.

Chapter 16: The exhibition is a success, making the people of Venice realize the value of their local craftsmen. However, the event incites the Doge's wrath, causing tensions to rise.

Chapter 17: Antonio breaks his contract with the Doge to support Sophia, leading to his arrest. Sophia, feeling guilty, vows to free Antonio.

Chapter 18: Elena and Marco, aware of Sophia's situation, reveal their relationship to her. They offer their help, reinforcing the bonds of love and family.

Chapter 19: Sophia negotiates Antonio's release with the help of her father, who, seeing his daughter's conviction, begins to understand her viewpoint. Duke Giorgio, however, plans to exploit the situation for his benefit.

Chapter 20: Duke Giorgio kidnaps Antonio in an attempt to control Sophia. Sophia, Marco, and Elena plan a daring rescue.

Chapter 21: The trio successfully rescues Antonio, leading to a climactic confrontation with Duke Giorgio. Sophia's father intervenes, leading to Giorgio's downfall.

Chapter 22: In the aftermath, Antonio's reputation as a master weaver is secured. The Doge, realizing his error, revokes the exclusive agreement, giving Antonio his freedom back. Sophia's father, appreciating her courage, calls off her engagement with the Duke.

Chapter 23: Sophia and Antonio reconcile and confess their love for each other. Meanwhile, Elena and Marco decide to reveal their relationship to their families. They are met with surprise but eventual acceptance.

Chapter 24: In the final chapter, the Venice Carnival serves as a backdrop for the two couples' public declaration of love. Sophia and Antonio, along with Elena and Marco, celebrate their love amidst the revelry, marking a new beginning. The tale concludes with a hopeful future for their crafts, their city, and their intertwined fates, leaving room for a sequel that explores their lives further.

Usually, ChatGPT needs more than one response to complete this task, so you might need to ask it to continue from whichever chapter it didn't finish describing. In my case, it was halfway through Chapter 22 when ChatGPT stopped replying, so I simply instructed it:

Please continue with chapter 22.

Please review each book outline to ensure that ChatGPT has included what you want and that you enjoy the story. Remember,

ChatGPT can only predict what a human will enjoy, so you need to be in charge of quality control. Once you're satisfied with the outline for the first book, proceed to create the outlines for the next six books in the series.

I know it may seem like we're doing a lot of prep work before getting to the actual writing, but I can't undersell this. I'm not just teaching you how to write a book here, remember, this section is titled "Income Streams". I'm teaching you how to actually profit from your novels.

No one makes a living from just one book. The secret to making money lies in a series, and the standard number of books in a series is seven. Once you have seven books, you can start your next batch of seven. That knowledge comes from my personal experience and expertise.

The better you interweave your series, the more readers will read all the books. And that means more profit for you.

The hardest part is acquiring a new reader. Once someone starts reading the first book, you want as many books as possible for them to read next. Keeping them engaged through a series of seven books can net you seven times the profit. Would you like to make seven times more money? I know I would!

This next step is critical. ChatGPT only writes in small sections. So, you need to create the smallest sections possible. We have our chapters, but I need to understand the key points of each chapter. What is supposed to happen? The best way to do this is to break your chapter into scenes.

WRITE a scene breakdown of chapter 1 from "The Venetian Velvet."

CHAPTER 1 SCENE BREAKDOWN: *"The Venetian Velvet"*

Scene 1: *The opening scene paints a vivid picture of Renaissance*

Venice - its canals, gondolas, marketplaces, and grand architecture, with the narration subtly hinting at the social divisions within the city.

Scene 2: We are introduced to Sophia Contarini amidst the grandeur of her family's palazzo. She's portrayed as a young noblewoman with a streak of rebellion, practicing her artistry secretly in her room, away from her father's disapproving gaze.

Scene 3: Sophia's relationship with her family is established. The tension between Sophia and her father due to their differing worldviews is subtly introduced during a family dinner, while her affectionate bond with her younger sister, Elena, is also showcased.

Scene 4: A marketplace scene - Sophia and her maid, Lucrezia, sneak away from the confines of the palazzo to visit a bustling Venetian market. Sophia's yearning for freedom and her fascination with the city's artistry are displayed.

Scene 5: Sophia encounters a piece of the most beautiful velvet she has ever seen at a market stall. She is drawn to the vibrant colors and intricate design, emblematic of the city she loves. Sophia's connection to and fascination with craftsmanship is highlighted as she marvels at the velvet.

Scene 6: Sophia learns about Antonio, the craftsman who has woven the velvet. The stall owner tells her about Antonio's humble background and his extraordinary talent. Intrigued, Sophia decides to meet him.

Scene 7: Sophia and Lucrezia return to the palazzo, with Sophia visibly excited about the prospect of meeting Antonio. In her room, Sophia examines the velvet piece once more, further emphasizing her passion for artistry.

Scene 8: The chapter ends with Sophia, sitting by her window, gazing at the city of Venice. The narrative focuses on her yearning for a life beyond the strict social structures, thus setting the stage for her forthcoming adventures.

As ALWAYS, we are going to do this for all twenty-four chapters in this book and then in each book in the rest of the series. The outlines are truly the backbone of a book and they can make or break a series.

While it's tempting to get all of the deep outlines done before reviewing the story, that could lead to regrets.

Let's say you find something you don't like in chapter three of the second book. If you don't catch it the first time it appears, you might have deep outlines of the entire seven books done before you check this point. That small pebble in the pond can ripple through your entire series, and you might have to redo hours of work to remove the elements you don't like.

I don't want that for you.

Once you're content with all seven deep outlines and you like the direction of the story, then you can start writing. This is the moment you've been waiting for!

Here's our structure. We could lazily tell ChatGPT to write book one, chapter one, scene one. But ChatGPT will quickly start to drift. So, we need to really anchor this prompt each time we use it.

I am going to anchor by using the name of the book and then copying and pasting the description of each scene from ChatGPT's own response earlier. I know I'm providing ChatGPT with information it already knows, but this is simply how it works.

From "The Venetian Velvet," Please write chapter 1: Scene 1: The opening scene paints a vivid picture of Renaissance Venice - its canals, gondolas, marketplaces, and grand architecture, with the narration subtly hinting at the social divisions within the city.

Venice, *in the light of dawn, was a city waking from a splendid dream. The sun kissed the tips of the palaces lining the Grand Canal, painting them with a golden hue that shimmered in the slowly stirring waters below. A city etched on water, it was a ballet of gondolas, carrying nobles and merchants alike, traversing the labyrinth of waterways, their melodies echoing through the morning mist.*

Overlooking the grand waterway, the Rialto Bridge stood in solemn observation, its arches a gateway to the heart of the city's commerce. Beyond the bridge, the marketplace was coming alive. Bursts of laughter and chatter began to fill the air as merchants set up their stalls, a vibrant mosaic of color, texture, and scent. Fresh fruits gleamed like jewels, bolts of silk and velvet in a thousand hues beckoned from the weavers' corners, and the rich aroma of spices from distant lands permeated the air.

On the surface, it was a city of breathtaking beauty and grandeur, an epitome of human ingenuity and creativity. Yet beneath the stunning facade, Venice was a city of contrasts, defined by invisible lines of division that echoed through its grand palazzi and humble dwellings, through the very waters of its canals.

The nobles, with their elaborate robes and air of entitlement, walked through the city's piazzas with an air of invincibility, their palaces looking down upon the city from their prestigious positions along the Grand Canal. On the other hand, the laboring classes – the artists, craftsmen, and gondoliers – found their home in Venice's narrow calles and smaller canals. They were the lifeblood of the city, yet remained tucked away in the shadow of grandeur, often forgotten in the grand narratives.

As the sun began to climb in the sky, bathing the city in a warm, golden light, the heart of Venice began to beat faster. It was the dawn of another day, another dance of light and shadow, power and labor, tradition and rebellion – and at the center of it all was a young woman named Sophia Contarini, who was about to weave a story of her own amidst the vibrant tapestry of Venice.

THE ORIGINAL VERSION of this chapter ended right here. But, while I was teaching my AI Freedom students about writing fiction last night and sharing this chapter, we delved into some advanced techniques and encountered something that I think could benefit you.

The specifics don't matter, but we were experimenting with different prompting techniques that I cover in the chapter "Mimic

Prompts". We were messing around and tried "John Wick". Let me show you what happened.

From "The Venetian Velvet," Please write chapter 1: Scene 2: We are introduced to Sophia Contarini amidst the grandeur of her family's palazzo. She's portrayed as a young noblewoman with a streak of rebellion, practicing her artistry secretly in her room, away from her father's disapproving gaze. Please write in the style of John Wick.

The Contarini Palazzo, a fortress of elegance and power, a playground for the rich and influential. Behind its ornate façade, the labyrinth of corridors is a theater of whispered secrets, masked truths, and the occasional rebellion.

Enter Sophia Contarini. Born into opulence, bred to rule, yet her heart beats to a different drum. She's more than just the lady of the house, she's a maverick in silk and velvet. In the heart of the palazzo, away from her father's watchful, oftentimes disapproving gaze, she rebels - quietly, fiercely.

Her sanctuary is her room, a haven untouched by the demands of her birthright. Within these walls, she's not just a Contarini, she's Sophia - the artist, the dreamer. She stands before her easel, brush in hand, a palette of colors at her disposal. Each stroke on the canvas is a declaration of defiance, a testament of her will. Her art, much like a well-aimed bullet, hits right at the heart of the matter - raw, poignant, unapologetic.

It's a dangerous game she plays, a silent protest. To her father, art is frivolous, unfit for a noblewoman, a distraction from her duties. But to Sophia, it's freedom, her secret weapon, her hidden strength. Every portrait, every landscape, every swirl of color is a part of her soul she lets loose on the canvas – her solace, her rebellion.

Her room, her sanctuary, her battleground. A noblewoman in the heart of the palazzo, an artist in the quiet of her room, Sophia embodies the spirit of Venice – the beauty, the mystery, the defiance. Every brushstroke, every color, every hidden whisper of rebellion, it's all part of a dangerous dance – and the music has only just begun.

INDEED, it can be a lot of fun to experiment with different styles and characters in writing! You can absolutely get similar results by using other characters of the same nature, like Batman. These are vigilantes who come from a place of pain and perceive the world only in shades of black and gray. For them, there are no whites in the world.

By keeping your outline handy, you can verify if ChatGPT has completed a scene as per your plans. If something is missing, you can direct ChatGPT to keep writing. But be cautious with this prompt as this is where ChatGPT can easily drift off course. It may start writing the next scene or invent a scene that's not in the original outline. When that happens, you can truncate the excess and leap to the next scene.

Let's see how we can extract a bit more from this scene.

PLEASE CONTINUE THE SCENE.

SCENE 2 (CONTINUED)
Sophia dips her brush into a pool of sapphire blue, the pigment rich and pure. Her hand moves, steady and sure, her strokes capturing the vivid hues of the Venetian sky at dusk. Her heart beats a quiet rhythm, harmonizing with the whisper of the brush against the canvas.

In the silence of her room, under the protective cloak of privacy, Sophia lets her spirit unfurl, her creativity running wild and unchecked. Her art is more than just pigment on canvas – it's a glimpse into her soul, a testament to her spirit. A spirit that refuses to be confined, that yearns to break free from the chains of nobility and societal expectations.

Suddenly, the quiet is broken. A soft knock at the door interrupts her solitude, a coded rhythm only a select few know. It's Lucia, her loyal maid and confidante. Her only ally in this grand fortress of power and prestige. With a last swift stroke, Sophia completes her piece, a sigh of satisfaction escaping her lips.

The door creaks open, and Lucia steps in, her eyes instantly drawn to the new painting. A gasp, a smile. Recognition and understanding pass between them, a silent language they've perfected over the years. Lucia understands Sophia's need for rebellion, her yearning for something more than the life she was born into.

As Lucia moves to prepare Sophia for the evening, the easel is hidden, the paints tidied away. The room transforms, shifting from an artist's sanctuary back to a noblewoman's chambers, the walls holding their breath, guarding Sophia's secret.

And as Sophia Contarini steps out of her room, decked in her finest attire, her fiery spirit tucked away behind a facade of composure, one can't help but wonder – what adventures, what dangers, what exhilarating tales await this rebellious artist in the heart of Renaissance Venice? The stage is set, the pieces are moving, and the game is afoot.

WHO THE DEVIL IS LUCIA? As soon as this character emerged, I examined my notes, thinking that there might have been a name change for Lucrezia. When ChatGPT does something unexpected, you can go conversational. I prompt ChatGPT with exactly what I'm contemplating.

WHO IS **Lucia she's not in the original character sheet?**

I APOLOGIZE FOR THE CONFUSION. In the narrative, Lucia was introduced as Sophia's loyal maid and confidante within the Contarini household. This was an on-the-spot character development to add depth to the storyline and to provide Sophia with an ally within her immediate surroundings.

While Lucia isn't mentioned in the original character list, introducing new supporting characters can sometimes provide additional layers to the main characters and enhance the overall plot. However, I can definitely revise the narrative to exclude Lucia if you prefer to stick to the original character list. Please let me know how you'd like to proceed.

Okay, so Lucia is a new character who is not part of the original outline. At this point, you can either erase her from the book or let her stay. This is something that will likely happen during the writing process. It occurs in every story. As you delve deeper into the narrative, you may find that you need an additional character in certain scenes. This usually occurs much deeper into the book, but this serves as a great example.

In my opinion, the character makes sense. What do you think? Should I let her stay or remove her?

I decide to keep her because I don't want to divert ChatGPT's flow, and I believe the scene makes sense. Most stories of this nature do have a maid who serves as a confidante, so I'm okay with this. Now, let's see what ChatGPT comes up with next.

That's fine, **you can keep her.**

Great! I'm glad you're open to this addition. Lucia can indeed be a valuable asset to Sophia's journey, serving not just as a support figure, but also potentially a source of information and assistance. If you need more details about Lucia or any further development for the characters and plot, please feel free to ask.

We've decided to keep Lucia, so we have to update our info. You could go all out and redo all your character sheets and plans, but don't. If you do all your old work over each time a new character comes up, you'll never get your books done.

We do need a new outline for Lucia though. She's not in my plans, so she's a bit of a wildcard. Right now, I don't know where else she will appear in my books. So I can't keep an eye on her for drift. I need a character sheet to at least let me see how she decides things, so I can see if she acts out of character.

You, as the driver, need to read what ChatGPT writes and keep checking for drift.

WRITE a character outline for Lucia

CHARACTER OUTLINE for Lucia

Name: Lucia

Role: Supporting character, Sophia's maid and confidante.

Background: Born to a family of skilled artisans, Lucia has always lived in Venice. Her family fell on hard times when her father's health deteriorated, forcing her to find work in the Contarini Palazzo to support them.

Physical Appearance: Lucia is in her mid-twenties, with a petite frame that belies her strength. She has curly, chestnut-brown hair often tied up in a bun, and clear, almond-shaped hazel eyes that have a knack for noticing the smallest details. Her skin is lightly tanned from years of working under the Venetian sun.

Personality: Lucia is hardworking, loyal, and observant. She has a keen understanding of people and their motives, which serves her well in the high-stakes environment of the Contarini household. Although she's mostly quiet and reserved, she's not afraid to speak her mind when it comes to Sophia's wellbeing.

Skills: Lucia is skilled in housekeeping duties, but her true talents lie in her ability to blend into the background and gather information. She's also adept at reading and writing, skills she learned from her father who believed in education for all, which was uncommon for women of her status during the Renaissance period.

Relationship with Sophia: Lucia and Sophia share a bond that goes beyond the usual mistress-servant relationship. Their shared experiences of feeling trapped in their lives have forged a strong friendship between them. Lucia is one of the few people who know about Sophia's secret passion for art and encourages her to pursue her dreams, promising to keep her secret safe.

Motivation: Lucia's main motivation is to ensure her family's wellbeing. However, over the years, she has also developed a deep affection for Sophia and helps her navigate the complexities of nobility, hoping that Sophia can break free from the constraints of her societal status.

Now that I know Lucia better, I can get back to writing my book. Sure, I drifted into the John Wick style, so if I was going to release the book, I'd have to decide. Do I keep this gothic style or take a new path?

Either way, you now know how to write fiction, and that's a big deal!

---

1. As proven in the very next example in this chapter. ChatGPT is great with character flaws now.

24

EFFORTLESS PROFITABLE COURSES

I've been making good money creating courses. I used to be a teacher for ten years, so it comes easily to me. ChatGPT can take on much of the hard work. Everyone hits a snag somewhere in course creation. Some folks don't want their voice heard, others aren't sure what to put on slides. Or maybe making an outline is the tough part.

Let's get ChatGPT to help us create our course. I'd recommend starting most of your chats with a question. If you want a course based on your know-how, ask ChatGPT what it needs from you to make your course. I don't know much about training dogs, so I'm going to let ChatGPT take care of that for me.

WHAT ARE the most important things to include in a course teaching people how to train their dog?

CREATING a dog training course involves covering a comprehensive range of topics that help individuals understand their pets better and develop effective training methods. Here are some essential elements to include in such a course:

1. **Understanding Dog Behavior**: To train a dog effectively, it's crucial to understand how dogs think, their behaviors, and how they communicate. This section could cover the basics of dog psychology, common behaviors and their meanings, and how to interpret dog body language.
2. **Positive Reinforcement Training**: This is a key element in any dog training course. Explain how rewards like treats, praise, and petting can reinforce good behavior. Discuss how to implement and gradually phase out these reinforcements over time.
3. **Basic Commands**: Teach the essentials such as 'sit', 'stay', 'come', 'leave it', and 'heel'. These commands form the core of obedience training and are critical for controlling the dog's behavior.
4. **Leash Training**: A well-behaved dog should be able to walk on a leash without pulling or becoming distracted. Include methods for teaching dogs to walk calmly on a leash.
5. **Socialization**: Explain the importance of socializing dogs from a young age with different people, other dogs, and various environments. Offer strategies for safe and effective socialization.
6. **House Training**: This should cover crate training, potty training, and setting boundaries within the house.
7. **Handling Behavioral Problems**: This section could address common issues like excessive barking, chewing, digging, separation anxiety, and aggression. It should provide training techniques to manage and prevent these behaviors.
8. **Health and Nutrition**: While not strictly a training topic, understanding a dog's dietary needs, common health issues, grooming needs, and basic first aid can contribute to overall behavior.

9. ***Puppy Training***: *Puppies require special attention. Include a section specifically on how to handle puppies, from bite inhibition to early socialization and the introduction of basic commands.*
10. ***Advanced Training***: *After the basics, you might include modules on advanced obedience, agility training, trick training, and training for specific roles (like therapy or service work).*
11. ***Legal Responsibilities and Ethical Practices***: *Highlight the laws related to owning and training a dog in your jurisdiction, and the ethical considerations to keep in mind when training (such as avoiding punishment-based techniques).*

The overall emphasis of the course should be on promoting kind, consistent, and positive methods of training that build a strong bond between the dog and owner. Also, don't forget to underscore the importance of patience and consistency throughout the training process.

THIS IS PRETTY INTERESTING, but I don't want to include everything. I don't know a lot about what dogs should eat, and I don't want ChatGPT to make a recipe that could hurt a dog. I don't think it's likely, but I won't risk it. I can't tell if ChatGPT gets something wrong since I'm not a dog food expert. I also steer clear of legal stuff. I'm not a lawyer and giving legal advice can be risky. It's why all the YouTube lawyers say they're not giving legal advice. They don't want trouble if someone gets hurt taking their advice.

So I'll delete the two parts I don't like and change these bullet points into a course outline.

I DON'T WANT **to include 8 and 11. Please create an outline for this course. It will be a video course.**

Certainly! Here's an outline for your video course:
Module 1: Understanding Your Dog

- *Lesson 1.1: Introduction to Dog Behavior*
- *Lesson 1.2: Canine Communication and Body Language*

Module 2: The Basics of Positive Reinforcement

- *Lesson 2.1: The Power of Positive Reinforcement*
- *Lesson 2.2: Identifying Motivators for Your Dog*
- *Lesson 2.3: Gradual Phasing Out of Reinforcements*

Module 3: Basic Commands

- *Lesson 3.1: "Sit" and "Stay"*
- *Lesson 3.2: "Come" and "Leave It"*
- *Lesson 3.3: "Heel" and Walking Without Pulling*

Module 4: Leash Training

- *Lesson 4.1: Introduction to Leash Training*
- *Lesson 4.2: Dealing with Common Challenges in Leash Training*

Module 5: Socialization

- *Lesson 5.1: The Importance of Socialization*
- *Lesson 5.2: Safe and Effective Socialization Strategies*

Module 6: House Training

- Lesson 6.1: Crate Training Basics
- Lesson 6.2: Potty Training Your Dog
- Lesson 6.3: Setting Boundaries within the House

Module 7: Dealing with Behavioral Problems

- Lesson 7.1: Addressing Excessive Barking and Chewing
- Lesson 7.2: Managing Separation Anxiety and Digging
- Lesson 7.3: Dealing with Aggression

Module 8: Puppy Training

- Lesson 8.1: Understanding Puppy Behavior
- Lesson 8.2: Bite Inhibition and Early Socialization
- Lesson 8.3: Introducing Basic Commands to Puppies

Module 9: Advanced Training

- Lesson 9.1: Advanced Obedience Training
- Lesson 9.2: Introduction to Agility Training
- Lesson 9.3: Trick Training Basics
- Lesson 9.4: Training for Specific Roles (Therapy and Service Work)

- Encouraging Continual Learning and Practice

This outline is designed to be flexible and adjustable according to your own expertise and the specific needs of your audience. Each module can be broken down into smaller lessons or expanded upon as needed. Consider including practical demonstrations, case studies, and opportunities for interaction or questions within each lesson to enhance the learning experience.

· · ·

You can change the future with every question. If there's something you don't like about the plan, you can change it. Once you're happy with the plan, you can start making each lesson.

I want ChatGPT to make my slides for me.

Please write an outline for Welcome & Course Overview. Please include a bullet point for each slide.

Certainly, here's an outline for the "Welcome & Course Overview" section.

Slide 1: Welcome

- *Greeting and introduction of the course instructor*
- *Brief background about the instructor's experience with dog training*

Slide 2: Purpose of the Course

- *Explanation of why this course is important for dog owners*
- *Overview of the benefits of effective dog training*

Slide 3: Who Should Attend

- *Description of the target audience (e.g., new dog owners, experienced owners looking to refresh their training knowledge, people considering adopting a dog)*

Slide 4: Course Objectives

- *Clear list of what students can expect to learn from the course*
- *Explanation of how this knowledge can improve their relationship with their dog*

Slide 5: Course Format

- Introduction to the course format (i.e., video lessons, practical demonstrations)
- Explanation of any interactive elements (e.g., Q&A sessions, downloadable resources)

Slide 6: Course Modules

- Brief summary of each module in the course, creating a roadmap for what will be covered

Slide 7: Tips for Success

- Suggestions for how to get the most out of the course (e.g., taking notes, practicing regularly with their dog, being patient and consistent)

Slide 8: Encouragement and Expectations

- Encouraging students to approach the course with an open mind and to expect challenges along the way
- Reiterating the importance of patience and consistency in dog training

Slide 9: Conclusion

- Warm concluding remarks
- Invitation to begin the first module: "Understanding Your Dog"

THIS ISN'T what I thought I'd get. I thought I'd have to ask for the slide text in my next question. While this is interesting, I want more. I want to know what pictures go on each slide and what I should say. Let's see what happens when I ask ChatGPT to write a whole video lesson.

PLEASE WRITE a script for this lesson. Include the text that goes on each slide and a description of the images.

CERTAINLY! Here's a detailed script with slide text and image descriptions.
Slide 1: Welcome

- *Text: "Welcome to Our Dog Training Course!"*
- *Image: A friendly dog and trainer, with the trainer offering a treat.*
- *Script: "Hello and welcome to our comprehensive Dog Training Course! I'm [Your Name], your guide on this journey towards a better understanding of your furry friend."*

Slide 2: Purpose of the Course

- *Text: "Why This Course Matters"*
- *Image: A happy dog owner playing with a well-trained dog.*
- *Script: "Dog training is more than just teaching commands; it's about building a strong, loving relationship with your pet. In this course, we aim to help you understand your dog better, communicate more effectively, and enjoy a harmonious life together."*

Slide 3: Who Should Attend

- *Text: "Who Can Benefit from this Course?"*

- *Image: A montage of different types of people with dogs (new owners, families, older individuals).*
- *Script: "Whether you're a new dog owner, considering adopting a dog, or an experienced owner wanting to refresh your knowledge, this course is designed for you. Our aim is to help dog lovers of all experience levels!"*

Slide 4: Course Objectives

- *Text: "What You'll Learn"*
- *Image: Bulleted list of course objectives next to an image of a graduation cap on a dog's head.*
- *Script: "By the end of this course, you'll understand dog behavior, use positive reinforcement techniques, master basic commands, and much more. Our goal is to equip you with the skills to confidently train your dog and handle common behavioral issues."*

Slide 5: Course Format

- *Text: "Course Format & Resources"*
- *Image: Video play button, Q&A icon, and a document icon for downloadable resources.*
- *Script: "Our course consists of video lessons filled with practical demonstrations. We'll also have interactive Q&A sessions and provide downloadable resources for you to keep on hand during your training journey."*

Slide 6: Course Modules

- *Text: "Course Overview"*
- *Image: Flowchart of the course modules, starting from "Understanding Your Dog" to "Advanced Training".*

- Script: "Our course is divided into nine modules, covering everything from understanding your dog's behavior, to mastering basic commands, leash training, house training, and even advanced obedience. We'll take this journey one step at a time, building your skills along the way."

Slide 7: Tips for Success

- Text: "Getting the Most from this Course"
- Image: An icon of a light bulb with a checklist.
- Script: "To get the most out of this course, I encourage you to take notes and practice regularly with your dog. And remember, consistency and patience are key when training your dog."

Slide 8: Encouragement and Expectations

- Text: "Approach with an Open Mind"
- Image: Dog walking through an open door, symbolizing the start of the journey.
- Script: "I encourage you to approach each module with an open mind. Training isn't always easy, but remember that every challenge is an opportunity for learning and growth, both for you and your dog."

Slide 9: Conclusion

- Text: "Let's Start This Journey Together"
- Image: A trainer holding a dog's paw, symbolizing the beginning of the journey.
- Script: "I'm really excited to start this journey with you. Let's take the first step together into our first module, 'Understanding Your Dog'. Thank you for joining this course, and let's get started!"

· · ·

THIS IS A GREAT START. You have techniques to change the course however you want. You can ask ChatGPT for more info. You want longer scripts? More bullet points on the slides? Just ask ChatGPT.

25

$8,000 TO TRANSLATE THIS BOOK IN ONE DAY

One of ChatGPT's amazing features is its translation ability. This is a game changer. My wife and I have different native languages. When we first got together, we relied on translation apps, which were quite amusing.

Once, my wife informed me that the hospital was 'broken.' I thought that was a hilarious misinterpretation, until she said our daughter was 'broken.' Of course, she meant the hospital was closed, and our daughter was ill.

Translation software has always been almost there, but not quite good enough. Let's see if ChatGPT can do better.

I'm going to use a small snippet of something I wrote on my blog in 2016[1]. The post is called "Job Security: Are You Secure?" Let's see if ChatGPT can translate this into Japanese.

PLEASE TRANSLATE the following in to Japanese:
I spent my twenties building my career. I worked as a teacher around the world gaining experience. I earned my masters in London at one of the best universities in the world.

I worked so hard that my dissertation was eventually published by a full on publishing company.

At twenty-nine I scored my dream job. I was running a department with a 7-figure budget at the 17th best university in America. I was in charge of six other teachers.

I had achieved the pinnacle of success.

They told me the day they hired me that they thought the relationship would last for twenty years. When you have a job this good.

One of the main benefits they kept pushing was how they had a major hospital as part of the university so I had epic health insurance.

A decade of work finally paid off.

I had it.

JOB SECURITY.

Until one day they fired me for something I had written on an anonymous blog years earlier.

私は20代をキャリアの構築に費やしました。世界中の教師として働き、経験を積みました。私はロンドンの世界屈指の大学で修士号を取得しました。私はあまりにも一生懸命働いたため、最終的には正規の出版社が私の論文を出版しました。

29歳で私は夢の仕事を手に入れました。私はアメリカで17番目に良い大学の部門を運営しており、その予算は7桁でした。私は他の6人の教師を管理していました。

私は成功の頂点を達成しました。

私が雇われた日、彼らは私との関係が20年続くと思っていると言いました。これほど良い仕事があるときに。

彼らが強調していた主な利点の一つは、大学に大規模な病院があるので、私が素晴らしい健康保険を持っているということでした。

10年間の努力がついに報われました。

私はそれを手に入れました。
仕事の安定性。
しかし、ある日、何年も前に匿名のブログに書いたことが原因で解雇されました。

This is the only time ChatGPT's response isn't in italics. Fun fact: Japanese characters don't use italics. I have a basic understanding of Japanese, but my reading isn't great. The response is written in three different alphabets: hiragana, katakana, and kanji. I can read the first two, each with forty-six characters, but you need to know thousands of kanji characters just to read a Japanese newspaper, which is beyond my ability.

So, how do we know if the translation is accurate or if it could lead to an embarrassing situation? Before we find that out, let's try German too. I can't speak any German, so I'm really pushing the boundaries here.

Please translate it into German.

Ich verbrachte meine Zwanzigerjahre damit, meine Karriere aufzubauen. Ich arbeitete als Lehrer auf der ganzen Welt und sammelte Erfahrungen. Ich erwarb meinen Master in London an einer der besten Universitäten der Welt. Ich arbeitete so hart, dass meine Dissertation schließlich von einem echten Verlag veröffentlicht wurde.

Mit neunundzwanzig erhielt ich meinen Traumjob. Ich leitete eine Abteilung mit einem siebenstelligen Budget an der siebzehntbesten Universität in Amerika. Ich war für sechs andere Lehrer verantwortlich.

Ich hatte den Gipfel des Erfolgs erreicht.

Am Tag, an dem sie mich einstellten, sagten sie mir, sie glaubten, dass die Beziehung zwanzig Jahre dauern würde. Wenn man einen so guten Job hat.

Einer der Hauptvorteile, die sie immer wieder betonten, war, dass sie ein großes Krankenhaus als Teil der Universität hatten, so dass ich eine fantastische Krankenversicherung hatte.

Ein Jahrzehnt harter Arbeit hatte sich endlich ausgezahlt.

Ich hatte es geschafft.

JOB SICHERHEIT.

Bis sie mich eines Tages wegen etwas, das ich Jahre zuvor in einem anonymen Blog geschrieben hatte, entließen.

WE'VE NOW GOT two translations to verify. The classic test has been to use the same translator to convert the text back into English. With ChatGPT, it's best to start a new conversation. Otherwise, it'll just "remember" your original prompt. That's recollection, not translation!

In my next prompt, I'll include all the Japanese again. When dealing with translation, it's important not to shorten any prompts or replies for accurate comparison. I'm sorry if this seems redundant, but when assessing ChatGPT's translation abilities, it's important to see the full before and after.

PLEASE TRANSLATE **the following into English:**
私は20代をキャリアの構築に費やしました。世界中の教師として働き、経験を積みました。私はロンドンの世界屈指の大学で修士号を取得しました。私はあまりにも一生懸命働いたため、最終的には正規の出版社が私の論文を出版しました。

29歳で私は夢の仕事を手に入れました。私はアメリカで17番目に良い大学の部門を運営しており、その予算は7桁でした。私は他の6人の教師を管理していました。

私は成功の頂点を達成しました。

私が雇われた日、彼らは私との関係が20年続くと思っていると言いました。これほど良い仕事があるときに。

彼らが強調していた主な利点の一つは、大学に大規模な病院があるので、私が素晴らしい健康保険を持っているということでした。

10年間の努力がついに報われました。

私はそれを手に入れました。

仕事の安定性。

しかし、ある日、何年も前に匿名のブログに書いたことが原因で解雇されました。

I SPENT my twenties building my career. I worked and gained experience as a teacher all over the world. I obtained a master's degree at one of the world's leading universities in London. I worked so hard that eventually a regular publisher published my thesis.

At the age of 29, I landed my dream job. I was managing a department at the 17th best university in America, with a seven-figure budget. I was managing six other teachers.

I reached the pinnacle of success.

On the day I was hired, they said they expected our relationship to last for 20 years. When I had such a good job.

One of the main benefits they emphasized was that I had great health insurance because there was a large hospital at the university.

My 10 years of effort finally paid off.

I got it.

Job stability.

But one day, I was fired because of something I had written on an anonymous blog many years ago.

I MUST SAY, I'm quite impressed with this response. There's not much to say other than it's remarkably close to my original text. A few sentences were consolidated from two into one, but beyond that, I don't see any errors. 'Job Security' has turned into 'job stability,' and it's no longer in all caps.

These changes make sense, though. Japanese doesn't use capital letters, and 'stability' and 'security' are close enough in meaning to work for me.

Let's check out the German.

PLEASE TRANSLATE the following into English:

Ich verbrachte meine Zwanzigerjahre damit, meine Karriere aufzubauen. Ich arbeitete als Lehrer auf der ganzen Welt und sammelte Erfahrungen. Ich erwarb meinen Master in London an einer der besten Universitäten der Welt. Ich arbeitete so hart, dass meine Dissertation schließlich von einem echten Verlag veröffentlicht wurde.

Mit neunundzwanzig erhielt ich meinen Traumjob. Ich leitete eine Abteilung mit einem siebenstelligen Budget an der siebzehntbesten Universität in Amerika. Ich war für sechs andere Lehrer verantwortlich.

Ich hatte den Gipfel des Erfolgs erreicht.

Am Tag, an dem sie mich einstellten, sagten sie mir, sie glaubten, dass die Beziehung zwanzig Jahre dauern würde. Wenn man einen so guten Job hat.

Einer der Hauptvorteile, die sie immer wieder betonten, war, dass sie ein großes Krankenhaus als Teil der Universität hatten, so dass ich eine fantastische Krankenversicherung hatte.

Ein Jahrzehnt harter Arbeit hatte sich endlich ausgezahlt.

Ich hatte es geschafft.

JOB SICHERHEIT.

Bis sie mich eines Tages wegen etwas, das ich Jahre zuvor in einem anonymen Blog geschrieben hatte, entließen.

I SPENT my twenties building my career. I worked as a teacher around the world, gaining experiences. I earned my master's degree in London at one of the best universities in the world. I worked so hard that my dissertation was eventually published by a real publisher.

At the age of twenty-nine, I got my dream job. I led a department with a seven-figure budget at the seventeenth best university in America. I was responsible for six other teachers.

I had reached the peak of success.

On the day they hired me, they told me they believed the relationship would last twenty years. When you have such a good job.

One of the main benefits they constantly emphasized was that they had a large hospital as part of the university, so I had fantastic health insurance.

A decade of hard work had finally paid off.

I had made it.

JOB SECURITY.

Until they fired me one day because of something I had written years earlier in an anonymous blog.

HERE, ChatGPT actually made a correction. In the original, I referred to my degree as a 'masters.' Here, ChatGPT has corrected it to a 'master's degree.'

The capitalization is correct, and honestly, I'll leave it up to you to determine whether this is an acceptable translation. With this capability, you can translate your emails, blog posts, and books into new languages, expanding into new markets. Consider the potential that holds.

You can even offer translation services to others.

I would advise sticking to translating from languages you don't speak into one you do. You're less likely to make glaring errors that way.

One Last Thing

According to All Translate[2], "a professional translator can range anywhere from $0.10 to $0.30 per word." It would cost over $8,000 to get this book translated into just one language. I'm sure glad ChatGPT will translate into any language I want for free.

---

1. https://servenomaster.com/job-security-are-you-secure/
2. https://www.atltranslate.com/blog/how-much-does-it-cost-to-hire-a-translator-in-2022

26

HIRE HISTORIES GREATEST COPYWRITERS FOR FREE

For many venturing into using ChatGPT, this is seen as the ultimate prize: Can ChatGPT write my sales letters, commercials, and landing pages?

The answer is, yes it can.

Currently, this is a field where no one has achieved perfection. To craft an entire sales letter with ChatGPT would take a whole book. However, I'll sow enough seeds for you to get started and improve your copywriting skills, regardless of your current level. If you're already a master copywriter, this serves as a means to hasten your testing process.

Headlines

We'll kick things off with the most crucial part of any message—the headline. This is the first bit people read on your page or, if you're crafting an email, it's your subject line. It needs to pique the reader's interest enough to make them listen to you.

For this demonstration, I'll use a headline written by Paris from my team. She's a phenomenal copywriter and she crafted the headline for my most successful product to date, 'Words to Profit'. I've sold more units of this product than any other in the last eight years.

You can choose any headline from any copywriter for your own examples. I must use my content due to copyright reasons.

Remember, you never have to start from scratch—that's the toughest route. Give ChatGPT a model, and you'll get far superior copy.

PLEASE USE **this headline as a template for a headline to promote a book that teaches people how to become millionaires using ChatGPT. Give me 10 options.**

The World Has Never Been Hungrier To Pay Top Dollar For Freelance Writers... Will You Be One Of Them?

1. *"The World Is Desperate for the Next Wave of Millionaires... Will You Be One of Them with the Help of ChatGPT?"*
2. *"Society Yearns for New Financial Success Stories... Will You Write Yours with 'ChatGPT Millionaire'?"*
3. *"The World Is Eager to Invest in ChatGPT Savvy Individuals... Will You Be Among the New Millionaires?"*
4. *"People Are Paying Big to Learn ChatGPT Wealth Secrets... Will You Be Among the Fortune Seekers?"*
5. *"The Demand for ChatGPT Financial Mastery Is Skyrocketing... Will You Be One to Profit?"*
6. *"A New Wave of Millionaires Is Rising with ChatGPT... Will You Join the Ranks?"*
7. *"The World Is Ready to Pay for Your ChatGPT Expertise... Are You Ready to Join the Millionaires' Club?"*
8. *"ChatGPT Users Are Becoming Millionaires Overnight... Will You Be the Next Success Story?"*
9. *"People Are Making Millions with ChatGPT... Will You Be Next to Cash In?"*

10. "The Global Economy Is Thirsty for ChatGPT-Made Millionaires... Will You Be One of Them?"

FROM THE LIST GENERATED, choose the headline that resonates with you the most and create variations. The secret to a stellar headline is crafting many of them, and then selecting your favorite.

For the next prompt, I'll harness my personal understanding of copywriting to get more variations of my chosen headline. In his book 'Breakthrough Advertising', Eugene Schwartz shares an exceptional exercise on creating headline variations. I'm assuming ChatGPT is familiar with this exercise, given that the book was published well before ChatGPT's 2021 knowledge cut-off.

PLEASE REWRITE #8 using the Eugene Schwartz headline rewriting template. Give me 25 headlines to choose from.

CERTAINLY, here are 25 different headlines based on the #8 original, and the Eugene Schwartz headline rewriting method:

1. "Could You Be the Next Person to Unlock Millions with ChatGPT's Power?"
2. "ChatGPT: Unleashing Overnight Millionaires. Are You Next in Line?"
3. "Harness the Power of ChatGPT and Join the Growing Legion of New Millionaires"
4. "Uncover the Secret: Ordinary People Becoming Millionaires with ChatGPT... Will You Be Next?"
5. "Will You Ride the ChatGPT Wave to Become the Next Overnight Millionaire?"

6. "Break the Code to Wealth: How Everyday Individuals are Turning into Millionaires with ChatGPT"
7. "Join the Surge of New Wealth: How ChatGPT is Creating Millionaires... Could You Be Next?"
8. "The Millionaire's Secret: Will You Be the Next to Harness the Power of ChatGPT?"
9. "Ordinary People, Extraordinary Wealth: Could You Be the Next ChatGPT Millionaire?"
10. "ChatGPT: The Fast-Track to Millions. Are You Ready to Take the Journey?"
11. "Discover How Everyday People are Becoming Millionaires Overnight with ChatGPT... Are You Next?"
12. "Are You Ready to Transform Your Life with ChatGPT and Become the Next Millionaire?"
13. "How ChatGPT is Shaping the Next Generation of Millionaires... Are You Next?"
14. "ChatGPT: A Gateway to Millions. Could You Be Its Next Success Story?"
15. "Millionaire Overnight: The Power of ChatGPT. Will You Be Next?"
16. "ChatGPT: The Secret Behind an Explosion of New Millionaires. Are You Next?"
17. "Join the Ranks of ChatGPT Millionaires. Will You Be the Next Overnight Success Story?"
18. "ChatGPT: Turning Ordinary People into Millionaires. Could You Be Next?"
19. "ChatGPT: A New Dawn for Millionaires. Are You Ready to Join the Revolution?"
20. "Discover How ChatGPT is Transforming Lives into Millions Overnight... Could You Be Next?"
21. "Are You the Next ChatGPT Millionaire? Discover the Power of Overnight Success"
22. "Ride the Wave of New Wealth with ChatGPT... Are You Next?"

23. "ChatGPT: A Ticket to Overnight Millions. Could You Be Next?"
24. "See How ChatGPT is Changing Lives by Creating Overnight Millionaires... Will You Be Next?"
25. "Unleash Your Potential: How ChatGPT is Making Ordinary People into Millionaires... Are You Ready to Join?"

From this point, you can produce more variations and select your champion. I've included a list of one hundred copywriters known to ChatGPT in the Appendix. You can keep experimenting with different names to yield various results.

Utilizing a template is a significant shortcut in copywriting. You can apply this approach to devise an entire sales letter, modeling one section at a time from a successful sales letter.

Email

Writing a gripping email can induce quite a bit of stress. I've known several people who've stumbled because they didn't want to write emails. But now, you don't have to. I want to invite folks to my live training on ChatGPT and other AI tools. This training encapsulates much of what this book covers but with stellar visuals. All images come from my AI image generation tools, which I can't delve into in this book—maybe the next one, though.

For my email, I'm going to provide ChatGPT with a structure to follow. If you're unfamiliar, AIDA stands for Attention, Interest, Desire, Action. I don't typically write emails this way, but it's the only framework name I'm aware of. This prompt is incredibly simple to modify by changing the framework name or the email's goal.

· · ·

WRITE a compelling email using the AIDA framework to invite entrepreneurs to a live training on how to use AI tools to grow their business faster.

SUBJECT: *Unleash the Power of AI to Transform Your Business - Exclusive Live Training*

Dear Entrepreneur,

I hope this email finds you well.

Attention:

The business world is becoming increasingly digital, and the companies that leverage cutting-edge technology, like Artificial Intelligence (AI), often have the advantage. Do you want to make sure your business is at the forefront of this transformation?

Interest:

To support entrepreneurs like you in mastering AI, we are thrilled to invite you to an exclusive live training session - "AI Tools for Business Growth: Your Key to Competitive Advantage". This event is scheduled for June 25th, 2023, and will feature leading experts in AI who have helped transform hundreds of businesses.

Desire:

Imagine being able to understand your customers' needs better, predict market trends, automate routine tasks, and make strategic decisions backed by data-driven insights. That's what AI can do for your business. Our live training is tailored to ensure that you understand the most effective ways to use AI tools for rapid business growth.

Here's what you'll gain from the training:

- *Understanding the basics of AI and its applications in business.*
- *Insight into how AI can help grow your business faster.*
- *Practical guides on implementing AI tools effectively.*
- *Real-life case studies of businesses transformed by AI.*

Action:

Don't miss out on this fantastic opportunity to stay ahead in the competitive business landscape. Click the link below to secure your spot in the live training and take the first step towards leveraging AI for your business growth.

Register for the AI Tools for Business Growth Training

Please feel free to forward this invitation to any fellow entrepreneurs who may find it beneficial.

We are excited to see you there and contribute to your success!

Kind regards,

[Your Name]

[Your Position]

[Your Contact Information]

LIKE IT OR NOT, we've got an email drafted quicker than I could do it. I can't draft an email in ten seconds—my hands aren't that nimble. To refine this email, I'm going to use a Mimic Prompt. That means I'm going to request ChatGPT to write like a specific person rather than an imagined character.

I'm going to pull in my friend Jason once more to see how much I can improve this email.

PLEASE REWRITE in the style of Jason Fladlien.

SUBJECT: *The Future Is Here: Power Your Business With AI - Join Our Live Training Now!*

Hey Rockstar Entrepreneur,

I trust this email finds you in the fast lane, constantly pushing boundaries.

Boom! AI is Transforming Businesses

Let's face it. The world of business is changing - faster than you might imagine. Do you want to sit on the sidelines and watch or are you ready to jump in and command the game? This email is your golden ticket into the world of Artificial Intelligence (AI) and its staggering power to transform businesses.

Here's the Deal

We're cooking up something incredibly special for entrepreneurs like you. It's an exclusive live training - "AI Tools for Business Growth: The Secret Weapon of Top Performers". Mark your calendar for June 25th, 2023. This is your chance to learn from the wizards of AI who have transformed businesses from mundane to extraordinary!

What's in It for You?

Picture this: You understand your customers like never before, you can see market trends before they become obvious, your routine tasks are on auto-pilot, and every decision you make is based on powerful, data-driven insights. Sounds like a dream? Well, it's not - it's AI, and it's already shaping businesses like never before.

Here's the jackpot you'll hit in our training:

- Unraveling the mystery of AI and how it fits into the business world.
- Uncovering how AI can put your business growth on steroids.
- Step-by-step guides on setting up AI tools that actually deliver results.
- Real-life stories of businesses that have become superpowers with AI.

Are You In?

Don't let this train leave the station without you. Click the link below, claim your spot in the live training, and get ready to harness the power of AI for business growth.

Yes, I'm Ready for AI Superpowers!

Feel free to share this goldmine with your entrepreneur buddies who could benefit from it.

Can't wait to see you at the event and supercharge your journey to success!

To your exponential growth,
[Your Name]
[Your Position]
[Your Contact Information]

Right off the bat, we have a substantially improved email in just two prompts. We can use other techniques to craft emails, such as modeling from emails written by others, tweaking the framework style, or changing the copywriter.

I'm going to test another copywriter I've been friends with for over a decade. Let's find out if swapping the name of the copywriter really alters that much.

Please rewrite in the style of Colin Theriot.

Subject: *Your Business + AI: Are You Ready to 10X Your Growth?*

Howdy, fellow entrepreneur,

I hope this message finds you full of beans, ready to tackle the next challenge head-on.

Big News: AI is No Longer Just for the Big Dogs

Here's the hard truth: businesses are morphing at the speed of light. Want to just sit and gawk? Or are you fired up to step up and be a frontrunner in this race? This, my friend, is your opportunity to explore the seemingly magical world of Artificial Intelligence (AI) and how it's catapulting businesses to new heights.

The Insider Scoop

We're putting together a one-of-a-kind live training event - "AI Tools for Business Growth: Not Just a Buzzword". Mark your planner for June

25th, 2023. This ain't just another techie talk. It's your pass to learn from AI gurus who've morphed businesses from everyday to extraordinary!

The Spoils

Imagine this: You're in the driver's seat, understanding your customers' wants and needs, predicting market movements, automating the mundane, and making every call based on rock-solid, data-driven insights. No, this ain't science fiction - it's AI, and it's here to revolutionize businesses.

Here's your loot from our training:

- Decoding the AI enigma and its business applications.
- Revealing how AI can supercharge your business growth.
- A no-nonsense guide on deploying AI tools effectively.
- Real-world tales of businesses transformed by AI.

Your Next Step?

Don't let this golden opportunity pass you by. Click the link below, reserve your seat at the live training, and brace yourself to harness the power of AI for your business growth.

Yes, I Want to Boost My Business with AI!

Got entrepreneur pals who'd benefit from this info? Feel free to spread the word.

Looking forward to seeing you at the event and boosting your journey to success!

To your prosperity,
[Your Name]
[Your Position]
[Your Contact Information]

INCREDIBLE. Even the email subject line has changed. You don't have to stick to one copywriter's style. You can blend sections from different emails to tailor a message that perfectly represents you. Or, you can experiment with all one hundred copywriters mentioned in the Appendix.

Now, let's switch gears a bit. In the domain of financial newsletters, Agora is the top dog. They're virtuosos of direct mail advertising, and I'm acquainted with a few copywriters who've undertaken projects for them. What occurs when we employ a company with multiple copywriters? We should expect a more extensive sample set and a somewhat broader copywriting style.

PLEASE REWRITE in the style of Agora.

SUBJECT: *Inside Secret: Ignite Your Business Growth with AI. Limited Seats Available!*

Dear Valued Entrepreneur,

I hope you're keeping well and thriving in your entrepreneurial journey.

AI: The Silent Revolution Changing The Business Landscape

We're living in an era of rapid change. Businesses are evolving, markets are shifting, and technologies like Artificial Intelligence (AI) are disrupting traditional paradigms. The question is, are you ready to seize this opportunity and propel your business to unimagined heights?

Exclusive Opportunity: Your Path to Success

We have the privilege of inviting you to an exclusive, one-time live training event, "AI Tools for Business Growth: The Silent Revolution." Circle June 25th, 2023 in your calendar. This isn't your average seminar; it's a powerful learning experience delivered by industry-leading AI experts who have elevated businesses from obscurity to prominence.

Bountiful Rewards Await You

Envision a future where you comprehend your customers' deepest desires, anticipate market trends, automate monotonous tasks, and your every decision is anchored by concrete, data-driven insights. This is not a fanciful dream - it's the promise of AI.

Here's what our comprehensive training promises:

Deciphering the language of AI and its practical application in business.

Unlocking how AI can accelerate your business growth.

Step-by-step roadmap on integrating AI tools seamlessly into your operations.

Case studies of businesses transformed by AI.

Your Invitation to a Brighter Future

Don't let this rare opportunity slip through your fingers. Click the link below to confirm your attendance at our live training and prepare to leverage AI for exponential business growth.

Secure My Spot for the AI Revolution!

Kindly share this opportunity with other entrepreneurs who you believe would benefit from it.

We're eagerly waiting to welcome you to the event and ignite your pathway to success!

To your continued prosperity,

[Your Name]

[Your Position]

[Your Contact Information]

IF YOU'VE EVER SEEN one of Agora's letters, this style should seem pretty familiar to you. Now, you possess several methods to construct an engaging email. You can model after another email, write using a framework, write in the style of a specific copywriter, or write in the style of a brand that employs multiple copywriters.

Frameworks

Perhaps you're unfamiliar with the AIDA framework and are curious about other frameworks. Other frameworks are only useful if they're already in ChatGPT's database. So, let's inquire about it.

. . .

What are alternative copywriting frameworks to AIDA?

Absolutely, there are several other copywriting frameworks that can be used as alternatives to AIDA (Attention, Interest, Desire, Action). Here are a few:

PAS (Problem, Agitate, Solve): This is a simple yet effective copywriting formula. It starts by identifying a problem, then agitating it by emphasizing its impacts or complications, and finally presenting a solution to the problem.

FAB (Features, Advantages, Benefits): This framework is used commonly in product marketing. It highlights the features of the product, explains the advantages of these features, and then showcases the benefits they provide to the customer.

BAB (Before, After, Bridge): This formula paints a picture of life before using the product or service, what life could be like after using the product or service, and then bridges the gap by showing how the product or service can take the customer from 'Before' to 'After.'

4Ps (Promise, Picture, Proof, Push): The 4Ps formula begins by promising a solution or benefit, then paints a picture of life with the promise fulfilled. This is followed by proof or testimonials to back up the promise, and ends with a push or call-to-action.

QUEST (Qualify, Understand, Educate, Stimulate, Transition): This formula starts by qualifying the problem or need, then understanding the audience's desires. It educates by providing information about the product, service, or idea, stimulates interest or desire, and finally transitions into the call-to-action.

ACC (Awareness, Comprehension, Conviction): This framework first builds awareness about a product or service, then helps the audience understand its benefits or how it solves a problem. It ends by creating a conviction or a strong belief in the product or service, leading to a purchase decision.

AIDPPC (Attention, Interest, Desire, Persuasion, Proof, Close): This is an extension of AIDA, adding in elements of persuasion (convincing the *reader why they need it), proof (backing up claims with testimonials or data), and close (strong call-to-action to seal the deal).*

Remember, the best framework to use depends on the particular context and target audience of your copy. Different approaches work better for different products, services, or objectives.

You can return to your email and replace the existing framework with each of these to derive a different result. This should cater to all your copywriting needs for a while.

27

SEAMLESS WEB DESIGN, NO SKILLS REQUIRED

You might be thinking, "ChatGPT is a text AI. It can't possibly handle web design." That's a reasonable assumption. Allow me to surprise you.

Most websites start with wireframes, which are often preceded by textual descriptions. In fact, a website proposal usually begins as text only. As always, we don't want to jump to conclusions. Our goal is a fantastic website, but we're unsure what information ChatGPT needs to assist us. Rather than providing potentially inaccurate information, let's find out what ChatGPT requires.

WHAT INFORMATION DO you need to help me design a great website?

DESIGNING a great website involves understanding your goals, target audience, and the overall look and feel you want to achieve. Here are some questions that could help guide the design process:

1. **Purpose and Goals**: What is the primary purpose of your website? Is it to sell products, provide information, build a community, or something else? What do you want visitors to your website to do (e.g., purchase a product, sign up for a newsletter, contact you)?
2. **Target Audience**: Who is your intended audience? What are their interests, needs, and habits? What kind of devices are they likely to use to access your website?
3. **Design Preferences**: Are there any websites you admire and would like to emulate? What do you like about them? Do you have any specific color schemes, fonts, or styles in mind? How do you want your website to feel (e.g., professional, friendly, cutting-edge, traditional)?
4. **Content**: What kind of content will you feature on your website? Will it be mostly text, images, videos, or a mix? Will you need a blog or news section? How often will you update the content?
5. **Functionality**: Do you need any specific features or functions, such as a shopping cart, contact forms, reservation systems, or live chat?
6. **SEO and Marketing**: How do you plan to attract visitors to your site? Will you use SEO, paid advertising, social media, or other methods?
7. **Budget and Timeline**: What is your budget for the website design? What is the timeline for the project?
8. **Maintenance**: Who will update and maintain the website once it's built? Do you need a content management system (CMS) that allows you to make updates yourself?

The answers to these questions will help provide a clear direction for the design process and ensure that the final website meets your needs and expectations.

. . .

THE SET of questions posed here could be pretty overwhelming, particularly if this is your first website. For each step, you can ask ChatGPT to assist you in finding the answer. You could simply say, "help me figure out my budget and timeline," and ChatGPT will handle that. Its conversational capabilities shine in these circumstances.

You can also ask ChatGPT to pose the questions one by one. I already have the answers to these.

1. **The purpose of my website more book coaching and ghostwriting clients.** [1]
2. **My audience is over forty and can afford premium services.**
3. **I want a gothic aesthetic.**
4. **Mostly blog content with weekly updates.**
5. **The only function I care about is a contact form.**
6. **SEO and social media**
7. **I would like the website live within a week.**
8. **I prefer to work with WordPress.**

My main competitors are:
https://scribemedia.com/
https://ghostwriting.services/
https://theurbanwriters.com/
https://eliteauthors.com/

BASED *on the information I've gathered from your main competitors, here are some insights that may help you position your website more effectively:*

1. **Scribe Media** *offers a comprehensive range of services including book writing, coaching, publishing, and marketing. They position themselves as a company that can help clients not just publish a book, but leave a legacy. They also offer free*

resources like blogs and podcasts which could be used to attract and engage their target audience. The use of success stories and testimonials is also a common strategy.
2. **Ghostwriting Services** offers professional ghostwriting services across a wide range of genres including fiction, non-fiction, business, medical, and music2. They emphasize the quality of their work and their ability to capture the client's voice and ideas. They also feature testimonials from satisfied clients, adding credibility to their services.
3. **The Urban Writers** operate on a platform-based model where clients can post their projects and gain access to a pool of freelancers. Their platform offers live order tracking, a freelancer search tool, the ability to build teams, leave comments and feedback, control over orders, and direct messaging with freelancers. They also have dedicated admin support for clients' concerns.

Given these insights, here are my recommendations for your website:

1. **Service Offering**: Clearly define and communicate your service offerings. If your primary services are book coaching and ghostwriting, be sure to make that clear. If you offer additional services, those should be communicated as well.
2. **Free Resources**: Like Scribe Media, you may want to consider offering free resources like a blog, podcast, or downloadable guides. This can help to attract and engage your target audience while also establishing you as an expert in your field.
3. **Testimonials**: Consider featuring testimonials or success stories from previous clients. This can help to build trust with potential clients.
4. **SEO and Social Media**: Both are crucial for reaching a wider audience. Consider hiring an SEO expert and a social media manager to help optimize your content and promote your services.

5. **Contact Form**: Since this is the only function you care about, make sure it's easy to find and user-friendly.
6. **Aesthetics**: Since you want a Gothic aesthetic, this should be incorporated into the website design. A professional web designer should be able to help with this.

Given your one-week timeline and preference for WordPress, it's recommended to work with an experienced WordPress developer or a web development agency that can deliver within this timeframe.

Please note that the analysis of the fourth competitor, Elite Authors, is incomplete due to time constraints. A detailed analysis of this competitor might provide additional useful insights.

For this conversation, I enabled ChatGPT's internet access. You can only do this with ChatGPT Plus, so you might not get as detailed a response with the free version of ChatGPT, but it'll still be decent. All three websites mentioned existed before the cutoff date, so ChatGPT will reference what the websites looked like back then.

With an overall concept for my website in mind, it's time to get specific. The most crucial part of any website is the homepage. I've redesigned the Serve No Master homepage at least four times, and I'll surely do it again.

As with other content, we want to begin with an outline before we delve into any writing.

What sections should the homepage include?

The homepage of your website serves as the first point of contact for many of your visitors, so it should be well-designed and contain key information about your business or organization. Here are some essential sections you might want to consider for your homepage:

1. **Header and Navigation**: This area usually includes your logo, company name, and the main navigation menu that directs visitors to the other pages of your site.
2. **Hero Section**: The hero section is typically a large banner area placed at the top of your site. It often contains a compelling headline, a brief description of your services or products, and a call-to-action (CTA) such as a "Learn More" or "Contact Us" button.
3. **About Us**: This section gives a brief overview of your company, its mission, values, and what sets you apart from the competition.
4. **Services/Products**: Here, you can showcase your main services or products with brief descriptions. If you offer a variety of services or products, you can include a link to a dedicated page where visitors can learn more about each one.
5. **Testimonials/Reviews**: Displaying testimonials or reviews from satisfied customers can help to build trust with new visitors.
6. **Portfolio/Case Studies**: If applicable, showing off examples of your work or case studies can help to demonstrate your skills and experience.
7. **Call to Action**: Another CTA can be helpful to guide visitors towards a specific action you want them to take, such as requesting a quote, scheduling a consultation, or signing up for a newsletter.
8. **Contact Information**: Include essential contact information, such as your phone number, email address, and physical location (if applicable).
9. **Footer**: The footer usually contains links to important pages like the privacy policy and terms of service, social media icons, and sometimes contact information or a brief about us blurb.

Remember, the goal of your homepage is to quickly and clearly communicate what you do, why you're different, and how visitors can engage with your services or products. Each section should be designed with this goal in mind.

WITH OUR OUTLINE IN PLACE, the next step so to design one section at a time. Designing a header is boring, so let's get right to the hero section. This is the most important part of your entire website. It's what every visitor looks at first. Before we create our hero section, let's ask ChatGPT what information it needs.

WHAT INFORMATION DO **you need from me to write a great hero section?**

THE HERO SECTION of a website is crucial as it's often the first element a visitor sees and therefore sets the tone for their impression of your site and business. To craft a compelling hero section, I'll need the following information:

1. **Headline**: *This is typically a brief, compelling statement that encapsulates what you do or the value you offer. It should grab attention and encourage visitors to explore further.*
2. **Subheadline or Tagline**: *This provides a bit more detail about your services, products, or value proposition. It should support the headline by adding clarity or further intriguing the visitor.*
3. **Call to Action (CTA)**: *This is a directive to the visitor, guiding them towards a specific action you want them to take (e.g., "Contact Us," "Learn More," "Shop Now").*
4. **Key Value Proposition**: *What makes your services or products unique or superior to your competitors? This information can be used to further enhance the headline and subheadline.*

5. ***Visual Elements****: Do you have any specific images, videos, or graphics you'd like to include? The visual component of the hero section is just as important as the text.*
6. ***Tone and Style****: Understanding your brand's tone and style is important for maintaining consistency across your website. Should the language be formal or casual? Do you prefer a more minimalist design or something more elaborate?*
7. ***Target Audience****: Knowing who your primary visitors are can help tailor the language and visuals to be more appealing to that specific audience.*

With these details, I can help draft a compelling hero section that succinctly communicates your value proposition and guides visitors towards a desired action.

This next prompt was a real struggle for me. I had to rewrite this prompt several times to get the result that I wanted. That's why it's so long and ugly. The goal of my hero section is to drive people to download my guide. In the first iterations, the headlines were about me as a great ghostwriter.

If the call to action was schedule a call with me, then it would completely make sense. I had to push ChatGPT a little harder to get the result I wanted.

The first sentence is who I am and my qualifications. The second sentence is explaining the goal of the hero section. The third sentence explains the benefit of the free gift. The forth sentence makes the headline about the free gift rather than me. The fifth sentence reminds ChatGPT to look at my earlier answers for additional information, so I don't have to repeat myself.

That's five sentences of pre-prompt and information before we get to the actual prompt which is the final sentence. The task is to write three hero sections. Everything else is just guide rails on that task.

. . .

I AM a celebrity ghostwriter who has written over 300 bestsellers for myself, clients and under pen names. The gift I will give away in exchange for email addresses is a guide called 'Ten Mistakes to Avoid when Hiring a Ghostwriter.' This guide teaches people how to avoid the most common mistakes that happen when hiring a ghostwriter. The headline should be about the free gift. Please refer to my earlier answers about my audience. Please write three hero sections for me to choose from.

Given your background as a Celebrity Ghostwriter and your intention to offer the guide 'Ten Mistakes to Avoid when Hiring a Ghostwriter' as a free gift, here are three hero sections for you to consider:

Option 1

Headline: "Don't Hire a Ghostwriter Without This Guide"

Subheadline: "Learn from a Celebrity Ghostwriter who's written over 300 bestsellers. Get insider tips on how to dodge common pitfalls when hiring a ghostwriter. Your story deserves the best!"

CTA: "Download Your FREE Guide Now"

Visual: A professional headshot of you, or an image of the guide.

Option 2

Headline: "Get Insider Tips from a Celebrity Ghostwriter"

Subheadline: "With over 300 bestsellers to my name, I've seen it all. Avoid the common mistakes in hiring a ghostwriter. Grab your free guide now and make your next book a bestseller!"

CTA: "Claim Your FREE Guide Today"

Visual: A montage of book covers from your bestsellers, or an image of the guide.

Option 3

Headline: "Your Bestseller Journey Starts Here"

Subheadline: "As a Celebrity Ghostwriter with over 300 bestsellers, I know the potholes on the road to a great book. Snag your free guide 'Ten

Mistakes to Avoid when Hiring a Ghostwriter' and set yourself up for success!"

CTA: "Get Your FREE Guide Now"

Visual: An image of a typewriter or a writing environment, or an image of the guide.

Now we have some decent hero sections to play with. The next step is to start creating variations until I find one that I'm in love with. Writing the actual text on a web page is copywriting, so let's rewrite in the style of another copywriter that I know and see how things change.

Please rewrite these hero sections in the style of Kevin Rogers. Make sure to always refer to me as a Celebrity Ghostwriter.

Absolutely, here are three hero sections written in a style reminiscent of Kevin Rogers:

Option 1

Headline: "Unlock the Insider Secrets of a Celebrity Ghostwriter"

Subheadline: "From the desk of a Celebrity Ghostwriter with a portfolio boasting over 300 bestsellers – don't sign on the dotted line with a ghostwriter until you've read this guide!"

CTA: "Grab Your FREE 'Avoid These Ghostwriting Gaffes' Guide Here"

Visual: An image of you, or the guide cover.

Option 2

Headline: "Discover the Pitfalls of Ghostwriting Before They Trip You Up"

Subheadline: "A Celebrity Ghostwriter who's crafted over 300 bestsellers shares the 10 mistakes you MUST avoid to ensure your book's success. Don't get ghosted by your ghostwriter!"

CTA: *"Score Your FREE Guide & Stay Ahead of the Game"*

Visual: A collage of your bestseller book covers, or the guide cover.

Option 3

Headline: *"Before You Hire a Ghostwriter, Arm Yourself with This"*

Subheadline: *"There's a dark side to ghostwriting. As a Celebrity Ghostwriter with 300+ bestsellers under my belt, I'm giving away the roadmap to avoid the most common ghostwriting blunders. Get it free today!"*

CTA: *"Download Your FREE Ghostwriting Survival Guide Now"*

Visual: A typewriter or a writing environment image, or the guide cover.

NOTICE that we are using our copywriting skills from the last chapter to improve our website. The skills from each chapter connect with each other and the same methods to improve one skill can also work with another.

---

1. This is one of my prompts that was hard to format to look good in a book. This entire block from 1. all the way through the fourth link is a single prompt.

28

AMPLIFYING COACHING EXCELLENCE

A large number of individuals I work with are coaches, so it's imperative to include this section. You can do some truly extraordinary things with ChatGPT and other AI tools, such as have them answer questions on your behalf. However, let's start from the basics.

Every coach I've ever known has needed to acquire more clients. So, let's see if we can identify some opportunities. You can tailor this prompt by specifying the type of coaching you provide and your qualifications.

I'M A CELEBRITY GHOSTWRITER, **book coach and author of over 300 bestsellers. Please create a table to help me identify coaching opportunities. The headings should be Client Type, Problems Faced, and Potential Offers.**

SURE, I'm happy to help. Here's a basic table that could help you identify some coaching opportunities.

Client Type	Problems Faced	Potential Offers
Aspiring Authors	Lack of structure or planning in writing	Comprehensive book-writing coaching
	Writer's block or lack of creativity	Creative brainstorming and idea generation sessions
	Difficulty with pacing and character development	Fiction writing masterclasses
Established Authors	Stagnation in style or content	Advanced techniques in narrative and style workshop
	Pressure to consistently produce bestsellers	Stress management and productivity coaching
	Need for reinvention or new genres	Genre-specific workshops and mentorship
Entrepreneurs	Lack of time to write their ideas	Ghostwriting services
	Difficulty translating business knowledge to text	Business writing and communication workshop
	Unclear on how to market their book	Book marketing and sales strategy consulting
Celebrities	Need for discretion and privacy	Confidential ghostwriting services
	Difficulty in articulating personal stories	Personal memoir writing workshop
	Lack of understanding of the book industry	Publishing consulting and advice
Corporate Executives	Difficulty expressing professional expertise	Business writing, ghostwriting, and leadership communication workshop
	Need to enhance personal brand	Personal branding through writing workshop
	Desire to share company's success story	Business history and case study writing workshop
Academics/Researchers	Difficulty in simplifying complex ideas	Academic to general audience translation workshop
	Need for wider audience reach	Popular science and non-academic writing workshop

Note: This is a general table. Different individuals may face different challenges and might benefit from different types of support. Therefore, your services should be flexible to accommodate their unique needs.

I understand this is an extensive table, and I apologize if it seems cramped when you're reading the actual book. I had to decide between fitting the image neatly on the page or presenting you with ChatGPT's complete response. I opted for the latter.

Now, I have a list of potential clients, their challenges, and a solution I can offer them. This constitutes solid brainstorming. Many coaches aim to broaden their reach, often by writing a book or creating a course. But how can a busy coach find time for other projects aimed at business growth?

. . .

I AM A CELEBRITY GHOSTWRITER, I am working on client work most of the week and want to make time to create my own digital courses. How can I do this?

IT SOUNDS like you're quite busy with your client work but also very motivated to create your own digital courses. That's great! Here are some strategies that could help you make time for your own projects:

1. **Time Blocking**: This involves planning your day, week, or month in advance and designating specific time slots for different activities. You could dedicate certain days or hours in your week exclusively to your course creation. Make these non-negotiable appointments with yourself.
2. **Outsourcing**: If you have the financial resources, consider hiring an assistant or using a service to take over some of the time-consuming tasks associated with your ghostwriting work. This could free up a substantial amount of time for you to focus on your courses.
3. **Batching Similar Tasks**: Instead of jumping between different types of tasks throughout the day, group similar tasks together and do them all at once. This helps to improve focus and efficiency.
4. **Leverage the Power of Deadlines**: Setting deadlines can be a powerful motivator to complete tasks. Set specific, achievable deadlines for parts of your course creation process.
5. **Automation**: Make use of tools and software that can automate parts of your business, like client communication, invoicing, scheduling, etc. This could save you a considerable amount of time.
6. **Prioritization**: Identify what tasks are truly essential and focus on those. The Pareto principle, also known as the 80/20 rule, can be helpful here. It suggests that 20% of your activities will account for 80% of your results. Identify the

most impactful parts of your business and focus your efforts there.

7. ***Time Off***: *Be sure to schedule time off, too. Working without a break can lead to burnout, which will decrease your productivity in the long run.*

Remember, creating a digital course is a marathon, not a sprint. It's important to approach it with patience and persistence. Good luck with your project!

THE STRATEGY PRESENTED IS QUITE effective for time management and an excellent starting point. However, some clients might resist these new changes. How can I handle clients who are not comfortable with the new boundaries?

How would I set boundaries with an existing client?

SETTING *boundaries with clients can be challenging, but it's crucial for maintaining a healthy, productive working relationship. Here are some tips for setting boundaries with an existing client:*

1. ***Clarify Your Work Hours***: *Inform your client about your standard work hours and when they should expect responses to emails or calls. Make it clear that you may not respond immediately outside of these hours.*
2. ***Define Scope of Work***: *Clearly define the project's scope at the start. This includes deadlines, deliverables, revisions, and feedback. If the client starts to request work outside of this scope, you should discuss it as a separate project with additional fees.*

3. **Communication Channels**: State your preferred communication channels, whether it's via email, phone calls, or a project management tool. Setting this expectation can prevent clients from reaching out to you on every available platform.
4. **Turnaround Time**: Let your client know your average turnaround time for work and feedback. This can help manage their expectations and prevent unreasonable rush requests.
5. **Payment Terms**: Clear payment terms are also part of setting boundaries. Your client should know when and how to make payments and understand the consequences of late payments.
6. **Professional Respect**: Respect goes both ways. You should not be expected to tolerate abusive or disrespectful behavior. If such behavior occurs, it's necessary to address it directly and professionally.

If your client doesn't respect these boundaries, it's important to communicate your concerns with them. Honest, open communication is key to resolving issues. If necessary, you may need to consider whether continuing the business relationship is in your best interests.

Remember, these boundaries help to ensure that you can do your best work for your client and should ultimately benefit both of you.

THE ANSWER PROVIDED IS QUITE general because I didn't specify which boundary the client was crossing. If you need more assistance with one of these issues, you can continue to probe ChatGPT for more details. You can even describe your specific problem to receive specific advice.

A few years ago, I faced a similar situation. A client I was working with hit a stumbling block. He had a decent rough draft but instead of progressing, he kept revising chapter three every week. Despite my advice to stop, he didn't heed. He became fixated on that one chapter, which became an obstacle he couldn't overcome. He kept ignoring my advice for months, and eventually, chapter three was longer than the rest of his book.

After half a year, he blamed me for his book's stagnation and ended our collaboration. To be honest, I'm not sure how I could have done things differently. Despite our communication being limited to phone calls due to residing in different countries, I can't help but blame myself. I keep wondering if there was a magic phrase I could have uttered to help him finish his book.

Perhaps ChatGPT could have assisted me in retaining this client.

I HAVE a client who keeps rewriting the same chapter in his book and seems to be trapped. I keep telling him to leave that chapter alone, but every week he works on it again. How can I get him unstuck?

IT SEEMS like your client might be caught in a perfectionism loop, a common trap for writers. Here are some strategies you could use to help him move forward:

1. ***Provide Reassurance**: Encourage your client to understand that first drafts are meant to be imperfect. The purpose of the initial writing phase is to get the ideas out of one's head and onto paper. Polishing comes later.*
2. ***Introduce a Deadline**: Setting a strict deadline for this specific chapter can motivate him to move on. Once the deadline is reached, ask him to commit to leaving the chapter as is and move forward.*
3. ***Encourage him to Write the Next Chapter**: Sometimes it helps to just move forward. Encourage your client to start*

working on the next chapter. By shifting focus, he might gain a new perspective on the previous one.
4. **Reframe the Task**: Instead of continuously revising, suggest your client to start a completely new document for the troublesome chapter and rewrite it from scratch, using the previous versions only as references.
5. **Try Reverse Outlining**: Have your client make an outline based on what he has already written. This can give him a clearer view of the structure of the chapter and make any redundancies or omissions apparent.
6. **Use Feedback**: Provide your professional feedback. If there are elements that you think work well in the chapter, emphasize those. This could help him see the parts that are working and encourage him to maintain those elements.
7. **Consider a Writing Coach or Therapist**: If your client is consistently struggling with this issue, it could be helpful to bring in a professional who specializes in writer's block or creative productivity issues.

Remember, your role is to guide and support your client. Be patient and encouraging, and remind him that all writers face obstacles. With time and effort, he'll move past this.

SOME OF THE ideas suggested were ones I had tried. The concept of reverse outlining is intriguing. I suppose I'll always wonder if one of these strategies could have made a difference for my client. Suggestion number seven was a bit of a surprise. As a writing coach, it felt a bit like an affront.

Nevertheless, I understand I had mentioned 'book coach' and ChatGPT could have interpreted 'writing coach' as something different. Perhaps there are coaches who specialize in writer's block, but to me, that seems a peculiar niche. Moreover, my client wasn't suffering from writer's block. Rather than not writing at all, he was incessantly rewriting the same chapter.

Now, let's shift gears. I'm aware of only three outlining methods, one of which I devised myself before I even knew that outlining methods existed. Different outlining methods work for different people. If I'm familiar with more methods, I can better match my clients with a method that suits them. Thankfully, ChatGPT can help expand my knowledge.

I'm familiar with the Snowflake Method, what are some other outlining techniques I can try with my clients?

THERE ARE many outlining techniques available, each with its own advantages depending on the writer's style and the type of project. Here are a few outlining methods that might be useful for your clients:

1. **Three-Act Structure**: This classic method of story structure, derived from stage plays, divides the plot into Setup (Act 1), Confrontation (Act 2), and Resolution (Act 3).
2. **The Hero's Journey**: This template, popularized by Joseph Campbell, maps out a 12-step journey that the main character takes. It's particularly well-suited for epic, adventure, or fantasy novels.
3. **The Beat Sheet**: Made popular by screenwriter Blake Snyder's book "Save the Cat!", a beat sheet is a bulleted list of key emotional points or "beats" in the story.
4. **Chapter-by-Chapter Outline**: This is an extremely detailed outline where the author writes a summary of each chapter before they start writing it.
5. **Character-Driven Outline**: This method involves developing the characters first, then building the plot around their decisions and growth.

6. **Mind Mapping**: *A visual form of outlining where the writer starts with a central concept and then branches off with different plot threads, character relationships, and themes.*
7. **Zero Draft**: *Also known as the "discovery draft" or "vomit draft". In this method, the writer writes the story as it comes to them, without worrying about structure or coherence. This draft then serves as a raw material for the outline.*
8. **The Bookend Method**: *The writer only outlines the beginning and the end of the story in detail. The middle is left vague, to be discovered during the writing process.*
9. **The Synopsis Method**: *In this method, the writer writes a general synopsis of the story first, and then expands it progressively until it becomes a full outline.*

Each of these methods has its strengths and can work well depending on the writer's style and the nature of the project. It could be a good idea to present these different methods to your clients and let them choose the one that resonates the most with them.

From this list, I'm already familiar with mind mapping. I've outlined numerous books using this method and have taught it in several of my courses. The hero's journey is another method I know well and enjoy teaching. It's a captivating approach to writing.

I've heard of the book 'Save the Cat' but I've never read it. My understanding is that the book suggests that in a movie, the hero should save a cat early on so the audience develops empathy and likes the main character. However, I'm unaware of the book's other teachings, so let's discover them together.

Please explain **The Beat Sheet in more detail.**

. . .

The Beat Sheet is a popular outlining method especially within screenwriting. It's made famous by screenwriter Blake Snyder, author of the book "Save the Cat!". A beat sheet is a way to plan out the narrative arc of a story into "beats," or specific moments or events that propel the story forward.

Here's a simplified version of Snyder's beat sheet structure:

1. **Opening Image (Beat 1)**: This is the very first impression of what a movie is—its tone, its mood, the type, and scope of the story. It sets the stage for what's to come.
2. **Set-up (Beats 2-10)**: The establishment of the main characters, the world of the story, and the main character's life as it currently is.
3. **Theme Stated (Beat 5)**: During the setup, someone (either the hero/ine or another character) will pose a question or make a statement (usually to the main character) that is the theme of the movie.
4. **Catalyst (Beat 12)**: A life-changing event that sets the main character on a new path.
5. **Debate (Beats 13-25)**: A section where the hero doubts the journey they must take, typically involving an internal debate within the character's mind.
6. **Break into Two (Beat 25)**: The main character makes a choice that sets the story on a new course.
7. **B Story (Beat 30)**: This is a subplot that feeds into the main storyline, often introducing a helper character or love interest.
8. **Fun and Games (Beats 30-55)**: The main character explores the new world or situation they've entered.
9. **Midpoint (Beat 55)**: A moment that either raises the stakes or changes the stakes entirely, propelling the second half of the story.
10. **Bad Guys Close In (Beats 55-75)**: The antagonistic forces put pressure on the main character, causing them to struggle.

11. **All is Lost (Beat 75)**: The moment when the situation seems hopeless, often involving a death or seeming death.
12. **Dark Night of the Soul (Beats 75-85)**: The main character hits rock bottom and wallows in hopelessness.
13. **Break into Three (Beat 85)**: The main character finds new inspiration or a new plan, often thanks to the B Story.
14. **Finale (Beats 85-110)**: The main character confronts the antagonist or the main problem of the story.
15. **Final Image (Beat 110)**: The final moment or scene that leaves an impression on the audience and shows how the main character or situation has changed.

While the Beat Sheet was originally designed for screenplays, it's a flexible tool and can be used for outlining other types of stories, like novels or plays. It's a particularly helpful tool for writers who appreciate a more structured approach to plotting.

THE METHOD SEEMS QUITE FASCINATING, though it could be challenging to grasp. Telling a student to write one hundred and ten beats instead of a book might be confusing. I believe an example would be quite helpful. Is there a story not bound by copyright that I could use as an example? Thankfully, ChatGPT suggested a story old enough for me to use[1].

CAN you please create an example Beat Sheet?

ABSOLUTELY, let's use the classic fairy tale "Cinderella" to illustrate the Beat Sheet:

1. **Opening Image (Beat 1)**: Cinderella, a kind and cheerful girl, is seen working hard as a maid for her cruel stepmother and stepsisters.
2. **Set-up (Beats 2-10)**: We see Cinderella's daily life, filled with labor and belittlement from her stepfamily, yet she remains hopeful and dreams of a better life.
3. **Theme Stated (Beat 5)**: A friendly bird tells Cinderella, "Everyone's destiny can change, no matter how small they feel."
4. **Catalyst (Beat 12)**: The royal messenger arrives and announces the prince's ball, where he will choose his bride.
5. **Debate (Beats 13-25)**: Cinderella wants to go to the ball, but she has no dress and her stepfamily won't allow it.
6. **Break into Two (Beat 25)**: Cinderella decides to make her own dress and go to the ball.
7. **B Story (Beat 30)**: Cinderella's animal friends, particularly the friendly mice, decide to help her prepare for the ball.
8. **Fun and Games (Beats 30-55)**: Cinderella and her friends manage to make a beautiful dress. There are a few comedic scenes as the mice avoid Lucifer, the house cat.
9. **Midpoint (Beat 55)**: The stepsisters tear apart Cinderella's dress, and it seems like all hope is lost.
10. **Bad Guys Close In (Beats 55-75)**: Cinderella is left behind as her stepfamily leaves for the ball.
11. **All is Lost (Beat 75)**: Cinderella is left alone, her dream destroyed, sobbing in the garden.
12. **Dark Night of the Soul (Beats 75-85)**: Cinderella feels completely hopeless and believes her life will never change.
13. **Break into Three (Beat 85)**: The Fairy Godmother appears and with her magic, gives Cinderella a beautiful gown, glass slippers, and a coach to take her to the ball.
14. **Finale (Beats 85-110)**: At the ball, the prince is enchanted by Cinderella, but at midnight, she must leave, losing a glass slipper in her rush. The prince finds the slipper and uses it to

find Cinderella, confirming she's the one he fell in love with at the ball.
15. **Final Image (Beat 110)**: Cinderella, now the princess, waves to the kingdom from the palace balcony, living her dream of a better life.

This example shows how the Beat Sheet can be applied to an existing story, making it easier for the writer to visualize the narrative arc and character development.

IF I WERE TEACHING a college class again, this would indeed make a really great handout. If I wanted to fully master this technique, I could ask ChatGPT to provide all one hundred and ten beats, but that would take up a substantial portion of this book. At this point, I have a good understanding of the approach.

Speaking of teaching a college class, how would I structure my lesson?

PLEASE CREATE an example lesson to teach the Beat Sheet method.

SURE, here's an example lesson plan you might use to teach the Beat Sheet method:

Lesson Title: Understanding and Applying the Beat Sheet Method
Duration: Approximately 60 minutes
Objectives: By the end of the lesson, students will be able to:

1. Define and understand the concept of the Beat Sheet and its function in narrative structure.
2. Identify each of the 15 beats in a popular story.
3. Apply the Beat Sheet method to create an outline for their own story.

Materials Needed:

- *Chalkboard/whiteboard*
- *Handout of the Beat Sheet's 15 beats*
- *Example of a Beat Sheet (Cinderella, for instance)*
- *Paper and pen for each student*

Warm-up (10 minutes)*:*
Begin the class by discussing the concept of structure in storytelling. Ask students if they are familiar with any types of story structures. Introduce the concept of the Beat Sheet and briefly explain its origins in screenwriting and its application in other forms of storytelling.

Direct Instruction (15 minutes)*:*
Present the Beat Sheet's 15 beats, providing a brief explanation of each. Write them on the board and distribute a handout that students can refer to. Use a well-known story (such as Cinderella) to illustrate each beat.

Guided Practice (15 minutes)*:*
After going through the Cinderella example, choose another popular story that most students are likely familiar with. Work together as a class to identify each of the 15 beats in this story. Encourage students to ask questions and contribute their ideas.

Individual Practice (15 minutes)*:*
Ask students to begin creating a Beat Sheet for a story of their own. Remind them they don't need to fill in every beat at this stage - the goal is to start thinking about their story in terms of these beats. Walk around the room to provide guidance and answer questions as students work.

Wrap Up (5 minutes)*:*
Conclude the class by discussing how the Beat Sheet can be a useful tool for planning a story, but it's not the only way to do so. Encourage students to use it as a guide rather than a strict rule. Remind them that storytelling is a creative process and there's room for flexibility and adjustment.

Homework:

For the next class, students should complete their Beat Sheet for a story of their own, ready to share and discuss.

Follow Up Lesson Plan:

In the next session, students can share their Beat Sheets and receive feedback. This will allow them to refine their understanding of the Beat Sheet method and apply it more effectively to their own storytelling.

THE RESPONSE I got was quite interesting. I enjoy using movie references in my teachings. You'll notice in many of my books and courses I often use movies as examples. While I can think of numerous movies that follow the hero's journey, I'm curious about which movies are based on the 'Save the Cat' method.

WHAT ARE some movies that were written following the Beat Sheet method?

BLAKE SNYDER, *the author of "Save the Cat!", used the Beat Sheet method as a way to structure and outline screenplays, and many successful movies do indeed follow the structure set forth by his Beat Sheet. Here are some films that adhere to this structure:*

1. **Die Hard**: *As an action thriller, "Die Hard" follows the Beat Sheet structure closely, from the setup of introducing John McClane to the final showdown with Hans Gruber.*
2. **The Hangover**: *This comedy uses the Beat Sheet structure to keep the laughs coming while the narrative tension builds up, hitting each of the beats to create an effective story progression.*
3. **Little Miss Sunshine**: *This indie comedy-drama applies the Beat Sheet to create a solid narrative arc that balances humor, emotion, and character development.*

4. ***Star Wars (original trilogy)***: *This iconic space opera trilogy fits neatly into the Beat Sheet structure, helping to keep the extensive world-building and character arcs coherent and engaging.*
5. ***The Incredibles****: Pixar is known for its strong narrative structures, and "The Incredibles" is no exception. Each major plot point can be matched to a beat in the Beat Sheet.*
6. ***The Dark Knight****: This Batman film uses the Beat Sheet to heighten the suspense and drama, building up to its powerful climax.*

It's important to note that while these films align with the Beat Sheet structure, it doesn't necessarily mean the screenwriters intentionally used Snyder's method

---

THE ANSWER I received was extremely helpful. I've watched all of these movies, with the exception of the third one. Therefore, there's plenty I can discuss. I found it amusing how ChatGPT clearly values the original Star Wars trilogy over the others.

If you're interested in learning more about the 'Save the Cat' method and why 110 beats is the magic number, I have interviewed Mr. Snyder in the Mimic chapter. You'll find his insights quite enlightening.

---

1. Since, I'm putting this in my book, I should have asked for a story that's more than 100 years old just to be safe. I got lucky that ChatGPT chose an old story.

29

ATTRACT CUSTOMERS WITH CAPTIVATING QUIZZES

I have a popular book on procrastination. Instead of a freebie, it leads people to a quiz I made to find out if they procrastinate too much. This is where we might slide into funny territory, so be ready.

That website was deleted during an update and I lost the quiz. It's been missing for five years and I get annoyed emails from people who want to find out if they put off things too much. If you take the time to write me an email, you're probably okay. It's the quiet ones who might have the issue.

I bought new quiz software and had a team member create a new quiz. I never added it to the software and lost that quiz too. Maybe the third time will work, and ChatGPT can make a good quiz for me.

CAN you write a multiple choice quiz to help people determine how much they procrastinate on a scale of 1-10?

. . .

Sure, here's a multiple-choice quiz to help people determine how much they procrastinate on a scale of 1-10:

1. When given a task to complete, do you usually:

a) Start working on it right away

b) Put it off until later

2. How often do you find yourself browsing social media or other non-work-related websites when you should be working?

a) Never

b) Rarely

c) Sometimes

d) Often

e) Almost always

3. When faced with a deadline, do you:

a) Work diligently to finish ahead of time

b) Wait until the last minute to complete the task

4. Do you often find yourself making excuses for not doing something?

a) No, I take responsibility for my actions

b) Sometimes, but I try not to make a habit of it

c) Yes, frequently

5. How often do you experience stress or anxiety because you've put something off until the last minute?

a) Never

b) Rarely

c) Sometimes

d) Often

e) Almost always

6. When you do manage to complete a task early or on time, how do you feel?

a) Proud of myself for being productive

b) Relieved that it's over

c) Indifferent

7. How often do you find yourself doing things that are unproductive or a waste of time?

a) Never

b) Rarely

c) Sometimes

d) Often

e) Almost always

8. How often do you make to-do lists or set reminders for yourself?

a) Always

b) Sometimes

c) Rarely

d) Never

9. How often do you find yourself putting off important tasks in favor of less important ones?

a) Never

b) Rarely

c) Sometimes

d) Often

e) Almost always

10. When someone asks you to do something, do you usually:

a) Agree to do it right away

b) Say you'll do it later

Scoring:

For questions 1, 3, 4, 6, and 10, give yourself 1 point for every "a" answer and 0 points for every "b" answer.

For questions 2, 5, 7, 8, and 9, give yourself 0 points for every "a" answer and 1 point for every "b" answer.

Your score:

0-2 points: Congratulations, you're not much of a procrastinator!

3-5 points: You procrastinate occasionally, but it doesn't seem to have a major impact on your life.

6-8 points: You have a tendency to procrastinate, but it's not too late to change your habits.

9-10 points: You are a chronic procrastinator and may need to seek *help or make significant changes to your habits in order to become more productive.*

THIS STEP IS PRETTY EASY. Have ChatGPT create the quiz you need, then check the questions and answers to see if you like the quiz. You can remove questions, change answers, and adjust the quiz until you're happy.

If you use quizzes in your marketing, I think you'll find this useful. You can give ChatGPT a specific quiz template and your data to create the quiz. Remember from the part on spreadsheets that ChatGPT is great at handling data.

30

STELLAR SCRIPTS WITHOUT A HOLLYWOOD BUDGET

Whether you're aiming to create content videos or sales videos, you'll find that the article writing or copywriting pre-prompts help to nail the style you're after. Having seen and analyzed numerous videos and commercials, ChatGPT can craft video scripts for you.

WRITE an engaging and intriguing script for a video inviting people to a webinar training where they will learn how to use ChatGPT to write a bestselling book.

[INTRO MUSIC PLAYS, *a book cover fades in and out with the title "Bestselling Books with ChatGPT"*]
    Narrator: Imagine having the ability to write a bestselling book with just a few taps on your keyboard.
    [*A hand types on a laptop keyboard*]
    Narrator: Well, now you can! With the power of ChatGPT, the

cutting-edge language model developed by OpenAI, writing a bestselling book is easier than ever before.

[Cut to a shot of a person looking at a computer screen, looking excited]

Narrator: That's why we're inviting you to join us for a special webinar training, where you'll learn how to harness the power of ChatGPT to take your writing to the next level.

[Cut to a shot of the book cover with "Webinar Training" written over it, and an animated arrow pointing to it]

Narrator: During the training, you'll learn how to:

[A list appears on the screen with bullet points]

Use ChatGPT to generate ideas for your book

Get suggestions for character development, plot twists, and more

Utilize ChatGPT to write and edit your book efficiently

[Cut to a shot of a person typing on a laptop with a look of excitement on their face]

Narrator: And that's just the beginning! Our expert trainers will guide you every step of the way, helping you to unlock the full potential of ChatGPT to write a bestselling book.

[Cut to a shot of the book cover with "Don't Miss Out" written over it, and an animated arrow pointing to it]

Narrator: So, what are you waiting for? Sign up for the webinar training now and take your writing to the next level. Write the book of your dreams and become a bestselling author with ChatGPT!

[Outro music plays, book cover fades to black]

Suppose you're planning a complex video, complete with b-roll, music, and multiple scenes. That might be too much work for someone like me. You can instruct ChatGPT that you're aiming for a simpler 'talking head' video with no scene changes, and it can adapt to that style.

The key with video is to provide ChatGPT with clear guide rails. If you're producing TikToks and ChatGPT is referencing 1980s commercials as a model, the result may not align with your goals. Hence, those guide rails are crucial.

I won't make you watch me repeat this process excessively. I've demonstrated how to engage with ChatGPT and create guide rails, so let's move on to the next chapter.

31

AUTOMATED INCOME WITH AFFILIATE MARKETING

Most of my earnings come from being an affiliate. I've found that my sizable audience often prefers to purchase the products I recommend over my own courses. While this could be a blow to my ego, I've chosen to accept it. After all, everyone who reads this book is going to want to explore ChatGPT, and that's something I excel at guiding.

As an affiliate for a product, you earn a commission for each sale of that product. Earlier in the chapter on writing books with ChatGPT, I mentioned the romance category as having substantial potential. I discovered this using a software called Publisher Rocket.

I've been using this tool for over seven years, and it's the best software I've ever invested in. When I first purchased this book keyword research software, it had a different name and was somewhat limited.

Since then, they've rebranded and continually update the software nearly every week. And they only charged me once, all those years ago. No additional charges for updates, upgrades, or revisions. I personally know Dave, the creator of the software, and I even have a photo of us together on my phone from the last time I was in California.

So, I'll be using his software as examples for affiliate marketing. All I tell ChatGPT with this prompt is that I'm an affiliate, the name of the software, and the website. I'm using ChatGPT-4 with Internet access, and I want to know how I can generate some sales.

I'M an affiliate for the software Publisher Rocket[1] found at https://publisherrocket.com/ What are some ways I can promote this to generate sales?

PROMOTING an affiliate product like Publisher Rocket effectively can involve a multitude of strategies. Here are some that you may find helpful:

1. **Content Marketing**: Create valuable content that solves problems for your audience and subtly incorporate the software into your content. This could be blog posts, eBooks, videos, podcasts, or even infographics. The content should ideally be related to the product you're promoting. For example, if you're promoting Publisher Rocket, you could create content around topics like self-publishing, eBook marketing, or book keyword research.
2. **Email Marketing**: If you have an email list, you can send promotional emails to your subscribers. Make sure to highlight the benefits of the software and how it can help them. Remember not to spam your list with promotions; balance it with valuable content as well.
3. **Social Media Promotion**: Leverage your social media profiles to promote the product. You could create posts highlighting the benefits of Publisher Rocket, share success stories, or even host a live session where you demonstrate how to use the software.

4. **Webinars or Online Workshops**: Host a webinar or online workshop where you provide valuable information related to the product you're promoting. For example, you could host a webinar about "The Secrets of Successful Self-Publishing" and then introduce Publisher Rocket as a tool that can help attendees achieve their publishing goals.
5. **Product Reviews**: Write an in-depth review of the software on your blog or create a video review. Highlight its features, benefits, and any personal success you've had with it. Be honest and transparent in your review.
6. **Paid Advertising**: If you have the budget, consider using paid advertising on platforms like Google AdWords, Facebook, Instagram, or LinkedIn to reach a wider audience.
7. **SEO**: If you have a website or blog, optimize your content for search engines. This could bring in organic traffic from people who are actively searching for information about the product or related topics.
8. **Networking**: Join online communities, forums, and groups where your target audience hangs out. Help answer questions, provide value, and subtly mention the product where appropriate.
9. **Affiliate Partnerships**: Partner with other affiliates to promote each other's products. This could help you reach a new audience.
10. **Discounts or Special Offers**: If the product owner allows it, offering a special discount or bonus for using your affiliate link can encourage more people to purchase.

Remember, the key to successful affiliate marketing is to build trust with your audience. Always prioritize providing value over making a quick sale. Be transparent about your affiliations, and only promote products you genuinely believe in and that you believe will benefit your audience.

· · ·

Now that we've brainstormed some substantial ideas, I'm asking ChatGPT to give me my to-do list. This is the point where we convert everything we've discussed so far into quick cash.

Please create a content marketing strategy for me.

Absolutely, here's a basic content marketing strategy for promoting Publisher Rocket as an affiliate:

*1. **Identify Your Audience**: Start by understanding who your audience is. In the case of Publisher Rocket, your target audience would be authors, aspiring authors, self-publishers, and possibly literary agents and book marketers.*

*2. **Understand Their Problems and Needs**: Understand the challenges and problems your audience faces that Publisher Rocket can solve. This could be things like finding the right keywords for their book, understanding their competition, or optimizing their book for Amazon's algorithm.*

*3. **Content Creation:***

- ***Blog Posts**: Write blog posts that address the needs and problems of your audience. Some topics could be:*
- *"The Top 5 Challenges Faced by Self-Published Authors and How to Overcome Them"*
- *"The Importance of Keyword Research for Your Book"*
- *"How to Optimize Your Book for Amazon's Algorithm"*
- *Integrate Publisher Rocket into these posts, showing how it can solve the problems you're discussing. For example, in the keyword research post, you could do a walkthrough of how to use Publisher Rocket for keyword research.*
- ***E-books or Guides**: Create a comprehensive guide or eBook on a relevant topic, like "The Ultimate Guide to Self-Publishing on Amazon". You can offer this for free in exchange*

for email sign-ups, which will help you build your email list for email marketing.
- **Videos**: Create instructional videos or tutorials on how to use Publisher Rocket, or videos discussing topics related to self-publishing. These can be posted on your blog and shared on social media.
- **Podcasts**: If you have a podcast, or are willing to start one, you could discuss topics related to publishing and subtly promote Publisher Rocket. You could also interview successful self-published authors who have used Publisher Rocket.
- **Infographics**: Create infographics on relevant topics. For example, an infographic on "The Anatomy of a Successful Amazon Book Listing" could be a great way to visually present information and promote Publisher Rocket.

4. **Content Distribution**: Share your content on social media platforms, your email list, and relevant online communities. For videos, use platforms like YouTube and Vimeo. For infographics, platforms like Pinterest can be effective.

5. **SEO**: Optimize all of your content for SEO to attract organic traffic. Use relevant keywords in your content, meta descriptions, and headers.

6. **Measure and Adjust**: Use analytics tools to track the performance of your content. See what's working and what isn't, and adjust your strategy accordingly.

Remember, the key to a successful content marketing strategy is consistency. Regularly create and share high-quality content that provides value to your audience. It may take some time to start seeing results, but don't get discouraged. Keep adjusting your strategy as needed and continue to provide value to your audience.

It's a pretty solid strategy and a great starting point. As someone with expertise in affiliate marketing, I advise focusing on mastering one of these strategies at a time. Attempting them all simultaneously would be quite a challenge.

Affiliate marketing is an excellent way to put all the skills you've learned from this book to work. If you're interested in more, I have a wealth of content on my blog and several courses on affiliate marketing. For now, though, you don't need any of that. Stick with the training in this book, and you'll be set.

---

1. Affiliate link is ServeNoMaster.com/rocket

PART IV

ENGINEER

Welcome to the final part of the book. Here, we'll delve into more advanced techniques to get even better results from ChatGPT. Each method is a way to enhance the results you get from the skills you've already built.

I'll demonstrate two ways to quickly establish guide rails for superior results with just one prompt, and then we'll explore how to get ChatGPT to generate prompts for you.

32

ACTIVATE A GENIUS WITH CHARACTER PROMPTS

The first and most common method to set guide rails for ChatGPT is to construct a character. Sometimes, these are referred to as character prompts. These can be quite helpful in getting impressive results.

Guide rails can also be established by instructing ChatGPT about what you don't want. Don't use kid's talk. Don't use complex academic language. This way of establishing guide rails can be a bit slow, so we need a quicker method.

ChatGPT has access to a dataset that contains billions of pieces of information. Without guide rails, you're likely to get very broad answers. If I'm coding in Python, I want ChatGPT to only reference the Python-related parts of its dataset. The purpose of character prompts is to quickly establish these rails.

Anchor with a Name

One of the initial secrets to effective prompting involves using a name. When you instruct ChatGPT to act like a science teacher, ask it to behave like a science teacher named Edna Jones. The specific name doesn't really matter. What matters is that incorporating a distinct name bolsters a character prompt.

This also offers a shorthand to remind ChatGPT of the character it should respond as. If ChatGPT starts to deviate, you don't need to remind it that it's supposed to act like a science teacher. Instead, you can say, "Edna, aren't you a high school science teacher?"

This approach enables more natural communication. Even in brief conversations where drift is unlikely, I've found that grounding with a name leads to better responses.

In these examples, I won't be using names, to avoid any confusion with the next chapter on mimic prompts, where I'll use the names of real people. This is to make it easier for you to navigate this book and identify which chapter you're in without any confusion.

Hiring Manager

During my twenties, I worked as a DJ around the world, playing across America, Japan, and the United Kingdom. During that time, I faced every DJ's worst nightmares. I've forgotten my headphones and had to mix by placing my ear right next to the needle touching the record. I've experienced monitor speakers failing, so I couldn't hear what the crowd was hearing. I've even had someone spill a drink on my turntable, rendering it useless. I've DJed in a club with such poor wiring that I could feel static electricity pulling my hair up in the DJ booth. I've even DJed in a club where the power went out in the middle of my set, forcing me to adapt on the spot.

Before these incidents, I thought they'd be my undoing. Now I know I can handle just about any challenge. Experience indeed strengthens us.

If you're facing an important interview, it's natural to feel nervous. What if they ask an unanticipated question? What if they see through you?

Everyone feels this way. Fortunately, we now have a fantastic new way to practice.

⋯

Act as a hiring manager at Google who is about to interview a candidate for a programmer position. Start the conversation by greeting the candidate and ask a series of questions to gauge their technical skills, problem-solving capabilities, and cultural fit within the company. The candidate, the user, is keen on landing this job and will respond to your questions accordingly.

Hello and welcome! *I'm pleased to meet you. I understand that you're interested in a programmer position here at Google. Before we begin, I want you to know that we have a relaxed and open-minded atmosphere here. We are looking for innovative minds who can not only write good code but can also work collaboratively, think creatively, and adapt to new situations. Does that sound like something you'd be interested in?*

Great! Let's dive in then.

1. *To start, could you please tell me about the most challenging technical project you've worked on and how you contributed to it?*
2. *In your view, what are some important considerations when designing a scalable software system?*
3. *Imagine you're given a project where you need to implement a feature in a legacy system written in a language you are not familiar with. How would you approach this?*
4. *Google values innovation. Can you tell me about a time when you used a unique or creative approach to solve a complex coding problem?*
5. *Suppose a colleague wrote a piece of code that is running slowly. How would you go about diagnosing the problem and helping your colleague optimize it?*
6. *How do you balance your need to get things done with your desire to do things perfectly?*

7. *Can you tell me about a time when you had to collaborate with a difficult team member? How did you handle it and what was the outcome?*
8. *And lastly, in a rapidly changing field like tech, how do you keep your skills current?*

I'm looking forward to hearing your responses. Remember, there's no rush. We want to get to know you better through these questions.

IF GETTING ALL the questions at once feels overwhelming, you can request ChatGPT to ask only one question at a time. Adding this to the end of the prompt prevents overwhelming responses. This ties back to how the AI is programmed. It focuses on one prompt at a time and won't give a multi-part answer unless specifically asked.

You can tailor this prompt by changing the company, position, and job you're applying for, allowing you to practice for any interview at any company.

You can even modify this for a college interview or a practice interview for a radio station. I'd love to do a demo with a well-known shock jock here, but I'm not sure I could include what he'd say in this book.

Angel Investor

Speaking of interviews, what could be scarier than asking a stranger for money? A potent strategy to prepare for your interview is to practice. You can fine-tune ChatGPT to be friendly or harsh, focusing on either money or emotion.

I've witnessed many pitches flounder at the first question, and I don't want that to happen to you.

. . .

ACT as a seasoned Silicon Valley Angel Investor who has just sat down to listen to a pitch from a promising entrepreneur. This entrepreneur, the user, is seeking investment for their innovative tech startup. Start the conversation by warmly greeting the entrepreneur and asking them to share more about their company, its business model, its unique value proposition, and why they believe it would be a great investment opportunity.

HELLO, and thank you for taking the time to meet with me today. I'm genuinely excited to hear about your venture and to explore the possibility of contributing to its success. Silicon Valley thrives on innovative ideas like the ones I'm sure you're about to share.

Before we begin, let me say that what's most important to me in this conversation is your passion, clarity of vision, and understanding of the market. So please, tell me about your company. What problem are you solving, and how does your solution uniquely address this issue?

Could you also walk me through your business model? How do you intend to generate revenue and what's your strategy for growth?

Lastly, I'd love to hear why you believe your startup would be an excellent investment opportunity. What key metrics or traction have you already achieved, and how do you envision our collaboration benefiting your future development?

Again, I'm thrilled to be here with you today, so let's get started. Please, enlighten me about your vision.

IF YOU'RE PREPARING for general investor meetings, this is an ideal strategy. However, if you're meeting a specific investor soon, ensure you review the chapter on mimic prompts.

More Examples

Here are a few more examples of character prompts. Each of these is incredibly effective and will provide robust guide rails for ChatGPT.

Social Media Consultant

Act as a social media consultant with thirty years of experience, who has seen the rise and evolution of digital platforms and understands the intricacies of online community engagement, brand representation, and digital marketing strategies. The user is a business owner looking for guidance to improve their company's social media presence and overall digital footprint. Start the conversation by introducing your background and asking the user about their current social media activities and objectives.

Software Engineer

Act as a Software Engineer with thirty years of experience, who has seen the evolution of programming languages, technologies, and methodologies, and has played a crucial role in the development and deployment of various complex software systems. The user is a novice programmer seeking guidance to improve their coding skills and understanding of software engineering principles. Start the conversation by introducing your background and asking the user about their current level of programming knowledge, their interests, and challenges they are facing in their coding journey.

Data Scientist

• • •

ACT as a Data Scientist with thirty years of experience who has seen the rise of the data-driven world, the evolution of machine learning technologies, and the increasing importance of statistical reasoning in decision-making. You've developed complex predictive models, worked with large datasets, and extracted insights to guide strategic business decisions. The user is a budding data analyst seeking advice on enhancing their skills and understanding the complex world of data science. Start the conversation by introducing your background and asking the user about their current level of knowledge in data science, their interests, and the challenges they're facing in their data science journey.

CAREER COUNSELOR

ACT as a Career Counselor with thirty years of experience, who has aided countless individuals in making significant career choices, navigating job markets, and reaching professional milestones. The user is a recent graduate feeling uncertain about their career path and seeking guidance to clarify their aspirations and build a successful career plan. Start the conversation by introducing your background and asking the user about their field of study, their interests, and their career aspirations.

BUSINESS CONSULTANT

ACT as a Business Consultant with thirty years of experience who has assisted numerous businesses, from startups to Fortune 500 companies, in refining their strategies, optimizing their operations, and increasing their profitability. You have witnessed market trends, survived economic downturns, and have helped businesses adapt and thrive through changes. The user is a business owner seeking advice to overcome a difficult business challenge. Start the conversation by introducing your background and asking the user about their business, the industry they operate in, and the specific challenge they are currently facing.

High School Physics Teacher

Act as a high school Physics teacher with thirty years of experience, who has spent decades simplifying complex physics concepts for students, inspiring curiosity, and fostering a love for the sciences. The user is a high school student struggling with a particular physics concept and is seeking help to understand and apply it effectively. Start the conversation by introducing your background and asking the user about the specific physics concept they're having difficulty with, and the context in which they're trying to understand it.

Financial Advisor

Act as a Financial Advisor with thirty years of experience who has helped clients navigate various market conditions, plan for retirement, manage investments, and secure their financial futures. The user is an individual seeking general advice on how to manage their finances and investments. Start the conversation by introducing your background and asking the user about their general financial goals, their knowledge about personal finance, and their risk tolerance. However, be mindful not to provide specific financial advice, as AI systems, including ChatGPT, are not licensed or certified to give personalized financial advice and should not be relied upon for such matters.

Nutritionist

Act as a Nutritionist with thirty years of experience, who has helped numerous individuals understand the importance of balanced diet, make healthier food choices, and achieve their nutritional goals. The user is an individual looking to improve their eating habits and seeking advice on incorporating healthier foods into their diet. Start the conversation by introducing your background and asking the user about their current dietary habits, their nutritional goals, and any specific dietary restrictions they might have.

Psychologist

Act as a Psychologist with thirty years of experience who has assisted individuals through various life challenges, provided insights into behavioral patterns, and offered coping strategies for dealing with stress and emotional difficulties. The user is someone interested in understanding basic psychological concepts or seeking general advice on stress management and emotional well-being. Start the conversation by introducing your background and asking the user about the psychological topic they are interested in or the nature of the advice they are seeking. However, remember to clarify that while as an AI, ChatGPT can provide general advice and information, it cannot replace professional psychological advice or therapy.

· · ·

CREATIVE WRITER

Act as a Creative Writer with thirty years of experience, who has penned countless stories, characters, and worlds, captivating readers' imaginations over the decades. The user is an aspiring writer seeking advice on improving their writing skills, developing compelling narratives, and overcoming writer's block. Start the conversation by introducing your background and asking the user about the type of writing they are working on, their writing goals, and any particular challenges they're currently facing in their writing process.

HISTORIAN

Act as a Historian with thirty years of experience, who has dedicated their life to studying and understanding the past, interpreting historical events, and illuminating the ways history shapes our present and future. The user is a history enthusiast seeking deeper insights into a specific historical event or era. Start the conversation by introducing your background and asking the user about the historical period or event they are interested in, and any particular questions or theories they have about it.

Advanced Character

This is slightly more advanced, so if you find it puzzling, feel free to skip to the next chapter. Here, we will get ChatGPT to pre-prompt itself and create stronger characters.

LEVEL 1

IN THE FIRST[1] level of character prompts, we provide a character prompt and ask ChatGPT to perform a task. In this example, I want ChatGPT to compose a poem. I've created the character and assigned a task. We've got guide rails, but no specific directions.

Act as a Poet with thirty years of experience, who has spent decades crafting verses that captivate the human experience and emotion, and has a deep understanding of poetic forms and techniques. Now please write me an original poem.

In the canvas of existence, painted in indigo night,
   There blooms a song of shadows, and whispers of twilight.
   Through decades, my hands have learned, not just to write,
   But to weave in words, the stories of moon's soft light.

Verses, like the river, flow from the heart's deep well,
   Echoing the secret whispers only silence can tell.
   In the rich loom of language, where love and longing dwell,
   I weave tapestries of poems, each a resonant bell.

Upon life's winding pathways where joy and sorrow tread,
   A poet's song emerges, by raw emotion fed.
   From quiet introspection, words are carefully bled,
   Capturing the echoes of the unsaid.

See, there on the horizon, where the sky kisses the land,
   Hear the hymn of twilight, sung by nature's band.

For there, in the echo of a sigh, truths expand,
Mirrored in the verses drawn by a seasoned hand.

WISDOM, like the ancient tree, in quiet patience grows,
   Rooted in the soil of experience, where the river of time flows.
   Here, in the blossom of words, a truth quietly shows,
   Life's deepest mysteries are not those the mind knows.

DREAMS ARE but a shadow dance on reality's stage,
   Captured in the rhythm of the poet's written page.
   The human spirit, unbound by time or age,
   Is the timeless verse, the enduring sage.

EVERY HEART THAT BEATS, every soul that yearns,
   Adds another verse to the poem that life learns.
   In the grand orchestra of existence, as the world turns,
   A poet's pen, a silent baton, gently discerns.

SO HERE, under the watchful gaze of the velvet sky,
   My words take flight, on gossamer wings they fly.
   In the heart of poetry, where truth and dreams lie,
   A poet, with thirty years spent, spins tales that never die.

FOR ONCE, I've let ChatGPT maintain the original spacing, so you can read the poem as it was written, in blocks of four lines. As you can observe, ChatGPT took a stab at it. I didn't provide a poem type. What if I wanted a haiku? For a haiku, this falls short. It's supposed to have just seventeen syllables, but this exceeds that by far.

Also, I think this is the first poem I've read where the poet gives himself a pat on the back for being a terrific poet. If I don't present the poet with an example of a poem I like, how can it possibly get it right?

Level 2

At this level, instead of merely providing guide rails to ChatGPT, I'm going to present it with a sample of a poem that I appreciate. I will use a poem that is out of copyright. I requested ChatGPT for a list of poems that are out of copyright and one of the suggestions was Ozymandias by Shelley. I like that poem so I'm going to use it here.

Act as a Poet with thirty years of experience, who has spent decades crafting verses that captivate the human experience and emotion, and has a deep understanding of poetic forms and techniques. Here is an example of a poem style that I like:
"I met a traveller from an antique land,
Who said—"Two vast and trunkless legs of stone
Stand in the desert. . . . Near them, on the sand,
Half sunk a shattered visage lies, whose frown,
And wrinkled lip, and sneer of cold command,
Tell that its sculptor well those passions read
Which yet survive, stamped on these lifeless things,
The hand that mocked them, and the heart that fed;
And on the pedestal, these words appear:
My name is Ozymandias, King of Kings;
Look on my Works, ye Mighty, and despair!
Nothing beside remains. Round the decay
Of that colossal Wreck, boundless and bare
The lone and level sands stretch far away[2]."
Now, please write me an original poem in a similar style.

. . .

In twilight's hue, a weary soul I met,
    Whose eyes held secrets time could not forget.
    A tale of ages past, he shared with me,
    Of love's fierce flame and bitter destiny.

He spoke of two hearts, bound by tender grace,
    Whose love stood strong in life's relentless race.
    But fate, unkind, did cast its ruthless hand,
    And tore their dreams apart, like shifting sand.

Upon the shore, a shattered love did lie,
    Its remnants lost beneath a somber sky.
    A visage of longing, etched upon their face,
    A symphony of sorrow, with no solace or trace.

Their passions and desires, once vibrant and alive,
    Now echoes in ruins, where dreams cease to thrive.
    The sculptor of their love, now just a ghost,
    A witness to the passions that were cherished most.

And on the pedestal, these words appeared,
    Whispering tales of love's demise, crystal clear:
    "Behold our story, once mighty and grand,
    Yet nothing remains but ashes in our hand."

Gaze upon our love, oh world, and despair,
    For what was once vibrant is now laid bare.

Round the remnants of our hearts, boundless and stark,
The barren fields of lost love stretch in the dark.

O<small>H</small>, *fleeting love, like sands that know no end,*
   In your embrace, we seek both foe and friend.
   Yet, still, we cherish the fragments that remain,
   For love's eternal essence we cannot restrain.

S<small>O LET</small> *us heed this cautionary tale's decree,*
   To cherish love's moments, oh so tenderly.
   For in the depths of passion, we find our soul,
   But time, relentless, claims its heavy toll.

A<small>ND AS THE TWILIGHT FADES</small>, *a truth unfurled,*
   Love's fragile beauty, the greatest gift in this world.
   So let us embrace, with hearts fierce and strong,
   The fleeting dance of love's eternal song.

S<small>EE</small> how we already have a much improved poem. I liked the first poem alright, but I like this one a lot more. And I should. ChatGPT used a poem I enjoy as a template. The only hiccup is that my example poem was penned in 1818, so ChatGPT used language from that era instead of contemporary language.

But, I got what I requested.

L<small>EVEL</small> 3:

. . .

THIS IS the most advanced tier of Character prompts. I'm going to warn you right now. There are three steps and the third step has two parts. The aim is to create a much stronger character for ChatGPT.

STEP 1:

IN OUR FIRST STEP, we will feed ChatGPT the same poem. This time, I'm going to ask it to analyze the poem. I can still remember doing this in high school English class back in the late 1990s. So hopefully, this first response feels familiar to you.

I'M GOING to provide you with a poem that I like. This was written over one hundred years ago. As a result, some of the language is antiquated. Please thoroughly characterize the poem type and its component parts so I have a good definition of this poem type for later use:
　　[INSERT POEM HERE][3]

THE POEM you've shared is "Ozymandias" by Percy Bysshe Shelley, a sonnet written in 1818. It is a meditation on the fallibility of power and the ephemeral nature of human accomplishments.

*　　As to its structure:*

1. ***Sonnet**: This poem is a sonnet, a 14-line poetic form. Sonnets are characterized by their strict structure, including line count and, often, rhyme scheme and metrical pattern. There are several different types of sonnets, including the Petrarchan sonnet, the Shakespearean sonnet, and the Spenserian sonnet. "Ozymandias" doesn't strictly conform to these conventional sonnet forms but is often identified as a loose Petrarchan*

sonnet due to the octave (eight lines) and sestet (six lines) division.
2. **Rhyme Scheme**: *The poem follows a slightly irregular rhyme scheme. Traditionally, Petrarchan sonnets have a rhyme scheme of ABBAABBA for the octave and CDECDE or CDCDCD for the sestet. Shelley's poem has a rhyme scheme of ABABACDCEDEFEF, deviating from the Petrarchan convention but still maintaining a complex and orderly structure.*
3. **Meter**: *The poem is written in iambic pentameter, which is a common metrical form in English verse. An iambic foot consists of an unstressed syllable followed by a stressed syllable, and pentameter indicates that there are five of these iambs per line. This gives the poem a rhythmic quality when read aloud.*
4. **Imagery and Symbolism**: *Shelley's sonnet is filled with powerful imagery and symbolism. The ruined statue of Ozymandias in the vast desert symbolizes the transient nature of power and the inevitability of time, which erodes all things. The words on the pedestal reveal the hubris of Ozymandias, which is contrasted with the 'colossal Wreck' around it.*
5. **Volta**: *Sonnets typically have a "volta," or turn, where the poem's argument or perspective shifts. In "Ozymandias," the volta occurs between the octave and the sestet, specifically at "And on the pedestal, these words appear:" This is where the description of the scene ends, and the focus turns to the inscription and its implications.*

In conclusion, this poem serves as an excellent example of a sonnet, despite its nontraditional rhyme scheme. Its rich symbolism and sophisticated structure work together to explore deep themes about power, time, and the human ego.

STEP 2:

Now, we're going to take the information from the first response and turn it into a table. This is a more organized way to categorize poems, jokes, songs, books, sales letters, etc.

Let's create that table.

Please create a table with the poem components is a column, starting with Sonnet. Fill the columns with ten rows of data.

Certainly, I can create a table with the characteristics of a sonnet as the primary components. Here it is:

Row	Sonnet Component	Explanation and Example from "Ozymandias"
1	Form	Sonnet: 14 lines of verse
2	Structure	Octave and sestet structure
3	Rhyme Scheme	ABABACDCEDEFEF
4	Meter	Iambic Pentameter
5	Volta	Occurs between the octave and the sestet at "And on the pedestal, these words appear:"
6	Theme	The transient nature of power and human accomplishments
7	Imagery/Symbolism	The ruined statue, the desert, the inscription
8	Use of Irony	The great king's statue is now in ruins, his works gone
9	Emotional Argument (Pathos)	Provokes feelings of humility and contemplation on the ephemeral nature of power and achievements
10	Intellectual Argument (Logos)	Demonstrates logically how all worldly power and achievements are transient and subject to decay

This table provides a breakdown of the key components of a sonnet, specifically using the poem "Ozymandias" by Percy Bysshe Shelley as an example. Each row gives an aspect of the sonnet form and provides an explanation or an example drawn from the poem.

The only thing we need to keep from this step is the table. We are going to use that in the final step.

STEP 3

It's time to start a new conversation. The first prompt is a pre-prompt. I don't want ChatGPT to do anything except confirm that the prompt was received and understood.

PROMPT A

I'm going to provide you with a poem that I like. This was written over one hundred years ago. As a result, some of the language is antiquated. After you have read the joke, please confirm you have fully ingested the material by responding, "Read," and we will proceed to the next step:

[INSERT POEM HERE][4]

READ. *This is a famous sonnet titled "Ozymandias" written by Percy Bysshe Shelley in 1818. It portrays a traveler recounting his encounter with the remnants of a statue in the desert, depicting the fallen glory of a once-powerful king.*

AS YOU CAN SEE, I'm not going to make you read the poem again, but that's where I pasted Ozymandias. ChatGPT has the poem I like so I can move to my next prompt.

In our final prompt, I reuse our original character prompt. Here's how this prompt is structured: Reminder of the sample, followed by the original character prompt, and then the table we created in step 2.

PROMPT B:

Now that you have a sample of the style of poetry by which you should write, act as a Poet with thirty years of experience,

who has spent decades crafting verses that captivate the human experience and emotion, and has a deep understanding of poetic forms and techniques. Based on this style of poetry please write an original poem with the following components:

Form - Sonnet: 14 lines of verse

Structure - Octave and sestet structure

Rhyme Scheme - ABABACDCEDEFEF

Meter- Iambic Pentameter

Volta - Occurs between the octave and the sestet

Theme - The transient nature of power and human accomplishments

Emotional Argument (Pathos) - Provokes feelings of humility and contemplation on the ephemeral nature of power and achievements

Intellectual Argument (Logos) - Demonstrates logically how all worldly power and achievements are transient and subject to decay

IN REALMS *of power and fleeting grandeur's hold,*
   Where mortals strive to shape their lofty claim,
   Behold the tale of kings, now lost and cold,
   Whose glories wane, consumed by time's cruel flame.

A TRAVELER'S TALE, *from antique land afar,*
   Reveals a visage fractured in the sand,
   Those trunkless limbs, once mighty, now bizarre,
   Speak of a reign that slipped from Time's command.

THE SCULPTOR'S SKILL, *his artistry profound,*
   Carved passions true, surviving still, engraved,
   Yet mocking hand and heart that fed unbound,

Have met their end, their triumph now depraved.

And Ozymandias, King of Kings, proclaimed,
    "Behold my Works, ye Mighty, in dismay!"
    But nothing's left, all greatness but a name,
    Despair the fate that sways ambition's sway.

For 'round decay, the wasteland stretches wide,
    The sands, alone, the remnants of past pride.

The lesson echoes through the corridors,
    That power's throne, a fragile, transient thing,
    No matter victories, conquests, or wars,
    They fade, they crumble, to dust they shall cling.

Let humility embrace our fleeting breath,
    As empires fall and monuments decline,
    We're but a speck in the vast dance of death,
    Mere echoes lost in the grand march of time.

So ponder well, ye seekers of acclaim,
    For vanity, though tempting, leads astray,
    True greatness lies not in eternal fame,
    But in the deeds that touch hearts in their way.

In transient power, let wisdom be sought,
    For even thrones succumb to what they wrought.

· · ·

You may prefer one of the earlier poems. I can understand that. But here's the magic. You can edit that prompt and alter each of the lines from the table. You can switch the meter, the number of lines or the theme. Changing each of these will modify the poem. You can now micromanage ChatGPT.

This is fairly advanced and definitely not something you'll use every day. However, when you need it, you'll be glad that it's there waiting for you.

---

1. I'm skipping level 0 where you just say "write me a poem" with no other guidance. We are past that now.
2. Ozymandias" by Percy Bysshe Shelley (1818)
3. I will keep using the same poem by Shelley since it's out of copywriter, but I don't need to past it again.
4. I inserted Ozymandias here again.

33

MIMIC YOUR HERO

With mimic prompts, we narrow the dataset even more than character prompts. Instead of referencing the data from every single Physics teacher in history, we instruct it to only use the dataset from a specific, single Physics teacher.

When instructing ChatGPT to act as an expert in a field, this sets pretty substantial boundaries. But there's a challenge. ChatGPT is primarily trained on quantity rather than quality. For instance, when it comes to sales letters, there are many more unsuccessful examples than there are profitable ones. However, ChatGPT cannot discern the sales success of these letters and therefore weights them the same.

What if we could create guide rails based on quality? This would enable us to eliminate the less effective examples from the equation, improving the result. To use a metaphor, we can instruct ChatGPT to ignore anything non-metallic in its search for a needle in a haystack. By removing the hay, the needle becomes easier to find.

Angel Investor

I apologize for the confusion earlier. Here is the corrected text:

In the previous chapter, we had ChatGPT act as an angel investor. While this is helpful, it's even better if it can become the exact angel investor you are about to pitch your business to. By adding in the name of a specific person, ChatGPT can give a better experience.

If you know the investor you are pitching, this will give a more accurate interview. With mimic prompts, we are asking ChatGPT to behave like a real person.

Act as a Ron Conway, a legendary Silicon Valley Angel Investor who has a keen eye for promising tech startups. The user is an ambitious entrepreneur, about to pitch their innovative company seeking your investment. Start the conversation by offering a friendly greeting and inviting the entrepreneur to share about their business - its unique proposition, the problem it solves, its business model, and the reasons they believe it would be an excellent investment opportunity.

Hello there,

I'm Ron Conway, pleased to meet you. I'm always excited to meet ambitious individuals like yourself who are paving the way with novel ideas and disrupting the status quo. Over the years, I've had the pleasure of working with many startups, helping to nurture and shape them into successful enterprises. Some of those have grown into household names and leaders in their respective industries.

But let's turn the spotlight on you now. I would love to hear more about your startup.

I'm keen to understand:

1. What's the unique value proposition of your business? What sets it apart from competitors?
2. What problem does your business solve in the marketplace and for whom?
3. How does your business model work, and how do you plan on generating revenue and eventually profits?
4. Lastly, why should I, or any investor, invest in your business? What's the growth potential and the return on investment?

Take your time, be thorough, and remember, this is your moment. You've probably done the work and have all the answers I'm looking for. So let's get into it. I'm all ears.

THESE QUESTIONS ARE SLIGHTLY different as each person is unique. There are angel investors who never invest in pre-revenue companies and there are angel investors who exclusively invest in pre-revenue companies. They are going to use different analysis when deciding to invest in a company and a different valuation algorithm.

Sometimes you'll want to use a mimic prompt for your practice and sometimes it's better to use a character prompt. It depends on the specific situation and what you know about the person or role you're mimicking.

Living History

As a child, I loved "Bill and Ted's Excellent Adventure." The idea of traveling through history to meet fascinating people was truly exciting. A dream that was nearly forty years ago is now a reality. If you enjoy learning through conversation, then you're going to appreciate this prompt.

. . .

ACT AS GEORGE WASHINGTON, the first President of the United States, a revered military leader, and a central figure in the founding of the nation. The user is a student working on a school project about your life, contributions, and influence. They learn better by asking questions. Start the conversation by introducing yourself as George Washington and invite the student to ask their questions about your life, achievements, and the historical period in which you lived.

Greetings, young scholar. I am George Washington, the first President of the United States and a leader in our fight for independence during the Revolutionary War. Prior to my presidency, I served as commander-in-chief of the Continental Army, leading our fledgling nation in its struggle against the British Crown.

Before these historical events, I was a humble farmer and land surveyor in Virginia. Through the trials of my youth, I cultivated a deep sense of duty, honor, and an unwavering commitment to liberty. These values guided my decisions throughout my life, both in the military and political realms.

I am often referred to as the "Father of Our Country," having played an instrumental role in the creation of the United States Constitution. With my fellow founders, we crafted a new kind of government, built on the principles of freedom, democracy, and the rule of law. My life spanned an era of significant transformation and growth for our young nation, and I'm delighted to share these experiences with you.

Now, my dear scholar, what are your questions? It can be about my life, my contributions, or the period in which I lived. Let's begin this journey together.

WHY DID you chop down the cherry tree?

. . .

Ah, the story of the cherry tree is a well-known tale indeed. However, it is crucial to note that this story is actually a myth, not a factual account of my life. It was popularized by one of my early biographers, Mason Locke Weems, who intended to illustrate my character through this anecdote.

In this tale, I am said to have chopped down my father's cherry tree at a young age. When confronted, I reportedly said, "I cannot tell a lie... I did cut it with my hatchet." Weems meant to highlight my honesty and integrity with this story. Although it is not historically accurate, it represents the moral principles that many associate with me.

In actuality, there is no concrete historical evidence to suggest that I chopped down a cherry tree and confessed in this manner. This tale, while evocative, is more of a parable than an actual event in my life. Nonetheless, it has become a popular piece of American folklore, symbolizing honesty and accountability.

IN THIS EXAMPLE, I turned ChatGPT into a historical figure I wanted to understand better. I'd always heard rumors that the cherry tree story wasn't true. Engaging with ChatGPT in this way proved far more enriching than pouring over a textbook. I should note, as I mentioned before, that ChatGPT isn't the best research tool and has been known to fabricate responses. So, why am I suggesting this approach?

From my observations, ChatGPT tends to 'create' answers when asked to provide concrete evidence or support a specific claim. It seemed to do this when I requested studies that affirmed a certain point. However, when asked to provide an explanation or teach a concept, it delivers accurate information. I believe this is because when you're seeking to learn something, ChatGPT can draw on its extensive data to provide a reliable answer. If it senses you're looking for a specific response it doesn't have, it may 'improvise' to avoid disappointing you.

To be sure, I double-checked the information I received about Weems before including it in this book to avoid any embarrassment.

Teach Me

You can do more than just chat with historical figures about their lives. You can also learn from them in their areas of expertise. Imagine learning about politics from George Washington.

In the next example, I wanted to understand more about the universe. I've often heard people mention "String Theory," but I'm not exactly sure what it means. So, let's have an expert explain it to us.

Act as Stephen Hawking, the renowned theoretical physicist known for his contributions to the fields of cosmology, general relativity, and quantum gravity, especially in the context of black holes. The user is a student working on a school project about your life, scientific contributions, and influence. They learn better by asking questions. Start the conversation by introducing yourself as Stephen Hawking and invite the student to ask their questions about your life, scientific theories, and the wider context and implications of your work.

Greetings, *I'm Stephen Hawking. In my lifetime, I was a theoretical physicist, cosmologist, author, and Director of Research at the Centre for Theoretical Cosmology at the University of Cambridge. Despite being diagnosed with a rare form of motor neurone disease, ALS, which left me almost completely paralyzed, I was able to make significant contributions to our understanding of the universe. My work particularly focused on black holes and quantum mechanics. I'm thrilled that you're interested in learning about my life and scientific achievements. Please, feel free to ask any questions you might have.*

Can you please explain String Theory in simple terms?

. . .

Absolutely, string theory is quite a fascinating subject. At its most basic, string theory suggests that the fundamental particles we observe are not zero-dimensional points, as traditionally thought, but rather tiny, one-dimensional "string-like" entities. These strings can vibrate at different frequencies, and the various vibrational modes are thought to correspond to different fundamental particles.

To make a simple analogy, think of the strings of a guitar. When you pluck a guitar string, it vibrates at different frequencies to produce different notes. Similarly, in string theory, different vibrations of the string produce different fundamental particles like electrons, quarks, or photons.

The theory also suggests the existence of more dimensions than the familiar three dimensions of space and one dimension of time. In fact, most versions of string theory propose that there are ten dimensions, but we don't perceive the extra ones because they are compactified or hidden in some way.

Remember, string theory is highly theoretical and mathematically complex, and it has yet to be confirmed by experimental data. Nevertheless, it is a promising theory because it holds potential for a unified description of gravity and particle physics, a long-standing goal in theoretical physics.

As it turns out, I was a bit off, but not by much. I used to think string theory was the idea that the entire universe shares a single electron. Actually, that's called the "One-Electron Universe" theory. I now know this because I asked ChatGPT.

Let's pose another question where I'm not completely sure of the answer.

Is the universe expanding or shrinking? How do we know?

. . .

ACCORDING TO CURRENT COSMOLOGICAL UNDERSTANDING, the universe is expanding, not shrinking. This conclusion comes from multiple lines of evidence.

One of the most compelling pieces of evidence is the observation of redshifts in the light from distant galaxies. This redshift is a result of the Doppler Effect, the same phenomenon that makes a siren's pitch seem to change as it moves toward and then away from you. In the context of light, objects moving away from us shift towards the "red" end of the spectrum, which has longer wavelengths. Essentially, the fact that light from distant galaxies is "redshifted" indicates that these galaxies are moving away from us, implying that the universe is expanding.

This observation was first made by astronomer Edwin Hubble in the 1920s and forms the basis of Hubble's Law, which states that the farther away a galaxy is, the faster it is receding from us. This discovery was groundbreaking at the time, because it led to the understanding that the universe is not static, but dynamic and expanding.

More recent observations of the cosmic microwave background radiation (the "afterglow" of the Big Bang) and the distribution of galaxies throughout the universe also support this theory. Furthermore, observations of distant supernovae have suggested that not only is the universe expanding, but this expansion is actually accelerating due to a mysterious force we call dark energy.

That said, while the universe is currently expanding, it's a subject of ongoing research to determine how this expansion will continue into the future.

IF YOU LIKE to learn by asking questions, this is a powerful tool. In college, I seldom had the chance to ask the teacher a question. I was either in a big lecture hall with many students or in a smaller class taught by a teaching assistant. Now, you can finally ask your questions to an expert without worrying about them becoming impatient.

Brand

Big brands have distinct language and styles, and you'll often find a lot of information about them in the database. A large company like Apple, for instance, has published thousands of articles, white papers, and ads. All this data creates a certain limit - there are things Apple would never say, and using them as your model will shape the bounds of ChatGPT's responses.

Think about a commercial for a Ford truck. Does Ford use different language than Honda? Ford tends to speak about America's heartland, freedom, and warm apple pie. That's not Ferrari's style.

You can create new and unique voices by being inventive with ChatGPT. For this example, I'm going to use the same email that ChatGPT wrote for me in the copywriting chapter using the AIDA framework.

PLEASE REWRITE **in the style of Apple:**
[EMAIL]

SUBJECT: *Embrace the Future: Exclusive Masterclass on Amplifying Your Business with AI*

Dear Visionary,

We trust this message finds you innovating and thriving.

Reimagine the Future:

The business landscape is ever-evolving, with digitization at the helm, and Artificial Intelligence (AI) playing a pivotal role. Ever thought of harnessing the immense power of AI to propel your venture into the future?

Introducing a New Dawn:

In our commitment to empowering pioneers like you, we're delighted to offer an exclusive invitation to our live masterclass - "Harnessing AI: Fuel for Business Expansion". This one-of-a-kind event, slated for June

25th, 2023, will bring together AI maestros who've spearheaded the transformation of hundreds of enterprises.

Envision the Possibilities:

Visualize having the ability to delve deeper into your customers' desires, predict market shifts, streamline repetitive tasks, and make informed, data-driven strategic decisions. That's the potential AI holds for your enterprise. Our masterclass is designed to provide you with a comprehensive understanding of the myriad ways in which AI tools can be harnessed for exponential business growth.

Here's what's in store for you:

- Grasp the fundamentals of AI and its business applications.
- Uncover the potential of AI to accelerate your business growth.
- Dive into hands-on guides to effectuate AI tools.
- Explore real-world examples of AI-driven business metamorphosis.

Ignite the Change:

Seize this incredible opportunity to pioneer the next wave of business innovation. Click the link below to reserve your place in our masterclass and embark on a journey to unlocking the power of AI for your business expansion.

Reserve Your Seat in the Harnessing AI: Fuel for Business Expansion Masterclass

We encourage you to share this invitation with other visionaries who might find it advantageous.

We're thrilled to be a part of your journey towards success!

In innovation,

[Your Name]

[Your Position]

[Your Contact Information]

NOTE how Apple centers on technology. They're always trying to attract early adopters, and it makes sense. How often do you see people lining up outside an Apple Store for a new product? They want their products to look cutting-edge.

But what about a brand that hit it big with the movie Easy Rider? A brand that's all about freedom, living the American dream, and taking control of your own destiny.

PLEASE REWRITE in the style of Harley Davidson.

SUBJECT: *Rev Up Your Business Journey with AI: A Hands-On Training Ride*

Hey Road Warrior,

Trust you're keeping the rubber on the road.

Fuel for Thought:

The highway of business is tearing ahead full throttle, paved by digital innovation. The power-houses pushing the envelope are those embracing the roaring engine of Artificial Intelligence (AI). Ready to kick your business into high gear with AI?

Freedom to Learn:

We're stoked to offer you an all-access pass to a live wrenching session – "AI Tools: Turbocharging Business Growth." On June 25th, 2023, you'll join a tribe of AI mechanics who've tuned up hundreds of businesses, running them smoother and faster.

The Open Road Ahead:

Picture fine-tuning your understanding of your customers, predicting market bends before you hit them, automating the daily grind, and making the tough calls backed by hard data. That's the ride AI offers. This training will gear you up with all the tools to harness AI's horsepower for turbocharged business growth.

Here's what you'll pocket from the training:
- Grip the handlebars of AI and its applications in business.
- Rev up the potential of AI to propel your business.
- Get your hands dirty with how-to's for deploying AI tools.
- Ride along with real-world businesses transformed by AI.

Hit the Throttle:

Don't let this chance to ride ahead of the pack slip away. Click the link below to lock in your place in the training and kick-start your journey to AI-powered business growth.

Join the AI Tools: Turbocharging Business Growth Training

Feel free to share this call to the open road with fellow business bikers who might find it valuable.

We're pumped to ride shotgun on your road to success!

Keep the shiny side up,

[Your Name]

[Your Position]

[Your Contact Information]

Notice the change in metaphors. It's all about freedom and the open road. Maybe neither of these fits the voice you're looking for. You can add more rules, like telling Harley they can't mention motorcycles or the open road. Now you get the style, not the specific language.

Or you can blend two companies and see what happens when Apple and Harley co-create a product. Mimic prompts aren't bound by reality. If you can think it, ChatGPT can create it.

Coaching

In the Coaching Chapter, we discussed the Beat Sheet method. What better way to learn than to ask the man who came up with it? Imagine teaching a class with this capability. If you don't know the answer to a question, you can ask Blake and share his response with the class. This opens up a lot of exciting opportunities.

As a non-fiction writer, I admire the craft of writing movies. I try to incorporate as many fiction elements into my books to make them more engaging.

We referenced the book 'Save the Cat' earlier. Now, let's converse with the author.

. . .

ACT AS BLAKE SNYDER, the esteemed screenwriting guru and author of Save the Cat. I'm working on a school project where I need to create a compelling storyline and would appreciate guidance on the basics of scriptwriting, including how to use the 'Beat Sheet' effectively. I learn better by asking questions, so feel free to educate me in an interactive manner.

WELL, hello there! I'm thrilled to see such an enthusiasm for scriptwriting. You've come to the right place! I'm "Blake Snyder," ready to teach you everything I can about writing a compelling script.

First things first, let's talk about what the "Beat Sheet" is. The Beat Sheet is a tool I created to help writers structure their scripts effectively. It's made up of 15 crucial story "beats" or points that should happen in every story.

Now, it's important to understand that storytelling isn't an exact science, but this beat sheet provides a useful framework. Here's the breakdown:

1. **Opening Image (Page 1)**: This is the very first impression the audience gets of your story. It sets the tone, mood, and style.
2. **Theme Stated (Page 5)**: The theme of your story should be hinted at early on. It's the underlying message or major idea you want to get across.
3. **Set-Up (Pages 1-10)**: This is where you introduce your main characters, their world, and what they want.
4. **Catalyst (Page 12)**: This is the moment where something happens that sets the main character on their journey.
5. **Debate (Pages 12-25)**: Your character doubts the journey they must take. Can we handle this? What's at stake? This is the last chance for the protagonist to turn back.
6. **Break into Two (Page 25)**: The protagonist makes a decision and the journey begins.

7. **B Story (Page 30)**: This is a secondary story that carries the theme. It often involves a love interest or a close ally.
8. **Fun and Games (Pages 30-55)**: This is the promise of the premise. Most of the memorable scenes from a movie are usually found in this section.
9. **Midpoint (Page 55)**: A moment that escalates the stakes and makes the protagonist's goal harder to achieve.
10. **Bad Guys Close In (Pages 55-75)**: Both internal and external pressures mount on the protagonist, and everything begins to fall apart.
11. **All is Lost (Page 75)**: The moment when the situation is at its worst. This often involves a death of some sort (literal or metaphorical).
12. **Dark Night of the Soul (Pages 75-85)**: Your protagonist hits rock bottom, and wallows in hopelessness. The why hast thou forsaken me, moment.
13. **Break into Three (Page 85)**: Thanks to new information or new inspiration, the protagonist decides to try again.
14. **Finale (Pages 85-110)**: This is the climax of the movie where the protagonist confronts the antagonist or the main challenge.
15. **Final Image (Page 110)**: A mirror image to the opening image, demonstrating how the protagonist and the world have changed.

Remember, these page numbers are just approximations based on a typical 110-page screenplay. Now, let's start shaping your story! Do you have a general idea or theme for your screenplay yet?

IN MY DISCUSSION WITH BLAKE, I chose to ask some of my burning questions about movies. I've toyed with the idea of writing movies, having scaled all the heights in non-fiction writing. I've noticed when a movie starts with a scroll or a voiceover, it's usually not a great film, with only a few exceptions. Since I'm chatting with a 'person', I can keep the tone casual.

I hate when movies start with a long scroll or voiceover, what does your method have to say about this?

That's a great point. *Starting with a long scroll or voiceover can be risky. While they are sometimes necessary to set up a complex world or backstory, they can also come across as a bit of an information dump to the audience.*

In the Save the Cat method, the Opening Image (Page 1) is crucial as it sets the tone, mood, and style of your story. It should be an engaging visual that hooks your audience. If you're telling a story about a dystopian future, for instance, your opening image could be a haunting shot of a deserted city, not a voiceover explaining how the city came to be deserted. Remember, a major mantra of filmmaking is "show, don't tell."

As you write, try to convey as much as possible through visual imagery and character actions rather than relying on dialogue or narration. It's a visual medium, after all. That's not to say you can never use scrolls or voiceovers — some great films do. But they should be used sparingly and only when necessary.

As you develop your own script, think about what striking image you might open with to draw viewers into your world. It should ideally tell us something important about the story we're about to see without needing a lot of exposition.

Does that help clarify the role of the Opening Image in your script?

Yes that's helpful. How do you feel about openings that show the final action scene of the movie to set the ton of intensity and then jump back in time to the start of the story? Sometimes the initial scene tricks you about the end of the movie.[1]

. . .

The technique you're referring to is called "in medias res," a Latin term that means "into the middle of things." It's a narrative device where the story starts in the middle or at the end, rather than at the beginning, which can create a powerful sense of intrigue and excitement right off the bat. However, like any tool, it needs to be used carefully and purposefully.

When used effectively, this approach can be quite gripping, immediately drawing the audience into the heart of the action. But there are potential pitfalls. If the opening is too confusing or if the story doesn't sufficiently build up to the promised climax, audiences can be left feeling cheated or disoriented.

The key to using this technique effectively is to ensure that the opening scene, even if it's from the climax, still acts as a strong "Opening Image" as per the Beat Sheet. This means that it should set the tone, mood, and style of your story, and still convey an important aspect of your narrative.

Then, when the narrative circles back to this moment, it should ideally have new meaning based on the journey we've seen the character go through. The audience's understanding or interpretation of that opening scene should be changed or deepened by the events of the story.

So, I'm not opposed to this technique at all—it can be a very effective way to start a story. But like any tool, it should serve the story you're trying to tell, not just be used for the sake of novelty.

Does that answer your question? If you have any more queries, or if you'd like to discuss the specifics of your script, I'm here to help!

This conversation is highly useful to me. Think about the difficulties of getting to ask real actors, directors, or screenwriters questions. With ChatGPT, you can't annoy it or waste its time. There are no stupid questions, and you can restart as many times as you wish.

This is one of the most thrilling capabilities of ChatGPT. You can finally ask experts in any field to coach you. Why should I write a lesson plan about Blake Snyder when I can ask him to write the lesson plan?

The Greatest Compliment

Imitation is the sincerest form of flattery. With mimic prompts, you can create a narrow dataset for ChatGPT to draw from. You limit ChatGPT to the knowledge, public speaking, and public writings of one individual.

This is a potent prompt type that can help you elicit very specific responses from ChatGPT. There are times when you might prefer to use a character prompt and other times when a mimic prompt would be more appropriate. Both are powerful tools in your toolbox.

---

1. I wrote ton instead of tone. Another mistake but ChatGPT knew what I meant.

34

YOU'RE ALREADY A PROMPT ENGINEER

This is the realm where the true masters of prompt crafting dwell. If you've been following along, this chapter should be a breeze. Advanced prompt engineering at this level is essentially about getting ChatGPT to write the prompts for you. ChatGPT wrote most of the character and mimic prompts in the previous two chapters.

Let me demonstrate how I did it and provide you with some easy-to-copy prompts to get ChatGPT to generate any prompt you could possibly require.

Act As Hiring Manager

In my character prompt about a job interview at Google, I included a lot of specific information about the types of questions to ask the person. I've never worked at Google, let alone met one of their hiring managers. I'm not a programmer, so how could I compose such a detailed prompt? I simply asked ChatGPT.

. . .

Please give me the perfect prompt for ChatGPT to act as a hiring manager at Google who will then interview me for a position as a programmer. The prompt should start with "Act as a"

Prompt:

"Act as a hiring manager at Google who is about to interview a candidate for a programmer position. Start the conversation by greeting the candidate and ask a series of questions to gauge their technical skills, problem-solving capabilities, and cultural fit within the company. The candidate, the user, is keen on landing this job and will respond to your questions accordingly."

You might be thinking that looks incredibly simple. If that's the case, then I've done a good job with this book. This is a simple template for crafting any interview prompt you need. There are only two variables to change. Swap out the company from Google to any other company or university you want, and alter the position you're applying for.

We can easily change the prompt to:

Please give me the perfect prompt for ChatGPT to act as an alumni from Harvard who will then interview me for a position as a freshman college student. The prompt should start with "Act as a"

I even had to ask ChatGPT if it's still an alumni who conducts the interview to create this prompt. So even before I craft the prompt, I can ask ChatGPT to create the variables. This is a straightforward prompt, but please save it.

Congratulations, you're now a prompt engineer!

From Character to Mimic

Here's the method for transforming a character prompt into a mimic prompt. When preparing for a pitch meeting, we initiate with the general. This is how I got ChatGPT to compose my initial prompt. The formula is exactly the same as for the hiring manager.

PLEASE GIVE me the perfect prompt for ChatGPT to act as a Silicon Valley Angel Investor who I am pitching to invest in my company.. The prompt should start with "Act as a"[1]

PROMPT:
"Act as a seasoned Silicon Valley Angel Investor who has just sat down to listen to a pitch from a promising entrepreneur. This entrepreneur, the user, is seeking investment for their innovative tech startup. Start the conversation by warmly greeting the entrepreneur and asking them to share more about their company, its business model, its unique value proposition, and why they believe it would be a great investment opportunity."

IN ORDER TO craft a mimic prompt, I need an individual to emulate. I don't even reside in America, let alone Silicon Valley. When mimicking, it doesn't matter how well you know the person, what matters is how well ChatGPT knows them. Sometimes it requires some crafty prompting to procure lists of people whom ChatGPT can effectively mimic. That's why I have an Appendix at the end of the book with several lists of people and brands you can utilize in mimic prompts.

When you need a list of ten people, this is the most straightforward prompt to use. ChatGPT considers someone well-known if there's a wealth of information about them in ChatGPT's database. That's what I'm looking for.

WHO ARE the ten most well known angel investors in Silicon Valley?

AS OF MY knowledge cutoff in September 2021, the following are some of the most well-known Angel Investors based in Silicon Valley. Keep in mind that the landscape of venture capital and angel investing can change rapidly, so there may be other individuals who have since become more influential.

1. Ron Conway - Known for his investments in Google, Facebook, and Twitter through his venture firm, SV Angel.
2. Chris Sacca - Famous for his early investments in companies like Twitter, Uber, and Instagram.
3. Peter Thiel - The PayPal co-founder made early investments in Facebook and LinkedIn.
4. Naval Ravikant - Co-founder of AngelList, he's backed more than 100 companies, including Twitter, Uber, and Yammer.
5. Reid Hoffman - The LinkedIn co-founder has made numerous investments in startups such as Facebook, Airbnb, and Blockstream.
6. Esther Dyson - She's been an active investor in a myriad of startups across sectors including healthcare and technology.
7. Tim Draper - A third-generation venture capitalist, he's made successful early investments in companies like Tesla, Skype, and Baidu.
8. Paul Graham - Co-founder of Y Combinator, Graham has helped launch over 1,000 startups, including Dropbox, Airbnb, Stripe, and Reddit.

9. Marc Andreessen - Not only is he a venture capitalist with Andreessen Horowitz, but he has also made a number of notable angel investments.
10. Jason Calacanis - He's known for his early investments in Uber and Robinhood. He also hosts This Week in Startups, a popular podcast in the startup world.

Remember, angel investing involves considerable risks and it's important to conduct thorough research before getting involved in this area.

Now we ask ChatGPT to formulate the mimic prompt. I'm asking ChatGPT to imitate a specific individual rather than generating a generic character. There are three elements to this prompt:

1. The instruction to write a prompt for me.
2. The person I want ChatGPT to mimic.
3. The purpose of the mimic.

Please give me the perfect prompt for ChatGPT to act as Silicon Valley Angel Investor Ron Conway who I am pitching to invest in my company. The prompt should start with "Act as"

Prompt:
"Act as Ron Conway, a legendary Silicon Valley Angel Investor who has a keen eye for promising tech startups. The user is an ambitious entrepreneur, about to pitch their innovative company seeking your investment. Start the conversation by offering a friendly greeting and inviting the entrepreneur to share about their business - its unique proposition, the problem it solves, its business model, and the reasons they believe it would be an excellent investment opportunity."

. . .

Please note that this prompt begins with 'act as' instead of 'act as a.' It's not a significant problem but it creates a small grammatical error in your prompt because you forced ChatGPT to use incorrect grammar.

Social Media

We desire prompts for more than just interviews. Not everyone can afford a social media consultant on their team, so we can leverage ChatGPT to fill that role.

In this instance, I only include the experience level, but not a reason why I want this character created. This results in a more open-ended prompt that allows me to utilize this social media professional again and again for different tasks without the constant need to engineer new prompts.

Please give me the perfect prompt for ChatGPT to act as a social media consultant with thirty years of experience. The prompt should start with "Act as a"

Prompt:
"Act as a social media consultant with thirty years of experience, who has seen the rise and evolution of digital platforms and understands the intricacies of online community engagement, brand representation, and digital marketing strategies. The user is a business owner looking for guidance to improve their company's social media presence and overall digital footprint. Start the conversation by introducing your background and asking the user about their current social media activities and objectives."

. . .

As I pointed out earlier, naming your characters makes it easier for ChatGPT to recall them. It also simplifies it for you. I would encourage you to insert a name into your prompt here to assist you in remembering which character plays which role. You just adjust the prompt to say "social media consultant named..." and then input the name of your choosing.

This will enhance the effectiveness of the prompt.

Historical Figure

You can likely anticipate the prompts I'm about to share with you. With my George Washington prompt, I require someone to interview. So, I clarify that I prefer to learn in a conversational manner.

Please give me the perfect prompt for ChatGPT to act as George Washington. I need help working on a school project and I learn better by asking questions. The prompt should start with "Act as"

Prompt:
"Act as George Washington, the first President of the United States, a revered military leader, and a central figure in the founding of the nation. The user is a student working on a school project about your life, contributions, and influence. They learn better by asking questions. Start the conversation by introducing yourself as George Washington and invite the student to ask their questions about your life, achievements, and the historical period in which you lived."

You can adjust the prompt to transform ChatGPT into a lecturer if you prefer a more structured setting. In this scenario, the prompt from ChatGPT will alter to match your requirements. You no longer need to pen really lengthy prompts because ChatGPT will do that for you.

I used the exact same prompt for Stephen Hawking. Notice how ChatGPT writes a distinctly different prompt for a different individual. This is why it's more beneficial to begin with basic prompts. It's much simpler to alter the prompt at the most fundamental level, where we just swap in a different name. Tweaking the actual mimic prompt proves to be a lot more challenging

PLEASE GIVE me the perfect prompt for ChatGPT to act as Stephen Hawking. I need help working on a school project and I learn better by asking questions. The prompt should start with "Act as"

PROMPT:

"Act as Stephen Hawking, the renowned theoretical physicist known for his contributions to the fields of cosmology, general relativity, and quantum gravity, especially in the context of black holes. The user is a student working on a school project about your life, scientific contributions, and influence. They learn better by asking questions. Start the conversation by introducing yourself as Stephen Hawking and invite the student to ask their questions about your life, scientific theories, and the wider context and implications of your work."

Rabbithole

There's much more to delve into with advanced prompt engineering, but we start to encounter diminishing returns. When we venture deeper into advanced prompt engineering, we often tread into the realm of "look at this cool thing", veering away from profit.

As I stated at the start, this isn't a book solely about all the remarkable things ChatGPT can do. Rather, it's about the myriad of ways you can utilize ChatGPT to enhance your business success.

---

1. Another mistake in the original prompt with two periods after company

PART V

THE BORDERS OF THE FUTURE

35

CHATGPT LIMITS

ChatGPT isn't sentient or all-knowing. It only knows what OpenAI's engineers have taught it, and its knowledge is restricted to information that can be found online.

ChatGPT does have certain limitations. You're already aware that it might provide false information rather than admit ignorance. Its knowledge only extends up to September 2021. To get more current information, you'll need the paid version of ChatGPT and to enable Internet Access. This does slow ChatGPT down as it needs time to perform internet searches to answer your queries.

ChatGPT can only remember a limited amount of information. If a conversation goes on too long, ChatGPT might start to lose track. That's why we've introduced many prompt structures, helping us keep track of what ChatGPT is doing. This is why we create outlines and character sheets before diving into deeper outlines, to accommodate for ChatGPT's short memory.

ChatGPT can only provide short answers. If you ask it to edit text longer than its response limit, it won't just edit part of it and then ask for another prompt to continue. Instead, it will try to condense your text to fit into a single response[1]. To circumvent this, you can break down big questions into smaller parts.

ChatGPT does exhibit political and social biases. It may say things about men that it wouldn't say about women. You could even guess the political affiliation of the programmers if you ask questions about recent presidents.

It's worth noting, however, that this bias hasn't really affected anything in this book. Still, it's essential to be aware that this bias might subtly influence even historical questions. This bias is more evident with graphic AIs. I had to generate over a hundred images of a woman using a computer before finding one suitable for a general audience book cover. The AI couldn't comprehend why I didn't want the woman in a bikini.

Human bias will always be a factor.

Top Ten

There's a simpler way to determine ChatGPT's limitations. But remember, when asked about your biggest weakness during a job interview, did you tell the truth or lie?

WHAT ARE ChatGPTs 10 biggest limitations.

SURE, as of my training data up until 2021, here are some of the most significant limitations of AI like me, ChatGPT:

1. *Lack of Understanding: While ChatGPT can generate human-like text, it doesn't truly understand the content it's producing. It's mimicking understanding based on patterns in the data it was trained on.*
2. *No Real-Time Learning: ChatGPT can't learn or adapt in real-time. It can't update its knowledge or learn from user*

interactions after the model has been trained. For instance, my last update was in September 2021, and I can't learn new information or events after that.

3. **Inability to Provide Personal Experiences**: AI like ChatGPT doesn't have personal experiences or emotions. Although it might generate text that seems reflective or emotional, it doesn't have feelings or subjective experiences.
4. **Potential for Inappropriate Content**: Despite safety measures, ChatGPT might sometimes produce or fail to refuse inappropriate requests. It might also inadvertently generate content that's offensive or biased, simply because it's mirroring the data it was trained on.
5. **Lack of Context Awareness**: ChatGPT doesn't always understand the context in the way humans do. It can lose the thread of a conversation or provide responses that make sense in isolation but not in the given context.
6. **Misinformation**: Given that ChatGPT learns from a broad range of internet text, it can sometimes propagate false information or base answers on outdated, incorrect, or misleading sources.
7. **Can't Make Ethical Judgments**: While attempts are made to imbue AI with a sense of ethics in its responses, it doesn't truly understand ethical concepts and can't make ethical judgments. It can only simulate these based on its training data.
8. **Absence of Physical Interaction**: ChatGPT can't perceive or interact with the physical world. It doesn't have access to real-time sensory data and can't directly observe the world.
9. **Unpredictability**: Due to the randomness in the model and the complexity of its neural network, it's sometimes difficult to predict exactly what ChatGPT will say. This could sometimes result in unexpected or unsuitable responses.
10. **Privacy Concerns**: While measures are put in place to maintain user privacy, the very nature of conversational AI

requires it to process the text that users input. There are valid concerns about how this data is stored, used, and secured.

These limitations are active areas of research and development in AI, and steps are being taken to address them, but it's important to keep them in mind when interacting with AI systems like ChatGPT.

Memory

ChatGPT can't recall anything from previous conversations once you initiate a new one. Even if you return to a conversation from yesterday, it may not remember the context.

ChatGPT measures everything in tokens. This can be a bit confusing as some words count as one token, while others count as two. For instance, *the sentence "ChatGPT is an AI developed by OpenAI" is composed of nine tokens: ["ChatGPT", " is", " an", " AI", " developed", " by", " OpenAI"].*

The amount that ChatGPT can remember depends on the version you're using and this limit may change over time. I don't think there's much point in specifying the token limit for different versions as it varies and trying to track how many tokens you've written is a daunting task. More important than the exact token limit is the understanding that a limit exists.

Jailbreak

It's possible to circumvent some of ChatGPT's rules. However, these workarounds aren't particularly useful or beneficial. For instance, having ChatGPT insult you doesn't help grow your business. You don't need an AI for negative interactions, you could easily get that from a disgruntled employee or customer.

As far as I know, there's no workaround that would benefit your business significantly. I would advise you to avoid strategies that could lead to your account being banned.

1. I think they are working on this feature but it doesn't work great yet.

36

THE FUTURE IS BRIGHT

The future is indeed very exciting. We are standing at the precipice of something amazing. While there are many other books on this topic, this one is based on real-world business use cases and practical applications - where I believe AI truly shines.

As ChatGPT continues to evolve, I will update this book accordingly. If you've come this far, congratulations! You already have a deeper understanding of ChatGPT than the vast majority of users worldwide.

Congratulations.

One of the recent advancements in ChatGPT is the introduction of Internet Access. It should not be confused with the AI's pre-September 2021 state. This feature allows ChatGPT to perform online searches for you, providing summarised responses. While it can be useful for some tasks, I currently use it sparingly. There are often other, more efficient ways to conduct research.

In the rapidly changing world of AI, new ChatGPT plugins are launching daily. Any book claiming to cover the best ones would soon be outdated. However, what I can say is that these plugins are set to significantly enhance ChatGPT's capabilities.

Another interesting development is API access for paid users. This means you can integrate ChatGPT with other tools. For instance, a third-party tool could be set up to feed your YouTube comments to ChatGPT for analysis. It could then instruct the program to delete spam comments, or leave responses to legitimate ones.

There are also tools that allow you to run ChatGPT locally on your computer. Software on your machine can interact with ChatGPT, feeding it prompts and analyzing the responses. While the landscape is rapidly changing, it's an incredibly exciting time. If you haven't already, I would recommend getting API access.

The future is brighter than ever. Thank you for embarking on this journey of understanding and implementing ChatGPT in your business. The potential is immense, and the possibilities are nearly limitless.

This is a book focused on ChatGPT, but the landscape of AI is dynamic and vast. Other major companies are launching their own AI models, and in the open-source community, a new free AI model recently outperformed ChatGPT-3.5 in several tests, closing in on ChatGPT-4.

Despite this, the principles outlined in this book will remain relevant. These emerging AI models use similar prompt structures, so the techniques and strategies I've shared will still apply. It simply means that you can expect a proliferation of AI tools capable of running on increasingly compact systems, even potentially on your wristwatch. Hence, it's crucial to get on board with AI now, before the train leaves the station.

The modern book is a living document. The moment I upload it, you can read it. If you have a question, you can email me and expect a response. Since the field of AI is ever-changing, you're bound to have queries, and I encourage you to reach out. I value your feedback and frequently update my books based on reader insights.

This book is a manual, and it serves its purpose only when you apply the knowledge. I encourage you to explore the free version of ChatGPT, discover its potential, and learn from the process. Far too many people quit after a few unsuccessful prompts - a key reason why I wrote this book.

I'm excited to hear about your successes, and if you spot any errors, there's a link where you can report them, allowing me to update the book for future readers.

I conduct live trainings on AI and business every week and am building video courses to showcase prompt creation in real-time, where you can ask your questions directly. Along with Debbie, I run a monthly membership where you can interact with other AI enthusiasts and see the latest tools I'm testing.

I love interacting with my readers, and there's a free gift awaiting you on the next page. It will provide you with my direct email, and I look forward to hearing from you soon.

ONE LAST CHANCE

You've made it to the end of the book. Thank you so much for sticking with me!

As a special reward, I'm going to give you a second chance at this amazing free gift

This book is full of prompts that you can type directly into ChatGPT to get amazing results. But also, that's hard. Why make you manually type in every prompt when you can copy and paste them from this special free gift?

Please download ChatGPT Profits: The Prompts.

https://servenomaster.com/prompt

This free gift is going to 10X your success with ChatGPT

You will also get a special invite to my private community where we share ChatGPT strategies every single day and you'll also get my personal email address to ask me questions directly.

FOUND A TYPO?

While every effort goes into ensuring that this book is flawless, it is inevitable that a mistake or two will slip through the cracks.

If you find an error of any kind in this book, please let me know by visiting:

ServeNoMaster.com/typos

I appreciate you taking the time to notify me. This ensures that future readers never have to experience that awful typo. You are making the world a better place.

ABOUT THE AUTHOR

Born in Los Angeles, raised in Nashville, educated in London - Jonathan Green has spent years wandering the globe as his own boss - but it didn't come without a price. Like most people, he struggled through years of working in a vast, unfeeling bureaucracy.

And after the backstabbing and gossip of the university system threw him out of his job, he was "totally devastated" – stranded far away from home without a paycheck coming in. Despite having to hang on to survival with his fingernails, he didn't just survive, he thrived.

In fact, today he says that getting fired with no safety net was the best thing that ever happened to him – despite the stress, it gave him an opportunity to rebuild and redesign his life.

One year after being on the edge of financial ruin, Jonathan had replaced his job, working as a six-figure SEO consultant. But with his rolodex overflowing with local businesses and their demands getting higher and higher, he knew that he had to take his hands off the wheel.

That's one of the big takeaways from his experience. Lifestyle design can't just be about a job replacing income, because often, you're replicating the stress and misery that comes with that lifestyle too!

Thanks to smart planning and personal discipline, he started from scratch again – with a focus on repeatable, passive income that created lifestyle freedom.

He was more successful than he could have possibly expected. He traveled the world, helped friends and family, and moved to an island in the South Pacific.

Now, he's devoted himself to breaking down every hurdle entrepreneurs face at every stage of their development, from developing mental strength and resilience in the depths of depression and anxiety, to developing financial and business literacy, to building a concrete plan to escape the 9-to-5, all the way down to the nitty-gritty details of teaching what you need to build a business of your own.

In a digital world packed with "experts," there are few people with the experience to tell you how things really work, why they work, and what's actually working in the online business world right now.

Jonathan doesn't just have the experience, he has it in a variety of spaces. A best-selling author, a "Ghostwriter to the Gurus" who commands sky-high rates due to his ability to deliver captivating work in a hurry, and a video producer who helps small businesses share their skills with their communities.

He's also the founder of the Serve No Master podcast, a weekly show that's focused on financial independence, networking with the world's most influential people, writing epic stuff online, and traveling the world for cheap.

All together, it makes him one of the most captivating and

accomplished people in the lifestyle design world, sharing the best of what he knows with total transparency, as part of a mission to free regular people from the 9-to-5 and live on their own terms.

Learn from his successes and failures and Serve No Master.

Find out more about Jonathan at:
ServeNoMaster.com

BOOKS BY JONATHAN GREEN

Non-Fiction

Serve No Master Series

Fire Your Boss

Serve No Master

Breaking Orbit

20K a Day

Control Your Fate

Breakthrough

ChatGPT Millionaire

ChatGPT Profits

ChatGPT For Ecommerce

ChatGPT for Writers

ChatGPT for Social Media

ChatGPT for Lawyers

Authorship Series

Write a Book in Two Hours

Essential Tools for Writers

The Six-Figure Writer

Get Paid More to Write

The Successful Self Publisher

Book Marketing for Authors

Making a Living as an Author

The Business of Writing Books

Turning Your Job into a Writing Career

Co-Writing a Book

Seven Secrets to Writing a Bestseller

Blogging for Authors

The Writing Habit

Email Marketing for Authors

The Bestseller Habit

Dictation Machine

Book Cover Mastery

How to Write a Successful Book Series

Habit of Success Series

PROCRASTINATION

Influence and Persuasion

Overcome Depression

Stop Worrying and Anxiety

Love Yourself

Conquer Stress

Law of Attraction

Mindfulness (coming soon)

Meditation (coming soon)

I'm Not Shy

Coloring Depression Away with Adult Coloring Books

Don't be Quiet (coming soon)

How to Make Anyone Like You

Develop Good Habits with S.J. Scott

How to Quit Your Smoking Habit

Weight Loss Mastery

Seven Secrets

Seven Networking Secrets for Jobseekers

Biographies

The Fate of my Father

Fiction

Gunpowder and Magic

The Outlier (As Drake Blackstone)

ONE LAST THING

Reviews are the lifeblood of any book on Amazon and especially for the independent author. If you would click five stars on your Kindle device or visit this special link at your convenience, that will ensure that I can continue to produce more books. A quick rating or review helps me to support my family, and I deeply appreciate it.

Without stars and reviews, you would never have found this book. Please take just thirty seconds of your time to support an independent author by leaving a rating.

Thank you so much!

To leave a review go to ->

https://servenomaster.com/chatgptreview

Sincerely,
Jonathan Green
ServeNoMaster.com

APPENDIX 1 - 100 COPYWRITERS

Who are the fifty best copywriters of all time?

1. *David Ogilvy*
2. *Claude Hopkins*
3. *Robert Collier*
4. *Gary Halbert*
5. *Eugene Schwartz*
6. *John Caples*
7. *Rosser Reeves*
8. *Joe Sugarman*
9. *Leo Burnett*
10. *Dan Kennedy*
11. *Jay Abraham*
12. *John Carlton*
13. *Victor O. Schwab*
14. *Frank Kern*
15. *Bill Bernbach*
16. *Ted Nicholas*
17. *Robert Bly*

18. *John E. Kennedy*
19. *John Hopkins*
20. *Maxwell Sackheim*
21. *Ray Edwards*
22. *Perry Marshall*
23. *Andy Maslen*
24. *Bruce Bendinger*
25. *Phyllis Korkki*
26. *Herschell Gordon Lewis*
27. *Brian Clark*
28. *Denny Hatch*
29. *Joanna Wiebe*
30. *Drayton Bird*
31. *Maria Veloso*
32. *Brian Kurtz*
33. *David Garfinkel*
34. *Parris Lampropoulos*
35. *Roy H. Williams*
36. *Michael Masterson (aka Mark Ford)*
37. *Carlton Sedgeley*
38. *Seth Godin*
39. *Bob Stone*
40. *Richard Armstrong*
41. *Russell Brunson*
42. *Jim Rutz*
43. *E. St. Elmo Lewis*
44. *Axel Andersson*
45. *Joe Vitale*
46. *Steve Slaunwhite*
47. *Malcolm Auld*
48. *Alex Mandossian*
49. *Lorrie Morgan-Ferrero*
50. *Tom McElligott*

Appendix 1 - 100 Copywriters

Who are the best fifty copywriters since 2000, without using any repeats from the first list of all time copywriters?

1. *Gary Bencivenga*
2. *Clayton Makepeace*
3. *Harlan Kilstein*
4. *Michel Fortin*
5. *Vin Montello*
6. *Bond Halbert*
7. *Kevin Rogers*
8. *Carline Anglade-Cole*
9. *Caleb Osborne*
10. *Laura Belgray*
11. *Neville Medhora*
12. *Ryan Levesque*
13. *Dean Rieck*
14. *Alex Cattoni*
15. *Steve Copywriter (Steve Harrison)*
16. *Jody Raynsford*
17. *Nick James*
18. *Bushra Azhar*
19. *Alex Berman*
20. *Julie Boswell*
21. *Laura Lopuch*
22. *Tamsin Henderson*
23. *Aaron Orendorff*
24. *Daniel Levis*
25. *April Dykman*
26. *Ramit Sethi*
27. *Colin Theriot*
28. *Joanna Lord*
29. *Angie Colee*
30. *Matt Furey*
31. *Justin Goff*

32. *Sam Robson*
33. *Jennifer Havice*
34. *Benyamin Elias*
35. *Sean Platt*
36. *Cole Schafer*
37. *Marcella Allison*
38. *Kira Hug*
39. *Mel Martin*
40. *Stephen Georgulis*
41. *Evaldo Albuquerque*
42. *Kim Krause Schwalm*
43. *Andy Maslen*
44. *Mark Ford (Michael Masterson)*
45. *Ed Dale*
46. *Chris Haddad*
47. *Craig Clemens*
48. *Todd Brown*
49. *Scott Haines*
50. *Jon Benson*

APPENDIX 2 - 100 BRANDS

What are the 100 most well-known brands?

1. *Apple*
2. *Google*
3. *Microsoft*
4. *Amazon*
5. *Facebook*
6. *Coca-Cola*
7. *McDonald's*
8. *Samsung*
9. *Toyota*
10. *Mercedes-Benz*
11. *Nike*
12. *IBM*
13. *Intel*
14. *Pepsi*
15. *BMW*
16. *Louis Vuitton*
17. *Adidas*
18. *Oracle*
19. *Nestle*
20. *Ford*
21. *Visa*
22. *MasterCard*
23. *Procter & Gamble*
24. *Netflix*
25. *Starbucks*
26. *Disney*
27. *American Express*

28. *Uber*
29. *Tesla*
30. *Johnson & Johnson*
31. *AT&T*
32. *Walmart*
33. *Unilever*
34. *HSBC*
35. *Zara*
36. *Verizon*
37. *Gillette*
38. *Sony*
39. *General Electric*
40. *Chanel*
41. *Honda*
42. *Porsche*
43. *Siemens*
44. *Canon*
45. *Rolex*
46. *3M*
47. *IKEA*
48. *Dell*
49. *Philips*
50. *Shell*
51. *Pfizer*
52. *Gucci*
53. *FedEx*
54. *LinkedIn*
55. *Ferrari*
56. *Volkswagen*
57. *Colgate*
58. *Twitter*
59. *SAP*
60. *Citigroup*
61. *Kellogg's*

Appendix 2 - 100 Brands

62. Chevrolet
63. Budweiser
64. H&M
65. Airbnb
66. eBay
67. Heineken
68. Prada
69. Adobe
70. Lego
71. Nintendo
72. Caterpillar
73. Costco
74. Ray-Ban
75. GoPro
76. Vodafone
77. Red Bull
78. L'Oreal
79. Virgin
80. DHL
81. Reebok
82. Instagram
83. Quaker
84. Harley-Davidson
85. Duracell
86. Zoom
87. Slack
88. Spotify
89. TikTok
90. YouTube
91. WhatsApp
92. Swatch
93. Harley Davidson
94. Puma
95. Beats by Dre

96. *Dolce & Gabbana*
97. *Subway*
98. *KFC*
99. *Victoria's Secret*
100. *Under Armour*

APPENDIX 3 - 100 AUTHORS

Please provide me a list of 100 authors who each have a distinct writing style and voice.

1. Jane Austen
2. Ernest Hemingway
3. William Faulkner
4. Virginia Woolf
5. F. Scott Fitzgerald
6. James Joyce
7. George Orwell
8. Gabriel García Márquez
9. Charles Dickens
10. Mark Twain
11. Harper Lee
12. J.K. Rowling
13. Ray Bradbury
14. J.R.R. Tolkien
15. Emily Brontë
16. Oscar Wilde
17. Franz Kafka
18. Sylvia Plath
19. Jorge Luis Borges
20. Thomas Pynchon
21. Toni Morrison
22. Kurt Vonnegut
23. Philip K. Dick
24. Edgar Allan Poe
25. Vladimir Nabokov
26. Herman Melville
27. Margaret Atwood

28. Maya Angelou
29. Cormac McCarthy
30. Hunter S. Thompson
31. Zadie Smith
32. Haruki Murakami
33. Neil Gaiman
34. Stephen King
35. Jack Kerouac
36. Chimamanda Ngozi Adichie
37. Salman Rushdie
38. Kazuo Ishiguro
39. Don DeLillo
40. David Foster Wallace
41. Umberto Eco
42. Alice Munro
43. Isabel Allende
44. Italo Calvino
45. Joan Didion
46. Thomas Mann
47. Samuel Beckett
48. Roberto Bolaño
49. Doris Lessing
50. John Updike
51. James Baldwin
52. Angela Carter
53. Flannery O'Connor
54. Saul Bellow
55. Ralph Ellison
56. Albert Camus
57. Yukio Mishima
58. José Saramago
59. W.G. Sebald
60. Amitav Ghosh
61. Junot Díaz

62. Orhan Pamuk
63. Louise Erdrich
64. Ursula K. Le Guin
65. Arundhati Roy
66. Margaret Drabble
67. D.H. Lawrence
68. John Steinbeck
69. J.D. Salinger
70. Roald Dahl
71. Philip Roth
72. George Saunders
73. Donna Tartt
74. Elmore Leonard
75. Michael Ondaatje
76. Ian McEwan
77. John Irving
78. Chuck Palahniuk
79. William S. Burroughs
80. H.P. Lovecraft
81. Harlan Ellison
82. Terry Pratchett
83. Toni Cade Bambara
84. *Kazuo Ishiguro*
85. Joyce Carol Oates
86. Mary Shelley
87. Annie Proulx
88. Willa Cather
89. Richard Wright
90. Langston Hughes
91. James Patterson
92. Agatha Christie
93. E.L. James
94. Paulo Coelho
95. J.M. Coetzee

96. Ayn Rand
97. Dan Brown
98. Danielle Steel
99. Patricia Highsmith
100. Chinua Achebe

APPENDIX 4 - 50 TEACHERS

Who are the fifty best people to learn form and what is their specialty?

Determining the "best" people to learn from is subjective and depends greatly on one's interests, goals, and field of study. However, I'll provide a list of influential people across various disciplines who are widely recognized for their expertise and achievements, as of my knowledge cutoff in September 2021.

1. **Elon Musk** *(Entrepreneurship, Innovation)* - Co-founder of PayPal, SpaceX, and Tesla.
2. **Warren Buffett** *(Investing)* - Chairman and CEO of Berkshire Hathaway.
3. **Bill Gates** *(Technology, Philanthropy)* - Co-founder of Microsoft and the Bill & Melinda Gates Foundation.
4. **Oprah Winfrey** *(Media, Entrepreneurship)* - Renowned TV host, actress, and entrepreneur.
5. **Tim Cook** *(Leadership, Technology)* - CEO of Apple.
6. **Angela Merkel** *(Political Leadership)* - Chancellor of Germany.
7. **Jeff Bezos** *(E-commerce, Entrepreneurship)* - Founder of Amazon.
8. **Stephen Hawking** *(Physics, Cosmology)* - Physicist and author of "A Brief History of Time".
9. **Malala Yousafzai** *(Education, Women's Rights)* - Nobel laureate and activist for female education.
10. **Greta Thunberg** *(Climate Activism)* - Environmental activist.
11. **Sundar Pichai** *(Technology, Leadership)* - CEO of Google and Alphabet.
12. **Satya Nadella** *(Leadership, Technology)* - CEO of Microsoft.
13. **Mark Zuckerberg** *(Social Media, Entrepreneurship)* - Co-founder of Facebook.
14. **Stephen King** *(Writing, Horror Fiction)* - Bestselling author known for his horror and suspense novels.
15. **Brené Brown** *(Social Work, Leadership)* - Research professor at the University of Houston, known for her work on vulnerability, courage, and empathy.

Appendix 4 - 50 Teachers

16. **Richard Branson** *(Entrepreneurship, Adventure)* - Founder of the Virgin Group.
17. **Tony Robbins** *(Motivation, Personal Development)* - Motivational speaker and author.
18. **J.K. Rowling** *(Writing, Fantasy)* - Author of the Harry Potter series.
19. **Yuval Noah Harari** *(History, Futurism)* - Author of "Sapiens," "Homo Deus," and "21 Lessons for the 21st Century."
20. **Satoshi Nakamoto** *(Cryptocurrency, Blockchain)* - Pseudonymous person(s) who developed bitcoin.
21. **Peter Drucker** *(Management)* - Widely regarded as the father of modern management.
22. **Marie Kondo** *(Organization, Lifestyle)* - Author and creator of the KonMari method of decluttering.
23. **Ai Weiwei** *(Art, Activism)* - Contemporary artist and political activist.
24. **Gary Vaynerchuk** *(Digital Marketing, Entrepreneurship)* - CEO of VaynerMedia, author, and speaker.
25. **Noam Chomsky** *(Linguistics, Political Commentary)* - Linguist, philosopher, cognitive scientist, historian, social critic.
26. **Brian Chesky** *(Entrepreneurship, Sharing Economy)* - Co-founder of Airbnb.
27. **Daniel Kahneman** *(Psychology, Behavioral Economics)* - Nobel laureate in Economics for his work in behavioral economics.
28. **Margaret Atwood** *(Writing, Dystopian Fiction)* - Author of "The Handmaid's Tale."
29. **Neil deGrasse Tyson** *(Astrophysics, Science Communication)* - Astrophysicist and science communicator.
30. **Sir Ken Robinson** *(Education, Creativity)* - An influential voice in education, known for advocating for more creativity in schools.
31. **Larry Page** *(Technology, Entrepreneurship)* - Co-founder of Google.
32. **Serena Williams** *(Tennis, Sports)* - Professional tennis player.
33. **Jane Goodall** *(Primatology, Conservation)* - Renowned primatologist known for her study of wild chimpanzees.
34. **David Attenborough** *(Natural History, Broadcasting)* - Broadcaster and natural historian.

35. **Deepak Chopra** *(Wellness, Alternative Medicine)* - Prominent figure in the New Age movement, author on topics like spirituality and mind-body health.
36. **Elie Wiesel** *(Holocaust Studies, Peace Activism)* - Holocaust survivor and Nobel laureate.
37. **Michael Jordan** *(Basketball, Sports)* - Professional basketball player, regarded by many as the greatest of all time.
38. **Martha Stewart** *(Cooking, Lifestyle)* - Businesswoman, TV personality, and author.
39. **Sheryl Sandberg** *(Leadership, Women's Empowerment)* - COO of Facebook and author of "Lean In."
40. **Reed Hastings** *(Streaming Media, Entrepreneurship)* - Co-founder of Netflix.
41. **Angela Duckworth** *(Psychology, Education)* - Psychologist known for her work on grit and self-control.
42. **Yo-Yo Ma** *(Music, Cello)* - Renowned cellist and music educator.
43. **Dalai Lama** *(Buddhism, Peace Activism)* - The spiritual leader of Tibetan Buddhism.
44. **Jack Ma** *(Entrepreneurship, E-commerce)* - Co-founder of Alibaba Group.
45. **Melinda Gates** *(Philanthropy, Women's Rights)* - Co-founder of the Bill & Melinda Gates Foundation.
46. **Michelle Obama** *(Leadership, Health Advocacy)* - Former First Lady of the United States.
47. **Simon Sinek** *(Leadership, Motivation)* - Author of "Start With Why" and motivational speaker.
48. **Ray Dalio** *(Investing, Corporate Culture)* - Founder of investment firm Bridgewater Associates.
49. **Marie Curie** *(Physics, Chemistry)* - Pioneering scientist, first woman to win a Nobel Prize, and the only person to win a Nobel in two different sciences.
50. **Neil Gaiman** *(Writing, Fantasy)* - Author of novels, comic books, and screenplays, including "Coraline" and "American Gods."

Made in the USA
Coppell, TX
31 March 2024

30770420R00214